Priceline.com® For Du

M000273975

Where to Go to Compare Rates

Before you bid on Priceline, check historical rates and get advice on **BiddingForTravel.com** (www.bidding fortravel.com) and **BetterBidding.com** (www.betterbidding.com). Then check competing rates on **Hotwire.com** (www.hotwire.com) and at least three of the following sites:

- **Expedia.com** (www.expedia.com)
- **Orbitz** (www.orbitz.com)
- **Travelocity.com** (www.travelocity.com)
- **Travelweb.com** (www.travelweb.com)
- **Quikbook Hotels** (www.quikbook.com; for hotels only)
- **SideStep** (www.sidestep.com)

And then go to individual airline, hotel, and car-rental Web sites (listed in Chapter 20), but especially these sites, which have fares that don't show up on most travel-agency sites:

- **Southwest Airlines** (www.southwest.com)
- **JetBlue Airways** (www.jetblue.com)
- **Independence Air** (www.flyi.com)

Getting in Touch with Priceline

Call Priceline at 800-774-2354 if you have problems. As of this writing, here are the steps to get through its voicemail menus:

1. **Choose option 1,** "for help with Priceline's travel related services."
2. **Choose option 1,** "calling regarding an offer you have already submitted."
3. **Enter your Priceline bid request number and hit the # button on your phone.**
4. **Enter your phone number and hit the # button on your phone.**
5. **Wait through about a minute of babble.**
6. **Choose option 4,** "for all other requests."
7. **Choose option 1,** "for further assistance."

   Victory! You're now on hold for a real, human operator.

Check, Check, and Check Again

When you get to the Please Review Your Request screen, print out your bid and check over:

- **The departure and arrival dates:** Are they the right months? The right days of the week?
- **The departure and arrival airports (for flights):** Are you comfortable with all of them?
- **The city zones (for hotels):** Are you comfortable with getting a hotel in *any* of these zones?
- **The car class (for rental cars):** If you want a four-door, did you pick full-size or larger?
- **Your offer price:** Make sure you didn't enter any extra zeroes ($150 and not $1,500, for example).

For Dummies: Bestselling Book Series for Beginners

Priceline.com® For Dummies®

Multiplying Your Bids

If your first bid is rejected, and you want to bid again and raise your price, Priceline requires you to change something about your bid. Fortunately, you can change your bid in several ways without adding options you don't want. When bidding for a hotel, you can get more bids by doing the following:

- **If you're looking for 4-star hotels, find and add zones with no 4-star hotels.** You'll have added a zone (satisfying Priceline) and so be able to raise your bid without having any chance of getting a hotel in the newly added zone, because it has no 4-star hotels (satisfying you).

- **If you're bidding on a room that you'll share with another adult, change the name of the bidder to the other person's name.** As long as you're both over 21 and you're both staying in the room, Priceline doesn't care.

- **Start a new bid with a different collection of zones and star levels.**

When bidding for a flight, you can get more bids by doing the following:

- **Add impossible airports (ones that have no flights to your destination).** You'll have added an airport (satisfying Priceline) and be able to raise your bid for your original itinerary, but you'll have no chance of getting a flight into the new airport (satisfying you). Go to www.itasoftware.com to find impossible routes.

- **Allow prop planes on your itinerary.**

- **Accept off-peak flights.**

- **Change your start city to another one that shares airports with your original start city.**

Hotel Chains and Star Levels

Typical U.S. hotel chains for each of Priceline's star levels include the following:

- **1 star:** Baymont Inn, Comfort Inn, Days Inn, Econo Lodge, Howard Johnson, Ramada Limited, Rodeway Inn, Sleep Inn, Super 8, Travelodge, and Wellesley Inns & Suites

- **2 stars:** Baymont Inn, Best Western, Candlewood Suites, Clarion, Comfort Inn, Days Inn, Fairfield Inn, Four Points Sheraton, Hampton Inn, Holiday Inn, Holiday Inn Express, Homestead Inn, Homestead Village, Howard Johnson, La Quinta, Microtel, Quality Inn, Ramada, Red Lion, Springhill Suites, TownePlace Suites, and Wellesley Inns & Suites

- **2½ stars:** AmeriSuites, Country Inn, Courtyard by Marriott, Doubletree Hotels, Hampton Inn, Hilton Garden Inn, Holiday Inn, Ramada Plaza, Residence Inn, Staybridge Suites, Summerfield Suites, Wellesley Inns & Suites, Wingate Inn, and Wyndham Gardens

- **3 stars:** Adam's Mark, Club Quarters, Crowne Plaza, Doubletree, Embassy Suites, Four Points Sheraton, Hilton, Holiday Inn, Hyatt, Marriott, Omni, Park Plaza, Radisson, Red Lion, Renaissance, Sheraton, and Wyndham

- **Boutique:** Kimpton Hotels

- **4 stars:** Embassy Suites, Hilton, Hyatt, Loews, Marriott, Omni, Renaissance, Sheraton, W, Westin, and Wyndham

- **Resort:** Hilton, Marriott

- **5 stars:** The Venetian, Waldorf Towers

For Dummies: Bestselling Book Series for Beginners

Priceline.com®
FOR
DUMMIES®

by Sascha Segan

Wiley Publishing, Inc.

Priceline.com® For Dummies®

Published by
Wiley Publishing, Inc.
111 River Street
Hoboken, NJ 07030-5774

Copyright © 2005 by Wiley Publishing, Inc., Indianapolis, Indiana

Published by Wiley Publishing, Inc., Indianapolis, Indiana

Published simultaneously in Canada

For general information on our other products and services or to obtain technical support, please contact our Customer Care Department within the U.S. at 800-762-2974, outside the U.S. at 317-572-3993, or fax 317-572-4002.

Wiley also publishes its books in a variety of electronic formats. Some content that appears in print may not be available in electronic books.

Library of Congress Control Number: 2004107903

ISBN: 0-7645-7592-9

Manufactured in the United States of America

10 9 8 7 6 5 4 3 2 1

1B/QY/RQ/QU/IN

WILEY

About the Author

Sascha Segan started bidding on Priceline.com in 1999 and stays in Priceline hotel rooms several times a year. He's the author of *Fly Safe, Fly Smart* (published by Wiley) and has contributed to a slew of *Frommer's* travel guides (published by Wiley). He's also the lead analyst for cellphones and PDAs at *PC Magazine*. In his spare time, he likes to fiddle with his TiVo and plot future escapes from New York.

Dedication

This book is dedicated to Leontine, who came to my desk every day for two years, reminded me to get out into the world, and gave me something to come back home to.

Author's Acknowledgments

All this travel stuff started with Stacy Lu believing in me, Rosemary Ellis giving me a chance, and Matt Hannafin pointing me in the right direction. Kelly Regan and David Lytle helped drag out the travel writer inside me, and Tom Heine came to me with an idea so crazy it was brilliant. Suma CM reminded me that yeah, other people find travel arcana fun, too.

This book wouldn't make any sense without Elizabeth Kuball's experienced and steady hand on the tiller, and it wouldn't be something you could trust without Jennifer Holst's keen and watchful eye. Finally, Sheryl Mexic, the world's greatest Priceline.com expert, taught me a lot of what I know about bidding, and I'll forever be in her debt for it.

Publisher's Acknowledgments

We're proud of this book; please send us your comments through our online registration form located at www.dummies.com/register/.

Some of the people who helped bring this book to market include the following:

Acquisitions, Editorial, and Media Development

Project Editor: Elizabeth Kuball

Acquisitions Editor: Tom Heine

Technical Editor: Jennifer Holst

Editorial Manager: Robyn Siesky

Media Development Supervisor: Richard Graves

Editorial Assistant: Adrienne Porter

Cartoons: Rich Tennant, www.the5thwave.com

Composition

Project Coordinators: Courtney MacIntyre, Nancee Reeves

Layout and Graphics: Andrea Dahl, Denny Hager, Stephanie D. Jumper, Michael Kruzil, Barry Offringa

Proofreaders: Carl Pierce, Brian H. Walls, TECHBOOKS Production Services

Indexer: TECHBOOKS Production Services

Publishing and Editorial for Technology Dummies

    Richard Swadley, Vice President and Executive Group Publisher

    Andy Cummings, Vice President and Publisher

    Mary Bednarek, Executive Acquisitions Director

    Mary C. Corder, Editorial Director

Publishing for Consumer Dummies

    Diane Graves Steele, Vice President and Publisher

    Joyce Pepple, Acquisitions Director

Composition Services

    Gerry Fahey, Vice President of Production Services

    Debbie Stailey, Director of Composition Services

Contents at a Glance

Table of Contents

Part II: Up, Up, and Away! Buying Plane Tickets on Priceline

Chapter 5: Straighten Up and Fly Right: Knowing Your Options

Chapter 6: Building an Airline Bid Strategy

Introduction

· ·

*I*f you travel, this book will save you hundreds of dollars. It may even save you thousands. That's a pretty good deal, huh?

Priceline is the ultimate bargain bin of travel agencies. It takes the extra rental cars, airline seats, and rooms that travel suppliers don't think they could possibly sell, marks them w-a-a-a-y down, and gives them to you for cheap.

How cheap? I've stayed in $220-per-night hotels for $55, and I've flown on $550 airline routes for $400. My mom got treated to the Shangri-La in Bangkok, a $200-per-night hotel, for $75. A recent in-depth study by Consumer WebWatch, a spin-off of *Consumer Reports,* found Priceline offered the best fares and rates more often than any other online travel site.

But Priceline terrifies many travelers. To use it, you have to guess at a good price and hand over your money before you know your airline, flight routing, hotel location, or car-rental firm. Priceline's Name Your Own Price approach (which should really be called "Guess Our Price"), spotty customer service, and no-refund/no-exchange policies scare many people away.

This book helps clarify Priceline's often-confusing requirements, explains its mysterious system, and helps you save lots of cash on airfares, hotels, and car rentals.

In these pages, I help you know exactly what you're getting from Priceline and show you how to get what you really want. I tell you how to bid as little as possible and still win the trip of your dreams. You'll be flying off with pockets stuffed with savings.

Conventions Used in This Book

In this book, I used a few special typefaces to make things clearer:

- ✔ Web addresses and e-mail addresses are in this typeface: `www.priceline.com`.
- ✔ Anything you have to type is in **bold.**
- ✔ Any new terms I'm introducing to you are in *italic.*

Foolish Assumptions

My grandma taught me that to assume makes an ass out of "u" and "me," but I assume a few things about you. Don't worry, though — I also tell you what to do if these things *don't* apply to you:

- ✔ **You have access to the Internet.** You don't have to own a computer, but you do have to be able to get online at home, at work, at a cybercafé, or at a library.

- ✔ **You have an e-mail account.** Again, you don't need to have e-mail access at home — you can sign up for a free Web-based e-mail through various sites such as Yahoo! or Hotmail.

- ✔ **You're pretty comfortable with surfing the Web.** You know how to print out a Web page, use the Forward and Back buttons in your Web browser, and know what links look like.

- ✔ **You're over 18 and have a credit or debit card.** You need some piece of plastic with your name and a Visa, MasterCard, American Express, or Discover logo on it. Priceline requires you to pay for your travel with one of those four cards.

If any of my first three assumptions don't apply to you, go buy a copy of *The Internet For Dummies,* 9th Edition, by John Levine, Carol Baroudi, and Margaret Levine Young (published by Wiley). The writers of that book will get you up to speed on Web surfing so you can get online and save money with Priceline.

I'm *not* assuming you've ever used Priceline before. I'm not assuming you've ever bought an airline ticket, or even that you've ever left your house. I'm guaranteeing, though, that after you see how inexpensive 4-star hotel rooms can be on Priceline, you'll want to leave your house a lot more often.

How This Book Is Organized

Think of Priceline as a shopping mall with three big stores: one sells airline tickets, one sells hotel rooms, and one sells rental cars. Priceline also has several little oddball shops selling other stuff around the edges.

This book has six parts — one big introductory part, one part on each of Priceline's main stores, one part on the other stuff Priceline sells, and one part full of fun lists. Each part stands on its own, so if you just want a hotel room, you can read Chapters 9 through 12 and ignore Chapters 13 through 15 completely, for example. Try to read Chapter 2 no matter what you do, though — it summarizes Priceline's triumphs and trade-offs and lets you decide whether Priceline is right for you.

Part I: What Priceline Can Do for You

In this part, I tell you what Priceline is, how it gets such cheapo fares, and why it's gotten some bad press in the past. In this part, you figure out whether Priceline is right for you, discover your rights as a traveler, and get a quick rundown of bidding — the core of the Priceline experience.

Part II: Up, Up, and Away! Buying Plane Tickets on Priceline

If you're trying to get on a plane cheaply, this is the part for you. I explain when Priceline is and isn't useful for buying airline tickets, and what you have to trade away in exchange for low fares.

Then you find out everything you need to know about airline bidding, including some neat tricks for letting you bend Priceline's rules so you can bid over and over again. Finally, you get some comforting words about what to do if things go wrong at the airport — or if your airline goes out of business.

Part III: Nabbing a Hotel Room with Priceline

Hotel rooms are the one Priceline product everyone should use. You usually get bigger savings than with airfares or cars, and the trade-offs are pretty minimal.

In this part, you find out all about star levels and zones, and I take a lot of the mystery out of figuring out what hotel you'll get when you bid. I show you tricks that will multiply your bids, so you can get your rooms for as little money as possible. I also tell you how to check into your hotel so you get the best room with the least fuss.

Part IV: Hot Wheels: Renting a Car through Priceline

This part walks you through the process of renting a car with Priceline. I explain Priceline's 11 car types, which are slightly different from the car types you get from other car-rental places. I tell you where you can pick up your car, and how much you should expect to save over renting from anyone else. Then I help you deal with the crabby car-rental counter people so you can make sure you get the car you ordered.

Part V: More Priceline Products

This is the part with the little oddball shops. Most importantly, this is the part where you can find out about using Priceline if you live in Canada, Europe, or Asia. If you live in the United States, you'll find out about buying air tickets and hotels together as vacation packages, as well as about Priceline's strangest product of all: mortgages. Yes, people buy mortgages from Priceline — and many people say they get really good rates.

Part VI: The Part of Tens

Everybody loves a good list. In this part, I have four of 'em for you. Here, you read about the best travel Web sites that *aren't* Priceline, get some great bidding tips (in case you don't want to read the 21 other chapters), and find out the best zones for hotels in 20 popular cities around the world. After all, just because you want to save money doesn't mean you've memorized the map of the city you're traveling to.

Appendix

At the end of the book is a glossary of common Priceline and travel terms, so you know the difference between a *round-trip flight* and an *open-jaw flight,* and what it means to use an *alternate airport* to get a *free rebid.* I define these terms throughout the book, too, but having somewhere to turn in case you forget is always nice.

Icons Used in This Book

When you flip through the pages of the book, you'll notice little pictures in the margin. These icons are there to draw your attention to specific kinds of information. Here's what they mean:

Knowledge is power. On Priceline, knowledge is money. When you see this icon, you know you'll find a strategy or approach that is sure to garner some serious savings.

Priceline does a lot of odd things, and this icon marks the ones that may trip you up. If you think you may forget one of these pearls of wisdom, dog-ear the page or attach a paper clip to it.

This icon helps you benefit from my mistakes. When you're elbow-deep in bidding, a few things can go wrong. I've seen them firsthand, so I can help you avoid them.

In five years of Priceline bidding, I've built up a lot of stories, as well as strategies I use in my own bidding. Gather 'round, fix yourself a drink, and let me tell you a tale. I'm pretty sure you'll like it.

When you see this icon, you're sure to find information that's interesting but not necessarily critical to your understanding of the topic at hand. If you're pressed for time, you can skip these paragraphs without missing out on anything crucial — but if you read them, you won't be disappointed.

Where to Go from Here

This book has six independent parts, so you can start pretty much anywhere. Depending on what you're shopping for, you may want to head for the parts of the book about airfares, cars, hotels, or even mortgages. Turn to the table of contents and pick out a chapter — you won't be confused no matter where you dive in.

All chapters are equal, but some chapters are more equal than others. Here's a starting point for every kind of Priceliner:

- **If you don't know anything about Priceline,** Chapter 2 is really, really important. That's where you get the skinny on Priceline's joys and let-downs, as well as where you decide whether Priceline is right for you.

- **If your trigger finger itches and you want to bid right now,** head for Chapter 7 (for airfares), Chapter 11 (for hotels), or Chapter 14 (for cars). I really suggest you go first to Chapter 5 (for airfares), Chapter 9 (for hotels), or Chapter 13 (for cars), though. You'll end up reading more, but you'll also end up a much smarter bidder, happier with what you get from Priceline and paying less than everyone else.

- **If you live outside the United States (or don't have a credit card with a U.S. billing address),** go to Chapter 18.

You can also join other Priceliners in two thriving online communities, where successful bidders swap stories, trade tips, and exchange the results of their bids. On both of the Priceline watchdog boards, you can find out what hotels you're most likely to get in a particular city, and you can get experienced Priceline bidders to give you specific, detailed strategies for bagging the best rates:

- **BiddingForTravel.com** (www.biddingfortravel.com) is the biggest and best of the Priceline watchdog boards. It has summarized tens of thousands of Priceline bids since 2000, making it a mandatory stop for everyone who wants to see what sorts of hotels and airline tickets people are getting on Priceline. It also helps you come up with bidding strategies, but one word of warning: The moderators are sticklers for their rules, even though they're also brilliant and informative. Read the board's Frequently Asked Questions (FAQs) first, follow their rules, and you'll do fine.

- **BetterBidding.com** (www.betterbidding.com) was started by a fellow who thought BiddingForTravel.com needed to lighten up. It's a smaller, friendlier, chattier board, where new Priceliners can get great tips on bidding. But it doesn't have anywhere near the depth of data that BiddingForTravel.com does.

I'm always up for a good Priceline story, though I may not have time to respond. Drop me a line at pricelinebook@saschasegan.com, and I promise I'll read your e-mail. You just may hear back from me, too!

Part I
What Priceline Can Do for You

The 5th Wave   By Rich Tennant

I just went onto Priceline.com and looked for a house to rent in Omaha that had some European charm.

In this part . . .

Yes, the rumors are true. You can save huge amounts of money on Priceline. Big buckets of money. Gouts of cash raining from the sky. Get out the rubber bands, because you're wallet's going to be so thick you'll need something to keep it from falling apart.

Of course, trade-offs are involved. But the trade-offs probably aren't as bad as you think. In this part, I help you judge whether Priceline is for you. You find out what your rights are and how to stand up for them. Then you take a whirlwind tour of bidding, because that's where the action happens.

Chapter 1

Have We Met? Getting Acquainted with Priceline

In This Chapter

▶ Understanding how Priceline works

▶ Comparing Priceline to the competition

▶ Weighing the pros and cons of Priceline

*P*riceline doesn't want you to read this book.

Its system of super-discounted travel relies on mystery: You can't know exactly what flights you're getting or exactly what hotel you'll be sleeping in.

I'm blowing the doors off Priceline's vaults and pulling out its secrets. Okay, maybe not all of them — Priceline holds a lot of information very close to its virtual chest. But when you put down this book, you'll know a lot more than Priceline gives away on its site.

The folks at Priceline refused to cooperate with this book, but I like to think they're secretly glad I'm putting the word out. Priceline is a marvelous way to save money on travel. In exchange for a little bit of mystery, you'll be able to take trips you never thought you could afford and stay in hotels that you could previously only tour the lobbies of.

Priceline has been working hard to improve its service over the past few years, and now is a great time to jump in and save. This chapter introduces you to Priceline — I show you around and get you familiar with the way it does business. After you're familiar with how and why Priceline can save you money, you'll be ready to bid on and win that trip of your dreams.

What Priceline Is and How It Works

Everything most people say about Priceline is wrong.

Priceline isn't an auction. You're not competing against other bidders. You don't really Name Your Own Price, and Priceline doesn't shop your prices around.

Priceline sells hotel rooms, airfares, and car rentals really cheaply by hiding the details. Priceline's products have fixed prices just like everyone else's — but it hides the prices from you. You have to guess them.

Travel gurus call Priceline's deals *opaque fares,* because you can't see the prices. Priceline isn't the only seller of opaque fares, but it's by far the largest.

In exchange for all the mystery, travel suppliers give Priceline really low rates — usually lower than everyone else's. That's because they see Priceline buyers as the most desperate, price-sensitive travelers anywhere, willing to give up all kinds of convenience for the absolute lowest price.

Priceline also sells regular airline tickets, hotel rooms, rental cars, and cruises. But the Name Your Own Price super-discounted rates are what made Priceline famous, and they're what you find out about in this book.

Building the mystery

Airlines and hotels want to sell their goods for as much money as possible. Fortunately for you, that's not always possible. Oftentimes, more airline tickets and hotel rooms are out there than people who are willing to pay high prices for them.

So airlines and hotels offer several levels of prices, depending on the hoops you're willing to jump through.

For example, airlines may have one, very high price for people who decide at the last minute that they absolutely need to travel. They have a lower price for people who can plan three weeks in advance. And they have an even lower price for people willing to stay over a weekend, because those travelers are probably bargain-hunting vacationers rather than cash-rich business travelers.

Even after all these discounts, though, some airline seats and hotel rooms are still left over. So the travel firms came up with the ultimate hoop: mystery fares and mystery hotel rooms. They decided to sell their last available seats and rooms at super-discounted prices to truly desperate bargain hunters, people who don't care what airline they're flying on or what hotel they're staying in.

Getting online with Priceline

To use Priceline, you need an Internet connection and a Web browser (such as Internet Explorer, Mozilla, or Netscape). You can use Priceline on either a PC or a Mac. You can bid on Priceline through a phone line or through a high-speed connection to the Internet — it doesn't matter — and you can use any Internet service provider (ISP). You can even bid on Priceline at work.

If you don't have Internet access at home or work, things are a little stickier. You can bid on Priceline using a computer at a public library or cybercafé, with a free e-mail address you get from Yahoo! (http://mail.yahoo.com), Hotmail (www.hotmail.com), or a similar service. But I don't advise it, because you have to enter your credit-card details into the computer while you're bidding, and who knows what sort of nasty hacker-like stuff that 17-year-old kid who last used the public computer did to it? Using a private, trusted machine is always best when entering credit-card details.

Those fares and rates are called *opaque,* because you can't see through them and find out your flight or hotel details before you buy. Priceline is the king of the opaque fare services, selling more opaque fares than anyone else. Hotwire.com, formerly run by five airlines and now owned by the folks who run Expedia.com, is the number-two seller of opaque fares. Expedia also sells some opaque fares.

Opaque fares and rates are a great way to save money. But Priceline found a way to squeeze even lower prices out of airlines and hotels: Name Your Own Price.

Guessing Priceline's price

Name Your Own Price is a lie. The reality is more like "Guess Our Price." It's a trick, a game to balance customers' savings with hotel and airline profits. If you play the game well, you'll save thousands of dollars. If you play it poorly, you'll pay through the nose.

Priceline's computers connect to the Worldspan reservation system, which lists Priceline rates that airlines and hotels set for tickets and rooms. When you submit a bid, Priceline checks your bid against its partners' Priceline rates. It grabs all the rooms, fares, or cars you can afford, and then, using a complicated computer formula Priceline has never explained to anyone, picks one of the bunch to give to you.

Many hotels have three different Priceline rates for the same room, so you can't predict which hotel you get by how much you bid. Experts have guessed (because Priceline isn't saying) that Priceline also throws a random element into the mix.

The Priceline rates may change every day, or they may remain the same for weeks or months at a time.

If you bid exactly at Priceline's price, the hotel gets its Priceline rate; Priceline gets its transaction fee; you get your room, flight, or car; and everybody walks away somewhat happy.

If you overbid, though, Priceline and the travel supplier pocket the difference and don't tell you. This book helps you get as close to the real Priceline rate as possible, saving you money.

Because some people overbid, travel suppliers are often willing to give Priceline even lower rates than they give to Hotwire and other opaque-fare sites. The profits reaped on overbids make up for the losses caused by smart bidders getting the lowest possible rate.

It's a complicated strategy, but it works. Priceline sold $360 million in travel during the first three months of 2004, and made a gross profit of $43.4 million. According to the company's financial reports, it expected bookings to grow by 50 percent as it moved into the 2004 summer travel season. In other words, Priceline is here to stay.

Priceline grows up: Travel the traditional way

Priceline offers "normal" airfares and hotels, too. Last year, it bought Lowestfare.com and Travelweb, two online travel agencies that sell airfares and hotels just as Expedia, Travelocity, and Orbitz do.

During 2004, Priceline started sprinkling its Lowestfare.com and Travelweb rates around its Web site. If you want to buy airline tickets, for instance, you have to go through a page of normal fares from Lowestfare.com, as shown in Figure 1-1. These fares may be better than Expedia or Travelocity — then again, they may not. Lowestfare.com is a travel agency just like any other — no better and no worse.

Similarly, when you click on links to buy one-way airline tickets, you get shunted to the Lowestfare.com travel agency.

Priceline also sells cruises through a partnership with NLG (a travel agency specializing in cruises) and sells travel insurance through American Home Assurance Company (a major travel insurer).

Figure 1-1:
The $290
Web fare on
this page
comes from
Lowestfare.
com,
Priceline's
traditional
travel
agency.

Priceline around the world

Priceline's idea worked so well in the United States that the rest of the world wanted in on it. But Priceline didn't want to just let foreigners use the U.S. Priceline Web site. Different laws control purchases in different countries, so other countries needed their own sites.

Priceline.co.uk (www.priceline.co.uk), for U.K. residents, came first. That site is wholly owned by Priceline and works just like Priceline.com for Name Your Own Price hotels — except that you pay in British pounds, not U.S. dollars.

The Asian conglomerate Hutchison Whampoa made a deal with Priceline to run several Priceline spin-offs in Asian countries. Priceline Hong Kong (www.priceline.com.hk; shown in Figure 1-2), Priceline Singapore (www.priceline.com.sg), and Priceline Taiwan (www.priceline.com.tw) all sell Name Your Own Price airline tickets from their home countries, along with hotel rooms all around the world. Because they're not entirely run by Priceline, they have their own quirks — you can demand nonstop flights, for instance, which you can't do on Priceline.com and Priceline.co.uk. They also offer hotel rooms in a slew of cities in Asia, Australia, New Zealand, and India, where Priceline.com doesn't sell rooms — so if you're heading to Auckland or New Delhi, you should check out Priceline Asia. Residents of more than two

---

Oh captain, my captain!

William Shatner, best known as Captain Kirk from *Star Trek,* has been the voice and face of Priceline since 1999. He doesn't need to find travel deals for himself — in past interviews, he's said he always flies first class. But Shatner's commanding presence and, most importantly, his sense of humor about himself have made him a great fit for the scrappy travel company. (How many celebrities would let a company sell bobble-head dolls of them on the Web?)

Shatner is something of a renaissance man himself. He's written successful science-fiction

novels and nonfiction books, supports a residential home for women recovering from alcohol abuse, starred in the only movie ever filmed in the Esperanto language, and speaks fluent French (he grew up in Montreal, Canada).

As Priceline shifts to selling "regular" airline tickets and hotel rooms as well as Name Your Own Price products, it's brought a second spokesman on board. Shatner says he's having a great time working with his old friend Leonard Nimoy, whom you may know as Mr. Spock.

Live long and prosper, Priceliners.

---

dozen countries are allowed to use Priceline's Asian sites (though if they're buying airline tickets rather than hotel rooms, they have to fly out of Hong Kong, Singapore, or Taiwan).

Figure 1-2:
Priceline Hong Kong sells airline tickets from Hong Kong to other cities, as well as hotel rooms around the world.

Suppliers versus consumers

Priceline loves smart bidders. Smart bidders use Priceline more often, so Priceline makes more money. If everyone in the world used Priceline, there would be a lot of happy people at Priceline's headquarters in Norwalk, Connecticut.

But there would also be a lot of very angry people in hotel and airline headquarters around the world. Priceline's travel suppliers *hate* smart bidders. Every smart bidder is another person who isn't buying more-expensive tickets, rooms, or rental cars through other means.

The suppliers don't want to kill Priceline. They just want to make sure Priceline knows its place, as a last-resort travel site.

Priceline stands on a knife's edge, trying to balance the desires of consumers and suppliers.

That's my theory as to why Priceline's system is full of loopholes. The loopholes attract smart, high-volume bidders who come back again and again. Sometimes, Priceline closes a loophole, because the travel suppliers don't like them.

For a while, Priceline had a friendly relationship with BiddingForTravel.com, the Priceline watchdog bulletin board, because they drove lots of business to Priceline. Then Priceline cut off contact with BiddingForTravel.com. The folks at Priceline wouldn't say why, but many people at the time thought it was because the suppliers didn't like Priceline getting all cozy with the smart-bidding crowd.

Seeing what happens when this book comes out will be interesting. If you happen to know any hotel-industry executives, don't tell them about it.

Non-Americans can also use the U.S. Priceline site by bending the rules. Priceline doesn't take any responsibility for what happens to you if you try, but plenty of Canadians have snuck across the barbed-wire border into the United States of Priceline. Jump ahead to Chapter 18 if you want to see the details.

How Priceline Stacks Up to the Competition

Priceline isn't the only travel agency on the Web. It's not even the only seller of opaque fares, or the only site where you can bid for travel. Hotwire, Expedia, Travelocity, and a whole bunch of smaller travel agencies all dabble in opaque fares, and SkyAuction.com and eBay both let you bid for travel.

But Priceline does let you get the lowest fares and rates for hotel rooms, the most often. An independent study by Consumer WebWatch, a spin-off of *Consumer Reports,* found Priceline had the lowest rates more often than any other Web site, with more than twice as many lowest rates as Hotwire.

Speedy growth and lousy service: Why many fear Priceline

Priceline started in 1998, at the height of the Internet boom, when the mantra on Wall Street was grow, grow, grow.

So Priceline grew. It tried to extend its Name Your Own Price offerings to groceries, phone calls, even gasoline. These attempts only served to confuse consumers as to what Priceline was all about — and to disappoint people when they failed. Priceline Mortgage is Priceline's only remaining non-travel product.

Priceline's customer service was also famously bad — so bad, in fact, that Priceline got kicked out of the Connecticut Better Business Bureau

(BBB) in 2000. A large part of the problem was that Priceline didn't explain its restrictions very well, which meant that many people were confused and disappointed when they didn't get the flights they wanted. Priceline's computers also used to give travelers some very strange routings, like New York to Chicago via Atlanta.

Don't worry: Priceline has turned itself around. It's back in good standing with the BBB. It's knocked some sense into its airline routing computers. It explains its restrictions better than it used to. And its customer service . . . well, I'll just say it isn't *famously* bad.

Priceline would have done even better in Consumer WebWatch's tests if the testers had used the tips in this book. The people at Consumer WebWatch got a hotel room on their first bid 46 percent of the time. If you win your first hotel bid, you're probably bidding too much. One of my key strategies is *rebidding* (using several bids to start low and then come up to meet Priceline's lowest acceptable price). So Consumer WebWatch's researchers probably could have bid even lower and succeeded.

All opaque sites are opaque, but Priceline is more opaque than others. The advantage of booking with another opaque site, or another bidding site, is that you know a little more than you do with Priceline. With other opaque sites, you'll see the price before you buy, so you can comparison shop. Other bidding sites will tell you exactly what you're bidding for, down to the precise airline or hotel name. Priceline is the most confusing, most complicated, and most mysterious way to book travel. It can be the most frustrating. But it's also usually the cheapest. Knowing less means saving more. Of course, if you'd rather know more and save a little less, the sites covered in the following sections can often provide fares lower than regular rates.

Hotwire.com

They're like Coke and Pepsi, or Hertz and Avis. Hotwire (www.hotwire.com) is Priceline's number-one competitor, and it's usually the site to beat when you're looking for airfares, hotels, and car rentals.

Hotwire sells opaque flights, hotel rooms, car rentals, and vacation packages, just as Priceline does. Like with Priceline, Hotwire's reservations are strictly nonrefundable, and you can't figure out your exact flight times or the name of your airline or hotel before you pay. Also just like with Priceline, you choose your hotel based on a star level and a neighborhood zone.

Hotwire is clearer than Priceline in several ways, though. First, it tells you its prices in advance — there's no bidding, no guessing, and no mystery there. It also tells you more about its hotels than Priceline does. For example, it tells you which hotels have pools, which have spas, and which are all suites (as shown in Figure 1-3).

And if you're buying a weekend vacation package for the next two weekends, you can restrict Hotwire to morning, afternoon, or evening flights. Priceline gives you a Playtime Guarantee that you'll spend 44 or 64 hours at your destination, but it doesn't let you specify your flight times.

Hotwire often rates hotels a little bit more generously than Priceline does. So a Priceline 4-star hotel may be a Hotwire 4½-star hotel. In other words, you can't always compare Priceline and Hotwire exactly.

Hotwire makes a great companion to Priceline, because you can check out prices on Hotwire, bid lower on Priceline, and then come back to Hotwire and accept its offer if Priceline can't beat it.

Figure 1-3: The little icons on Hotwire.com's hotel-selection screen tell you which hotels have pools — something you don't know before you pay with Priceline.

Want to know exactly what hotel you'll be getting with Hotwire? Better Bidding.com tracks the hotels people get on Hotwire. Of course, you could always get a hotel that's not on BetterBidding's list, but BetterBidding will help you narrow your possibilities.

Hotwire posts lists of all its airline and car-rental partners, and some of its hotel partners, on its Web site at `www.hotwire.com/travel-information/partners/index.jsp`.

If you buy a domestic airline ticket on Hotwire, you'll fly on one of the following airlines:

- Aloha Airlines
- America West Airlines
- American Airlines
- Continental Airlines
- Delta Air Lines
- Hawaiian Airlines
- Northwest Airlines
- United Air Lines
- US Airways

Northwest Airlines doesn't participate with Priceline, so you'll probably have better luck finding low fares from Northwest hubs like Minneapolis and Detroit on Hotwire.com.

If you buy an international ticket on Hotwire, you'll fly on one of the following airlines:

- Aeroméxico
- Air France
- Air New Zealand
- Alitalia
- America West Airlines
- American Airlines
- ANA
- BMI
- BWIA West Indies Airways
- Cathay Pacific Airways
- Continental Airlines

- ✔ Copa Airlines
- ✔ Delta Air Lines
- ✔ Finnair
- ✔ Hawaiian Airlines
- ✔ Iberia Airlines
- ✔ Icelandair
- ✔ KLM Royal Dutch Airlines
- ✔ LanChile
- ✔ LanPeru
- ✔ Lufthansa
- ✔ Mexicana
- ✔ Northwest Airlines
- ✔ SAS
- ✔ Singapore Airlines
- ✔ South African Airways
- ✔ Swiss International Air Lines
- ✔ United Air Lines
- ✔ US Airways
- ✔ Virgin Atlantic Airways

Neither Priceline nor Hotwire uses low-fare airlines like Southwest, JetBlue, Independence Air, or Virgin USA, any of which may have the lowest fares for domestic flights. And neither service uses British Airways, which may have great fares to Europe. This fact underscores the need to shop around and not just rely on one or two sources for airfares.

Hotwire.com car rentals will always come from Avis, Budget, or Hertz. Priceline uses those three services but also Alamo and National, so you can expect Priceline to have a wider range of available rental cars.

Neither Priceline nor Hotwire uses super-cheap rental-car companies like Enterprise, Rent-A-Wreck, and Thrifty, so you have to check those firms' prices independently.

Expedia.com

Expedia (`www.expedia.com`) is one of the nation's largest online travel agencies. It often has pretty good prices, because, with its huge size, it can negotiate special low rates from hotels and airlines.

Sometimes when searching for a flight on Expedia, you'll see something called a *Bargain Fare*. These are opaque fares, like the ones on Hotwire.com. Generally, with Bargain Fares:

✔ Your flight will leave between 6 a.m. and 10 p.m.

✔ You must agree to make one connection.

✔ The fare is totally nonrefundable — if you agree to it, you're stuck.

✔ You won't get frequent-flier miles.

✔ You'll fly on one of "20 name-brand airlines."

Don't worry too much about the airlines, Expedia doesn't disclose its list publicly, but it's a very above-board operation, and I trust it to put you on a big-name carrier.

Expedia's Bargain Fares are generally lower than regular published fares. It's competitive with Hotwire and Priceline.

To buy a Bargain Fare, click on it just like you would any other fare on Expedia. You'll only find out your exact airline and flight times after you pay your money, though.

You can't specifically search for or request Bargain Fares. You just have to get lucky. I've seen plenty of Bargain Fares in the past, but I couldn't find any when I was specifically looking for them for this book — that's luck for you. For more about Bargain Fares, see Expedia's Web site at `www.expedia.com/daily/highlights/bargainfares/default.asp`.

SkyAuction.com

Unlike Priceline, SkyAuction.com sells airline tickets and vacation packages in a real auction. You compete against other bidders, and the highest bidder wins. Also unlike Priceline, you usually see exactly what you're bidding for.

SkyAuction has a much smaller inventory than Priceline does, though. At any given time it may have a few dozen airline tickets and hotel rooms for sale — when Priceline has thousands. And the fine print in a SkyAuction sale can drive prices up way beyond what you bid. For example, in Figure 1-4, you can see that this ticket to Europe costs $300 or so — plus $50 if you're traveling on a weekend, plus $65 if you're going to Germany, plus $185 if you're flying from Chicago.

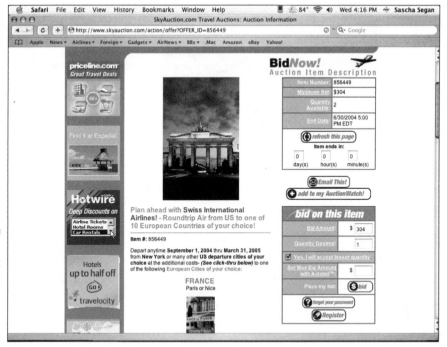

Figure 1-4:
Watch out
for the fine
print on
SkyAuction.
com.

As another example, SkyAuction was selling a ticket on Iberia Airlines to Europe, and the winner bid $400. But the fine print shows he'd be charged an extra $50 if he wanted to depart or return on a weekend, an extra $119 for taxes, and an extra $65 to $165 if he wanted to fly from any city other than New York. That means his $400 ticket could cost more than $700 — which isn't much of a deal!

Sure, SkyAuction has some bargains. But Priceline can probably beat 'em most of the time.

eBay Travel

I'm a travel expert, not an eBay expert. Greg Holden, on the other hand, is the author of *eBay PowerUser's Bible* (published by Wiley). I joined forces with him to check out eBay's travel section, shown in Figure 1-5.

If SkyAuction is an auction house for travel, eBay is a tag sale. All sorts of crazy stuff is on sale here from all sorts of people. How about two round-trip tickets to anywhere in the United States, starting at $79? Or a flight to anywhere in the world, starting at $89?

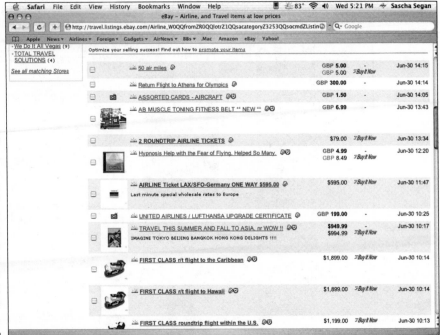

Figure 1-5:
eBay Travel
sells a wide
range of
tickets, but
buyers must
beware
of hidden
fees, fine
print, and
unreliable
sellers.

Some of these deals are real, and some are scams. Holden says eBay isn't widely known as a place to buy travel, so there's relatively little competition for the good stuff. You may turn up an incredible deal here.

Just be *very* sure you're getting what you asked for. Use eBay's Ask Seller a Question button to find out who the seller is. Is it a private person or a travel agency? If you're getting a certificate that must be redeemed for a flight, what's in the fine print? If you're getting a certificate issued by an airline, call the airline, describe the certificate, and find out if it's transferable — some airline certificates can't legally be signed over to another person.

If you're going to buy travel on eBay, look for two things above all others: a good feedback rating and Square Trade certification (Square Trade is an organization that certifies that a business has a commitment to provide good customer service and to treat people fairly). The feedback rating is much more important than Square Trade — so even if a seller has Square Trade, stay away if they have zero feedback. Greg Holden says:

> Feedback ratings are the most important thing to look at when purchasing from any seller on eBay and trying to judge their level of trustworthiness.

I would be wary of buying anything from anyone with a feedback rating of less than 5, and I would not recommend that anyone buy anything from a seller with a feedback rating of 0, because they may have just signed up with . . . eBay to unload these tickets and may be interested in cheating someone; you don't have any guarantees, at least. People with feedback ratings in the hundreds can generally be trusted. But take the time to scan the feedback comments; if there are more than two or three negative comments, you might want to shop elsewhere.

Square Trade means, first of all, that a seller is likely to be a business entity such as a travel agency rather than an individual (although individuals can get Square Trade certified). Actually, though, it really means the seller has paid money to get the seal, which does count for something. Square Trade certification isn't a guarantee that they will be reputable; it just means that, if you feel you have been cheated by this seller and there is a dispute of some sort, you can use Square Trade's resolution services to resolve the dispute through mediation.

Consolidator fares

Many travel agencies, both online and offline, have deals with major airlines where they hide the identity of the airline while you're shopping online, in exchange for very low fares.

For example, 1-800-FlyEurope (www.1800flyeurope.com) has great rates to Europe. It lets you pick your exact flight, and it lets you discuss the fare with its reservations agents in advance. But it doesn't advertise what airline its flights are on. (Often, the reservations agents will tell you if you call and ask.)

These *consolidator fares* aren't really opaque — think of them as translucent. With these fares, airlines are just being a little bashful. They don't want to trumpet these fares too loudly, in case people stop paying the higher fares they find elsewhere. But they want to make consolidator fares available for the real bargain-hunters.

Consolidator fares are mostly available on international routes, and many can be lower than Priceline fares — especially if they're offered by travel agents who specialize in one area of the world, as 1-800-FlyEurope does.

You can find a list of consolidators that serve your destination in the first chapter of any Frommer's Travel Guide (published by Wiley).

Online travel agencies

Online travel agencies like Expedia, Orbitz, Travelocity, Hotels.com, Quikbook. com, and AirlineConsolidator.com all have their own deals with airlines, hotels, and car-rental companies.

"Anything" goes

You can't earn frequent-flier miles on Priceline tickets, but you can earn eBay Anything Points. If you book your Priceline travel through www. ebay.com/travel, you can get up to 1,500 Anything Points (worth $15) for buying an airline ticket or hotel room, 500 Anything Points (worth $5) for booking a car rental, and 4,000 Anything Points (worth $40) for booking a vacation. You can use these points to buy items through PayPal on eBay.

Here's what Greg Holden, the eBay power guy, says: "I think [Anything Points] aren't that useful; they give you a credit on future purchases made on eBay and are only useful if you shop there a lot. Don't make a purchase based on them."

In various chapters of this book, I tell you which sites are the best to compare Priceline's rates to. You can find a summary of other travel-agency Web sites in Chapter 20.

No single online travel agency has the best rates all the time — not even Priceline! The more places you check, the more likely you are to get a deal.

Two programs you install on your PC can help summarize fares from a wide range of other travel sites, cutting down on your research time. Travelaxe (www.travelaxe.com) searches up to a dozen different hotel sites for the best rates. And SideStep (www.sidestep.com) brings together a slew of airline sites, including airlines like JetBlue and Southwest that don't appear on most travel-agency sites.

Airlines, car-rental firms, and hotels' own rates

Airlines, car-rental firms, and hotels would *really* rather you book directly through them than use a travel agency. That way, they don't have to kick back any money to the travel agencies — they can keep all the dough for themselves.

You find many exclusive deals available only on airline, car-rental, and hotel Web sites. The problem is, the suppliers' sites can be a pain to search. If six airlines fly on your route, you'll have to search six Web sites.

Find the lowest price you can on a regular travel-agency site such as Expedia or SideStep, and then go to that airline or hotel chain's own Web site to see if it can do better.

Several budget airlines, including JetBlue, Independence Air, and Southwest, don't appear on most travel-agency sites and don't participate with Priceline or Hotwire. You must use SideStep or go to those airlines' own sites to see their low fares.

Priceline usually has lower rates than hotels' own Web sites. But airlines and car-rental firms often beat Priceline with their own deals.

The Pros and Cons of Using Priceline

My dad would never buy a flight on Priceline. He's a stressed-out New York businessman who wants to fly out for the weekend on Friday night and back on Sunday night. Even if he takes a whole day off for his flights, he refuses to change planes — it's nonstop flights or nothing. He pays a little extra to fly the way he wants, when he wants.

My brother, on the other hand, thinks Priceline is great. He's a struggling actor in L.A., living month to month while he makes artsy indie films. If he's coming back to visit the folks, he can spare some time in exchange for some extra cash, and he's pretty flexible about how he gets home.

How about me? I rarely book flights on Priceline nowadays, but I love to book hotels with Priceline. I don't care whether I get stuck in the Marriott or the Intercontinental, just as long as I'm in a top-notch hotel downtown. And although I could probably afford a budget hotel on my own, I'd love to trade up to something plusher. Priceline even lets me stay in hotels when I don't have to. When my wife and I took a recent trip to Toronto, we stayed with friends one night and then spent our second night at the local Courtyard by Marriott for $36, including tax.

Priceline isn't for everyone. You have to be flexible, willing to do some research, and ready to accept Priceline's restrictions. If you're comfortable with its terms, you can save thousands of dollars on your travel. I have.

The pros: Great rates, solid partnerships

Priceline will get you a room at a name-brand hotel, a flight on a reliable airline, or a car from a big-name rental company for a really, really low price. Pluses to keep in mind when considering Priceline include the following:

- ✔ **You can trust Priceline's airline partners.** They're the biggest in the business, not little fly-by-night carriers.

- ✔ **Priceline can sit you in the lap of luxury for motel prices.** In many cities, you can get a Marriott, Sheraton, Westin, or Hyatt hotel room for as little as $50 a night.

✔ **Priceline can find you a luxury hotel in cities all over the world.** So you don't need to worry about what Asian budget hotels look like. (*Hint:* The rooms are pretty small.)

✔ **With Priceline, you can afford to take trips you never thought you could before.** You'll travel more, and you'll have more money to spend on food, fun, and friends.

The cons: Mystery, doubt, and inflexibility

If you think your travel plans have even the slightest chance of changing, don't use Priceline. Priceline locks you into your reservations, and makes changing them extremely difficult, if not impossible. Other downsides of using Priceline include the following:

✔ **You can't assume you'll get (or won't get) any specific flight or hotel.** If one of Priceline's partners is an airline you refuse to fly or a hotel you refuse to stay in, stay away.

✔ **Smart bidding is a lot of work.** You can't just jump online, punch in a number, and be assured of the lowest price. You need to do research, come up with a strategy, and spend some time pursuing the best rates.

✔ **You must agree to fly at almost any time of day or night.** If you're trying to get a flight after work or don't want to drag your kids to the airport at 6 a.m., don't bid for a flight on Priceline.

✔ **You must agree to change planes if necessary.** If your elderly grandmother can't handle connecting flights, bidding on Priceline isn't for her.

✔ **You can only guarantee space for two adults in a hotel room.** If you're trying to fit four people into one room, Priceline isn't for you.

✔ **You can't guarantee a nonsmoking hotel room, or one with a free airport shuttle, or one with a specific number of beds in the room.**

✔ **You don't get frequent-flier miles, hotel frequent-guest points, or car-rental loyalty points.**

✔ **One of the people traveling must be 18 years old for flights or 21 years old for hotels.** Sorry, college kids.

The Bidding Process

If you've ever seen the game show *The Price Is Right,* you're ready to use Priceline. Winning cheap travel on Priceline requires you to play Priceline's game, bidding as low as you can while still hoping you've guessed above Priceline's minimum price.

I go into bidding in depth in Chapters 7, 11, and 14, providing detailed screen-shots and step-by-step instructions. For now, though, I'll just let you dip your toes into the crucial steps of bidding:

1. **Research competing rates.**

   To guess the right price for Priceline, you need to know what other agencies are charging. By scouring major travel-agency sites; Priceline watchdog sites; Hotwire.com; and hotel, car-rental, and airline sites, you'll know what prices you're trying to beat.

2. **Enter where you want to go on Priceline's home page.**

   Whether you're flying, driving, or staying in a hotel, you always start at Priceline's home page (www.priceline.com), where you enter your cities and dates. Priceline can fly you anywhere in the world (as long as you're starting in the United States) and can find you hotels in dozens of worldwide cities, but you can only rent cars in the United States.

3. **Ignore Priceline's published rates.**

   For airfares and hotels, Priceline will funnel you through a screen of regular, published fares. The prices on this screen are just like any other ordinary online travel-agency prices, and the fares here have no bearing on what you can get if you bid. Ignore this screen and keep going.

4. **Decide on your criteria.**

   If you're trying to book a hotel, you need to decide what neighborhood zone and star level you want. If you're booking a flight, you get to choose the airports you're leaving from and arriving at. If you're driving away with a car, you need to figure out where you want to pick up the car and what kind of car you want.

   Knowledge pays off here. Knowing the city you're staying in lets you choose a hotel neighborhood or airport you're comfortable with, because some of Priceline's choices can be way out of town.

   Pore over the zone maps, and take a look at a travel guide such as the *For Dummies* guidebooks or Frommer's Travel Guides (both published by Wiley) if you don't know your destination well. Travel guidebooks always have neighborhood profiles and explanations of which airports are the best.

5. **Place your bid.**

   Enter how much you want to pay, and punch in your credit-card details. Now you're committed. If Priceline has a room, flight, or car at your price, you'll get it.

6. **Rebid if necessary.**

   If your first bid fails, don't worry. You can bid again by changing an element of your bid (like adding another neighborhood for hotels) or by waiting a few days. In Chapters 6, 10, and 14, I explain how you can keep rebidding over and over again, getting closer and closer to the ideal price for your trip.

7. **Travel!**

   Print out your confirmation page and head for the open road. It's time to travel with a full wallet and a happy heart.

What to Do if You Have a Problem

Priceline is not famous for great customer service. Priceline's customer service, alas, is known for sending unhelpful boilerplate e-mails and funneling you through the worst set of voice-mail menus in the Western world before you can talk to an actual human.

That said, you can still get satisfaction from Priceline if you're persistent and knowledgeable. In Chapter 3, I explain how to get through Priceline's voice-mail menus and talk to a real person. I've heard plenty of stories from people who've been rejected by Priceline's customer-service folks at first, and then gotten what they wanted after a dozen or so phone calls and e-mails.

Basically, you get what you pay for.

I've had better experiences with Priceline's customer service than most people. When I accidentally picked the wrong dates for a hotel reservation, Priceline fixed my problem without question.

Priceline says 80 percent of its customer-service problems come from people who don't understand what they signed on to. If you understand, for instance, that picking a Mid-Size car doesn't guarantee you a four-door, you'll have a much easier time dealing with Priceline's customer-service crew.

Airline, hotel, and car-rental staff can also create trouble for Priceliners — just as they can create trouble for any traveler. In Chapters 8, 12, and 15, I let you know how to minimize problems you may have when checking in, and what to do if you run into trouble.

Chapter 2

Is Priceline Right for You?

*P*riceline isn't for everyone. You pay for Priceline's savings in convenience and flexibility. Although most of this book is about saving big bucks with Priceline, this chapter tells you what you're getting into. If you're fully aware of Priceline's rules and regulations before you bid, you'll be happy with your hotel, flight, or rental car.

Priceline works by selling flights, rooms, and cars that travel companies can't get rid of by any other means. But you have to jump through hoops to prove you really need the savings. You may have to fly early in the morning, or you may get a smoking room when you really wanted nonsmoking. But you'll always get a flight on a major, full-service airline, stay in a name-brand or quality independent hotel, or drive away in a rental car from a big company.

I've flown more than a dozen times with Priceline and stayed in weeks' worth of Priceline hotels since 1999. I think the trade-offs are worth the savings. Read on to make your own decision.

Airline Tickets: Bending Over Backward

The good news, first: Using Priceline to get from Point A to Point B, within North America and Western Europe, is safe and cheap. Priceline only uses major, full-service airlines, and it doesn't send people on the crazy, roundabout itineraries it used to.

Yes, you'll get there alive

Priceline only uses, world-class, full-service airlines. (For a full list, see Chapter 5.) Its U.S. airlines are all big national carriers with solid safety records. Its foreign airlines are all national flag carriers from countries that have passed the U.S. Federal Aviation Administration's International Aviation Safety Assessment, except for one.

BWIA West Indies Airways is the national airline of Trinidad and Tobago, which didn't meet

U.S. safety standards as of April 2004. BWIA has never had a fatal accident, according to AirSafe.com. I consider it a safe airline. If you're queasy about flying with that airline, just don't bid Priceline for flights to Caribbean islands.

You can bid on Priceline with confidence that you'll fly on a leading global airline.

But you have to be really flexible to use Priceline for airline tickets — I'm talking Cirque du Soleil flexible. Priceline guarantees that it'll get you from Point A to Point B with one connection or fewer, but that's about it. You can't count on getting to your destination at any particular time, and you certainly can't ask for nonstop flights.

As you read this book, think about how much money means to you. Think of the worst-case Priceline scenario: a 6:05 a.m. or 9:59 p.m. flight with a three-hour layover somewhere halfway to your destination.

There's a 90 percent chance this scenario won't happen. But you must always bid Priceline as if it will. Any better result — and trust me, better results are likely — should come as a pleasant surprise.

Are you a threadbare student who's willing to cool your heels for a few hours to save $50? Maybe you're a working mom who is willing to put up with dragging your kid out of bed at 4 a.m. for $100. Or you're a small-business owner for whom time is money, but you'll pad your trip with a day on either end if it saves you $200 on airfare. Only *you* know what your Priceline savings threshold is. Lock on to it in your mind. As you shop around and bid, say, "I'm trading convenience for this much money." Does that feel good? If so, you'll make a great Priceliner.

In the following sections, I help you figure out when Priceline is a good choice — and when it isn't.

When to use Priceline

Certain trips are better for Priceline than others. If you're flying at the last minute, on an expensive route, or to a place Priceline often has a lot of tickets for, you'll probably end up a happy bidder. That doesn't mean you can't reap big savings bidding well in advance or on routes Priceline doesn't cover all that often — it's just a bit less likely that you will.

When you can be flexible

Trading time for money is what Priceline is all about. If you're flexible with your time, you can save big bucks on Priceline.

Before you bid for airline tickets, ask yourself four things:

- ✔ **Can I leave and return any time between 6 a.m. and 10 p.m. — even if it's 6:01 a.m. or 9:59 p.m.?**
- ✔ **If I'm flying internationally, can I leave and return any time — even 2 a.m., if necessary?**
- ✔ **Am I comfortable changing planes and maybe waiting an hour or two for a connecting flight?**
- ✔ **Would I rather save money than get frequent-flier miles?**

If your answers to all these questions are "yes," soldier on. You're a Priceliner.

For last-minute trips

Priceline is terrific for last-minute, spur-of-the-moment trips. If you're buying airline tickets well in advance, airlines' own sales often beat Priceline's rates. But prices balloon when you're less than a week away from flying. Priceline helps drag down those absurd last-minute fares to roughly the same level as advance-purchase fares.

For example, at the time of this writing, United was selling round-trips between Newark, New Jersey, and San Francisco for $198 plus tax — as long as you bought your ticket a week in advance. Try to get a flight for tomorrow, and United will charge you anywhere from $400 to $1,000. Meanwhile, out the back door, the airlines quietly slip Priceline lower fares up to the same day a flight takes off.

When airfares are high

Winter fares from New York to London run as low as $300. Try to buy the same ticket for July, and you may pay $600 if you book through normal means.

Priceline can help bring high-season fares down to more reasonable levels. You may not get that $600 down to $300, but $400 to $500 is certainly possible, especially on weekdays when airlines sometimes have trouble filling their planes.

For trips to popular Priceline destinations

Priceline doesn't release information on where its customers fly, so I've had to garner this from my own experiences and reports on various Internet bulletin boards. Based on what I've found, you're pretty likely to find great deals on Priceline if you're traveling to one of these destinations:

- ✔ Orlando
- ✔ Chicago
- ✔ New York
- ✔ Los Angeles
- ✔ Honolulu
- ✔ Toronto
- ✔ London
- ✔ Paris
- ✔ Amsterdam
- ✔ Frankfurt

Bidders have gotten cheap tickets for everywhere from El Paso, Texas, to Arcata, California, and you should be able to get deals to most major cities in Western Europe. This list is just a place to start — you can find great deals flying lots of places.

When you shouldn't use Priceline

Even if you're a frequent Priceliner, you're fighting against the odds if you try to use Priceline for some kinds of trips. If you're just looking for a weekend away, prices are generally low on your route, or you think you may have to change your plans, Priceline will probably be more hassle than it's worth.

For weekend trips

Never buy Priceline airline tickets for a weekend trip. If you try to buy tickets for Saturday and Sunday, you could get a flight leaving at 10 p.m. on Saturday and returning at 6 a.m. on Sunday. That's not much of a weekend!

To save money with Priceline on a three- or four-day weekend, buy an air-and-hotel package. Priceline's Playtime Guarantee ensures you'll spend at least 44 hours at your destination for a two-night trip and 64 hours for a three-night trip (unless you're going to Las Vegas, where, apparently, there are no guarantees).

That means if you book for Friday and Sunday, the worst-case scenario is flights that let you spend from 2 p.m. Friday to 10 a.m. Sunday at your destination, or 8 p.m. Friday to 4 p.m. Sunday. That's not so bad.

For last-minute trips, Priceline's Weekender packages even let you choose roughly what time of day you want to fly. See Chapter 16 for more on air-and-hotel packages.

When airfares are low

Airlines offer incredible sales nowadays through their own Web sites. If airlines are duking it out on your route, undercutting each other with great low fares and setting new records for cheap seats, Priceline won't be able to touch the fares they're offering. And if a low-fare airline like Southwest or JetBlue keeps prices low on your route, Priceline probably won't be able to beat them.

On the other hand, if last-minute fares look sky-high or the cheap seats are all sold out, it's time for Priceline.

Airlines deliver some incredible deals during *low seasons* (times of the year when fewer people are flying) for various destinations. Priceline isn't about to beat most super-low winter fares to Europe, or summer fares to the Bahamas. Even if no competitive airfare sale is going on, airlines typically cool it with the Priceline seats when their regular prices are at rock bottom.

When your trip can't be booked on one airline or with two stops

In order for Priceline to book a ticket, you must be able to fly your whole route on a single, Priceline partner airline. You can change planes, but you must stay on the same airline or one of its codeshare partners. And you must get there with no more than two stops each way.

This rule is more complicated than it seems because of *codeshares* (when one airline pretends to be another airline that it's friends with, selling seats on the second airline using the first airline's flight numbers). US Airways and United, for example, pretend to be each other all the time. Priceline counts codeshares as one airline.

The easiest way to check if Priceline handles your route is to punch your airports and dates into Expedia (`www.expedia.com`). Scroll down to the detailed list of flights. If all the flights show multiple airlines or more than two stops each way (as in Figure 2-1), forget about using Priceline.

When you may have to cancel or change your trip

Priceline tickets are nonrefundable and nonchangeable. That's not quite as bad as it sounds, but you should treat it as if it is. In other words, don't bid on Priceline if you think you may have to cancel or change your flight for any reason at all.

Stay away, scaredy-cats

Nervous flyers in the days after September 11, 2001, got no pity from Priceline. Although airlines will generally refund your money if they cancel your flight, neither the airlines nor Priceline will help you if you have vague fears that air travel may be dangerous.

Priceline's travel insurance (see Chapter 3) provides some protection against illness, car accidents on the way to the airport, or terrorist attacks at your destination. And, of course, if your airline cancels your flight and can't put you on another one, Priceline will give you your money back.

Using Priceline to connect with a cruise is a bad idea. If your cruise is cancelled, you'll be left in the lurch unless you bought good third-party travel insurance, like Travel Guard's Cruise Guard product (www.travelguard.com). Priceline's airline-ticket travel insurance doesn't cover missed cruise connections.

Even if you don't have travel insurance, Priceline may make a one-time exception and refund your money. Asking is always worthwhile.

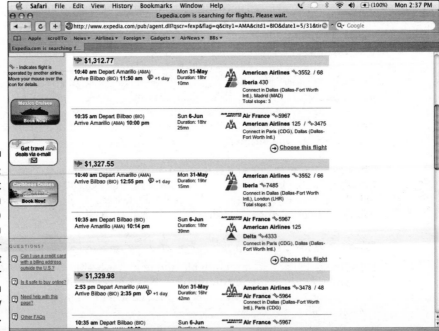

Figure 2-1: Forget about flying from Amarillo to Bilbao with Priceline — you can't get to your destination using only one airline.

If you want to book anything other than a standard round-trip flight

Priceline only books standard round-trip tickets. On Priceline, you can't buy a *one-way ticket* (a ticket taking you only from Point A to Point B), or a *three-legged ticket* (a ticket taking you from Point A to Point B to Point C, and then directly back to Point A), or an *open-jaw ticket* (a ticket taking you from Point A to Point B, and then from Point C back to Point A).

If one-way fares are very high on your route through the airlines, you can buy a round-trip ticket with Priceline and only use the first half. This strategy is called *throwaway ticketing,* because you're essentially using half of the ticket and throwing away the other half.

You can only throw away the *second* half of a ticket. If you miss the first half, your airline will automatically cancel the rest of your ticket.

Airlines hate throwaway ticketing. Even though it's legal for you to do, it lets you avoid insane airline fare policies. So airlines claim they'll dock your frequent-flier account if they catch you doing it. Realistically, they don't bother people who only rarely throw away tickets. To be on the safe side, don't give the airline your frequent-flier number if you plan to throw away your return ticket.

If you're someone Priceline won't accept

Sorry, kids: You must be 18 to fly solo with Priceline. That's because some airlines don't allow unaccompanied minors on the last flight of the day, and Priceline very well may put you on the last flight of the day. Under-18s can fly through Priceline if they're accompanied by someone older.

Priceline also rejects Canadians. It demands you have a credit card with a billing address in the United States, the United Kingdom, or one of the Pacific Rim countries where it does business.

Fortunately, many Canadians have found ways around Priceline's restrictions. One enterprising Canuck I spoke to managed to book 186 hotel nights with Priceline in an 18-month period. Turn to Chapter 18 for his secret.

For places Priceline usually doesn't fly

All Priceline flights must start in the United States (including Puerto Rico and the U.S. Virgin Islands). You can't use Priceline for flights *to* the United States from any other country, even Canada.

Don't bother with Priceline for tickets to India, Africa, or any but the largest South American and Asian cities. I've never seen a great Priceline deal to Australia. Eastern Europe is another weak area for Priceline.

Within the United States, if Northwest, Southwest, or Alaska Airlines dominates the city you're flying to, you're unlikely to find a great deal on Priceline. Those three airlines don't sell tickets through Priceline. So flights to Memphis, Minneapolis, and Nome will probably be pretty hard to find.

The nitty-gritty of flying with a Priceline ticket

Most airport procedures work just the same if you're flying on a Priceline ticket as if you're flying on any other ticket. You check in at the same counter, get the same seat assignment and fly on the same plane (of course!). You can even get *bumped* just like anyone else (which is when the airline sells too many tickets and you either volunteer to take a later flight or get forced onto one, in exchange for compensation).

But a few minor differences exist between your Priceline ticket and a non-Priceline ticket, mostly involving flying standby and using elite-flier privileges. They probably won't affect you, but I'd like you to know about them anyway.

Flying standby

If you want to pop on to an earlier flight on your day of travel, or slip onto a nonstop when you're ticketed for a one-stop flight, sometimes you can.

United Air Lines lets Priceline passengers stand by for earlier flights. Show up at the airport extra-early and tell the agent at the check-in counter that you'd like to stand by for an earlier flight. You'll be sent to the gate for the earlier flight, and if there's room, you're on your way.

For other airlines, allowing standby is entirely up to the agent you check in with. Technically, allowing standbys for Priceline customers is against airline policies, but it's been known to happen.

You have a better chance if you have carry-on luggage only, and you have an even better chance if you avoid the check-in counter, get your boarding pass from an electronic kiosk, go straight to the gate for the earlier flight, and try to persuade the gate agent to let you on board. Sometimes, it works.

Understanding upgrades and frequent-flier miles

Priceline tickets aren't eligible for frequent-flier miles, and I've never heard of anyone getting mileage on a Priceline trip. So forget about it.

Bumped in Barcelona

I got a round-trip ticket on Delta Airlines to Barcelona for $375 on Priceline. I came to the airport two hours before the flight, and when I got to the gate, I noticed there was a huge line at the counter — the flight was overbooked. So I offered up my seat. Not only did Delta give me $400 in flight credit for my ticket, it put me on an Air France flight that landed me in Barcelona only two hours later than I had planned. I actually *made* $25 on that ticket.

Elite fliers lose their upgrade privileges and, technically, aren't supposed to use priority check-in or boarding lines when they're flying on Priceline tickets. But realistically, you can still use your special line if you wave your elite card.

You can't buy upgrades to a Priceline ticket, but the all-powerful gate agents still have the power to upgrade you if they like you. Be nice to them, and see what happens.

Getting bumped

Priceline has no effect on whether you get bumped and, if you're smart, you can get more money in airline credits than you paid for your flight!

If you're interested in getting bumped:

1. **Show up at the airport about two hours before your flight.**

2. **Get to your departure gate as quickly as possible.**

3. **When the airline staff show up (usually 60 to 90 minutes before your flight), ask them if the flight is overbooked and whether they need people to be bumped.**

   Don't be shy!

4. **Ask what kind of compensation the airline is offering for passengers who are willing to be bumped to a later flight.**

   If they're offering a free ticket, find out if it's usable on any flight at any time, or only on a tiny number of seats on unpopular days.

5. **Make sure they'll be able to get you on another flight that pleases you.**

   Ideally, they should get you on a flight that arrives only a few hours later than your original flight.

6. **Sit back and enjoy your free ticket.**

Sleeping Tight in Priceline Hotels

Priceline can put you in 4-star hotels for 2-star prices, or even for less. I've saved thousands of dollars over the past five years using Priceline to book my rooms, and you can, too. But you need to go into Priceline with your eyes open, understanding what you can and can't guarantee. You'll find a lot more information on this topic in Chapter 9, but here's a quick rundown.

What you do and don't know about your hotel

It's no wonder Priceline's hotel business is booming. You give up relatively little to use Priceline for hotels, and the savings are huge.

When you bid on Priceline, you can choose your hotel's zone and its star level. A *zone* is a neighborhood or group of neighborhoods within a city. So you can demand that your hotel be downtown, or near the airport, or in a convenient suburb. Priceline's *star levels* let you lock down specific amenities or hotel brands. Do you demand luxury? Ask for a 4-star hotel, and you probably won't be disappointed.

You can get even more precise by going to BiddingForTravel.com (www.biddingfortravel.com) or BetterBidding.com (www.betterbidding.com). Those two sites list all the hotels their members win on Priceline, and you can get a pretty good idea of the four or five hotels you have the best chance of winning.

The one thing you can't pick, of course, is your specific hotel. Priceline adds and removes hotels from its lists all the time, so even if you've gotten the same hotel on three successive bids, you may get a completely different one for the fourth.

Feeling the love

A man I know proposed to his fiancée on a Priceline trip over Christmas 2003. First, he bagged airline tickets to Hawaii for $500, then got the 3-star Doubletree Alana for $56 per night. He called the hotel and told them he planned to propose. When he showed up, the hotel manager greeted him personally, showed him to an ocean-view room, and gave him goodie bags of local items. On Christmas night, the man brought his lady wine and roses, and she said yes.

His strategy for stretching pennies on his honeymoon? You bet — Priceline.

Bidding for hotels on Priceline requires a little bit of adventurousness. You must have an open mind to staying in a hotel you hadn't previously known about, maybe even on a block you hadn't expected.

When you shouldn't use Priceline

If you use Priceline to book a hotel, all you're guaranteed is a room. If you need a specific kind of room — such as a big room, or a nonsmoking room — or if you may need to cancel your room, Priceline isn't for you. Read these warnings to make sure you don't end up disappointed in your Priceline purchase.

When you're traveling as a family

Bringing a large brood? Priceline only guarantees space for two adults per room. Although many hotels will roll in a cot or even provide a sofa bed, you're taking the risk that you'll get a room with only one bed and no cot available.

Maximize your chances of getting a room that fits more than two people by bidding for a 2-star or 2½-star and checking which hotels in your zone people are winning on BiddingForTravel.com. In some zones, suite hotels appear frequently — and you can always fit three or four people in a suite. Alas, you can't be sure you'll get a suite, so bidding when you want one is always a bit of a gamble.

Never, ever, *ever* try to get a three-person room in New York, San Francisco, or downtown Chicago. All three cities are full of boutique hotels with closet-like rooms that barely fit two people.

When you need specific amenities

If you need a nonsmoking room, a first-floor room, a room with two beds, or a room in a specific location (for instance, you can't sleep if you're near the elevator), don't use Priceline.

Although you can usually get the kind of room you want, Priceline doesn't guarantee nonsmoking rooms, a specific number of beds, or any particular room location. See Chapter 9 for more on this topic.

In Priceline's defense, I've had hotels refuse my "guaranteed" requests even when I booked them over the hotel's own Web site.

When you think your plans may change

Just as with airline tickets, Priceline hotel reservations are nonrefundable. If you think you may have to cancel your room for any reason, buy Priceline's travel insurance (see Chapter 3) or just don't use Priceline at all.

Occasionally, Priceline makes one-time exceptions to its policy and refunds your money if things go dramatically wrong. Don't count on Priceline's generosity, though. You're better off thinking of Priceline rooms as totally nonrefundable, and to think of any refund as a potential gift.

When you're one of the people Priceline won't allow

If you're under 21, forget about using Priceline. Someone over 21 must be in each party of travelers staying at a Priceline hotel.

Residents of Canada also aren't supposed to be able to use Priceline, but plenty of Canadians have found ways around this rule. See Chapter 18 for more details.

Priceline for frequent guests

Signing up for hotels' frequent-guest programs really pays off with Priceline. Although you can't accumulate points on your Priceline room rate, you can get points for all the incidental purchases you make (like room service) and, in Hyatt hotels, your Priceline nights count toward qualifying for elite status.

Showing a frequent-guest card is the number-one thing you can do to get treated better on a Priceline reservation. Hotels respect room requests more often and even move bidders to club floors with bigger rooms and more amenities when Priceliners wield the power of frequent-guest programs.

Of course, nothing's guaranteed. But frequent-guest programs are free of charge to join, and the benefits are immense.

Driving Away for Less with Priceline Rental Cars

If you believe all rental cars are alike, you'll have a great time with Priceline. Priceline's cars come from five of the top U.S. car-rental firms: Hertz, Avis, Budget, National, and Alamo.

Hertz, Avis, and Budget commit to giving Priceline customers first-class service — they say you'll get the car you paid for, no matter when you arrive at the rental counter. Unfortunately, when I asked National and Alamo, they made no such assurances. But that shouldn't stop you from renting through Priceline — you just need to be on your toes to make sure you get the car you want (see Chapter 15).

Credit card versus debit card

Priceline will let you rent a car with either a credit card or a debit card. But using a debit card will reduce your chances of getting a car, because rental companies prefer credit cards.

Debit cards, otherwise known as *check cards,* take money directly from your checking account instead of charging it to an account you pay back later. Car-rental firms prefer credit cards because if you run off with their car, they can pursue you through your credit-card company.

Using a credit card protects you, too, because a federal law (the Fair Credit Billing Act) says you must get what you pay for when you use a credit card. So if your rental-car firm gets nasty, you can sic your credit-card company on them. You can't do that with a debit card.

Bottom line: If you can, use a credit card to book your car rental through Priceline.

Priceline lets you rent 11 types of cars, from economy to luxury. You can demand a convertible, or tool around in a pickup truck. You'll get your car at a time you request, in a location you want, with unlimited mileage included. For full details on Priceline's car options, see Chapter 14.

You can drive around the 50 states and Canada in your Priceline rental car. You just have to return it to the place you picked it up — Priceline doesn't allow one-way rentals.

Don't use Priceline if you plan to drive into Mexico. Four out of Priceline's five rental-car partners (all but Hertz) forbid you from driving into Mexico with a Priceline car, and there's no way to guarantee you'll get a Hertz rental.

When you should rent with Priceline

You can save the most with Priceline if:

- ✔ You're renting a bigger car, such as a mid-size or full-size vehicle.
- ✔ You need your car for several days.
- ✔ You're renting in the middle of the week (in other words, not picking up the car between Thursday evening and Sunday).

You can still find savings on smaller cars and weekend rentals. But rental-car companies' own Web sites and coupons can undercut Priceline's prices in those situations, so you have to be much more aware of competing rates.

When you should steer clear of Priceline

Like with hotels and airfares, there are a few situations in which renting cars through Priceline won't work for you. Check out the following sections to find out when you *shouldn't* get your rental car through Priceline.

When you need to pick up your car in an unusual location

Priceline lets you pick up your car at 190 airports in the 50 states, plus a few locations in the centers of cities. For example, you can pick your car up at BWI airport or in downtown Washington, D.C., but not in downtown Baltimore.

For a full list of cities where Priceline offers cars, go to `http://tickets.` `priceline.com/rentalcars/lang/en-us/city_list.asp`.

When you're under 25 years old

If you're over 25, you'll have no problem renting a car from Priceline.

Folks between 21 and 24 will find Priceline cars available in most cities, but not all. Of Priceline's rental-car partners, only Budget told me it will rent cars to 21- to 24-year-olds everywhere in the country. Avis said it will rent cars to those between 21 and 24 in New York state, Hertz nixed the youth crowd, and Alamo and National refused to say anything at all. So it's worth a try.

Kids between 18 and 20 can rent cars in New York City on Priceline. That includes LaGuardia and JFK airports, but not Newark Airport — that one's in New Jersey.

When you need a one-way rental

Priceline requires you to return your car to the same place you picked it up. So if you want to drive one-way cross-country, Priceline isn't for you.

When you think your plans may change

You guessed it: Just like hotels and airline tickets, Priceline car rentals are prepaid, nonrefundable, and nonchangeable. If you think your cousin Cliff may be able to lend you his car, but you won't know until you arrive in Miami, don't rent a car through Priceline.

If you're disabled

Priceline can't guarantee a car with hand controls. It'll try to find one for you, but if you need a car with hand controls, trying probably isn't good enough. Stay away from Priceline if you're disabled.

Understanding insurance and liability

Priceline rentals don't come with insurance. That puts you at the mercy of your rental-car company, which may charge huge sums of money for insurance.

If you own a car and have an insurance policy, you're probably covered for damage to a rental car within the United States (but not in Canada) and liability in case a passenger is injured. *Remember:* Be sure to check with your insurance company to be sure.

Some credit cards also give you some insurance coverage when you're renting a car; American Express is especially good with this.

Before you book with Priceline, find out which of your credit cards offers the best coverage. Call up your card issuer at the phone number on the back of the card and ask:

- ✔ Does it cover your destination?
- ✔ Will it cover additional drivers?
- ✔ How much liability coverage will it include if a crash injures passengers?

Then book your Priceline reservation with the credit card offering the best coverage.

Priceline for elite renters

Elite members of rental-car loyalty clubs give up all their privileges when they rent through Priceline. Technically, you're not supposed to be able to use express check-in, and you definitely won't get frequent-flier miles, loyalty points, or guaranteed upgrades.

Rental-car service issues

A few readers of Frommer's Travel Guides (published by Wiley) have reported bad attitudes from Alamo staff when renting cars through Priceline. When I confronted Alamo, it refused to offer any assurances that Priceliners *wouldn't* be treated as second-class citizens.

That said, the vast majority of Priceline rentals go well — and if you don't get what you paid for, you can enlist Priceline's help. See Chapter 15 for more.

Realistically, waving a gold renter card will still get you into the special express line. But all the other bonuses are still out. When you think about how much you're saving on Priceline, factor in the loss of your automatic upgrade.

Vacations: Paying for Knowledge

Priceline bundles together hotels, airfare, and rental cars into vacation packages — and then charges a big premium for telling you the name of your hotel and your exact flight times.

With Priceline's vacation packages, you choose your exact hotel by name. You find out in advance what you'll pay for a rental car, and you can often find out which airline you'll be flying on, at what times, before you plunk down your cash.

Sounds great, huh? Not so much. Priceline's partners tie savings to mystery. No mystery, no savings. Priceline's package prices compete well with other online travel agencies, but they're much higher than the prices you'd pay by bidding for your hotel, airfare, and car rental separately.

Still, there are situations in which you may want to buy a Priceline package. If Priceline offers a mystery airfare with your guaranteed hotel, you'll probably save money over booking your vacation elsewhere — though shopping around is always a good idea. Priceline's Weekender option, available for last-minute trips, guarantees you enough time to have fun at your destination, something normal Priceline airfare bidding can't provide.

Priceline Mortgages

Priceline sells mortgages? What's up with that?

Long ago, Priceline sold all sorts of crazy stuff. Groceries, gasoline, long-distance phone calls. Then the Internet bust hit, and Priceline came to its senses. But the mortgages remain.

The good: Low rates

Priceline sells mortgages in a partnership with EverBank, a Florida-based bank. (Priceline Mortgage is a joint venture between Priceline.com and EverBank.) EverBank is on the level, and Priceline Mortgage does, indeed, deliver really, really low rates and fees. It can't knock 40 percent off the cost of your mortgage, but home buyers have reported saving up to $1,500 in fees over local lenders.

Hey, where are the cruises?

Priceline sells cruises, but I don't cover them in this book. Priceline doesn't let you name your own price for cruises — it just made a deal with a regular, ordinary travel agency to sell cruises on its site. If you're looking for a cruise, pick up *Cruise Vacations For Dummies 2005* by Fran Wenograd Golden and Jerry Brown (published by Wiley). It's a great book all about cruises.

The bad: Slow responses

Borrowers also say Priceline Mortgage takes forever to close and can be extremely difficult to get in touch with. It's understaffed and overworked.

Only consider using Priceline Mortgage if you have at least 45 days to close, you're willing to keep your own library of documentation, and you're willing to pursue its processing people like a hawk.

Fortunately, Priceline doesn't lock you in to a loan the way it does with hotels, car rentals, and airfare. That'd be pretty insane, considering the 30-year commitment you're embarking on! You can back out with a $250 penalty.

Chapter 3

Knowing the Rules and Your Rights

Sometimes you have to fight the power. You have to stick it to the Man, and you have to stand up for your rights.

The good news is, as a Priceline traveler, you have the same rights as every other traveler (with a few exceptions). Sometimes those rights aren't easy to exercise, though. Hotel and car-rental desks can be staffed by petty tyrants more interested in proving their own superiority than giving you the room or car you deserve.

In this chapter, I tell you exactly what your rights are when you're dealing with airlines, hotels, car-rental firms, and Priceline itself. You discover how to extend your rights with travel insurance, and when to stand up and demand your due.

Your Rights as a Traveler

Believe it or not, you don't actually have the right to get what you paid for — but this has nothing to do with Priceline. Built in to the fine print of most travel purchases is the power to switch things around on you. Airlines can cancel your flights, hotels can move you to an entirely different building, and car-rental firms can change your ride.

According to John Hawks, executive director of the nonprofit Consumer Travel Rights Center, you have the right to get something *roughly equivalent to* what you paid for. So airlines must get you to your destination, hotels must put you up in a room as good as the one you bought, and car-rental firms must put you in a car at least as big as the one you asked for.

Airlines

Between Priceline's guarantees, airlines' customer-service contracts, and the law, there are a few things you can be assured of when you fly.

What Priceline guarantees you

Priceline guarantees you a ticket between airports you agreed upon, on a date you agreed upon. Unless you specifically agreed otherwise, you know your ticket:

- ✔ Will be on one of Priceline's partner airlines (for a full list, see Chapter 5)
- ✔ Will only force you to change planes once (though you can agree to two connections)
- ✔ Will only put you on jet planes (though you can agree to fly on propeller planes)

If you're flying within the United States, you're also guaranteed:

- ✔ No layover will last longer than three hours.
- ✔ Your flight will leave between 6 a.m. and 10 p.m. (though you can agree to fly at other times).

If the ticket you get violates any of these conditions, you're entitled to a refund from Priceline.

Your rights as a ticket holder

When you're holding a ticket (or an e-ticket receipt), you have the same rights as any ticket holder.

Your rights are listed in your airline's legally-binding Contract of Carriage, as well as by a non-binding Customer Service Commitment that all airlines put into place under federal pressure in late 1999. The Contracts of Carriage and Customer Service Commitments cover issues including:

✔ What the airline will do if your flight is delayed, your flight is cancelled, or you're involuntarily bumped

✔ What the airline will do if your plane gets stuck on the tarmac

✔ Your rights regarding lost, damaged, or delayed luggage

To find your airline's Contract of Carriage:

1. **Go to** www.onetravel.com.

2. **Click on Rules of the Air on the left-hand side.**

3. **Select your airline using the Links to Each Airline's Contract of Carriage drop-down list.**

4. **Click Go.**

On international flights, different regulations apply, and the contract is referred to as the *tariff rules*. Foreign carriers usually keep a copy of the tariff rules at city and airport ticket offices.

Your rights if your plane is delayed or your flight is cancelled

If your airline cancels or changes your flight more than a day before it's scheduled to leave, it has to put you on another flight — but that's about it. If it sticks you on a flight you don't want, you can call the airline and beg. Hopefully, it'll be merciful.

I bought a ticket from San Francisco to Las Vegas on US Airways a few months before I wanted to travel. About a month before my flight, US Airways called me to tell me it had cancelled my very pleasant 8:30 a.m. flight and moved me back to a very *un*pleasant 6:35 a.m. flight. I begged, I pleaded, but alas, I was at US Airways's mercy.

If your airline changes your schedule and it violates the terms of your Priceline bid — too many connections, say, or a domestic layover of more than three hours — Priceline will usually refund your ticket. Priceline isn't legally required to do so, but it's usually pretty understanding in these cases.

If you get to the airport and *then* find out your flight is delayed or cancelled, you have a lot more power — but you may have to stand up for your rights.

Each airline's Contract of Carriage has a rule, commonly referred to as "Rule 240" (though the lawyers call it something else). Rule 240 explains what an airline owes you if your flight is delayed or cancelled. Rule 240 is your legal right, and you should demand what it allows.

The major airlines' Rule 240 contracts are quite similar; they go something like this: If a flight is delayed or cancelled and the delay is *not* due to weather, labor disputes, terrorism, or certain other *force majeure events* (events that could not have been reasonably anticipated or controlled):

- ✔ **The airline *must* confirm you on its next flight to your destination on which space is available, at no extra cost.**

- ✔ **If that flight is not acceptable to you, the airline must confirm you on another airline's flight, at no extra cost.**

- ✔ **If none of these options are acceptable, the airline must refund your ticket, even if it's "nonrefundable," with no penalty.**

- ✔ **If a flight is diverted to an unscheduled point and the layover is expected to exceed four hours between 10 p.m. and 6 a.m., the airline must provide you with hotel accommodations.** If the flight is delayed at your origination or destination point, or diverted to an airport within the same metro area as your destination, the airline is not required to do so. The non-binding Customer Service Commitment may say the airline will provide accommodations if there's a delay caused by events within its control.

The ultimate force majeure

At 9 a.m. Eastern time, on September 11, 2001, I was on a plane traveling from Glasgow to New York, with a scheduled stop in Reykjavik, Iceland. I had bought my ticket on Priceline.

Landing in Iceland, I discovered all flights to the United States were cancelled. I stayed in Iceland for two and a half days; one night's hotel was paid for by the airline, and the second night was at a 50 percent discount. The Hotel Loftleidir in Reykjavik was set up as a center for displaced Americans, and Icelandair's second-in-command updated us in person every few hours on the status of American air space — and on the status of New York.

The moment the United States reopened its airspace, the stranded Americans hustled to the airport and jumped on to planes to North America. But too late! The FAA closed the airspace while we were over Greenland and forced us to land at Mirabel Airport, north of Montreal, Canada.

Icelandair then rustled up buses to drive American passengers across the border. I declined the eight-hour, midnight bus ride, went downtown, had a steak sandwich, crashed at a friend's house, and took Amtrak home the next day.

The September 11 attacks were known in the airline industry as *a force majeure* (an event that could not have been reasonably anticipated or controlled). All bets are off during a force majeure event. Icelandair wasn't required to do any of the things it did for me and the other passengers on September 11 — it wasn't even legally required to get me to my destination. But Icelandair decided to help us out anyway, and it didn't care how we'd bought our tickets.

Notice that Rule 240s almost never requires an airline to pay for meals, phone calls or other incidental expenses incurred because of a delay. But airlines may do so to show they love their customers. Be nice, be sympathetic, and ask. *Remember:* The gate agents are as harassed as you are, but their job is to help you.

If a delay causes you to miss a connection, the airline must put you on the next available flight.

Hotels

Priceline guarantees you a room of a certain star level in a certain zone of your destination city. It guarantees the room will be available no matter how late you arrive, and it guarantees the room will sleep two adults.

The star level of the hotel guarantees specific amenities. For example, a Resort-level hotel in a beachfront area must have beach access. For a full list of star-level guarantees, see Chapter 10.

It also guarantees that your room will be a standard, *run of house* room (in other words, the most common type of room or whatever's available at the time), not a special closet-sized room assigned only to Priceline customers. For example, in a document for hotel managers posted to the Web (www.utellportal.com/marketing/priceline), the Utell chain says "You will place the Priceline guest in a room comparable to (or better than) your 'best available' room assignment. You will welcome the Priceline guest just as you would welcome any other valued guest."

No other hotel chains have publicly released similar statements, but the Utell statement dovetails with what I've heard from Priceline in the past about what it tells its hotel partners.

Priceline doesn't guarantee how many beds the room will have — it could have one or two beds. It doesn't guarantee that it will be nonsmoking, accessible to the disabled, or in any specific location in the hotel. Your room could be smoky and sandwiched between the elevator and the ice machine.

If there's no room at the inn, the hotel must move you to another hotel of the same star level or higher, in the same zone of the city, and it must pay for your transportation to the new hotel.

Elite fliers, head to the back

The benefits of elite-flier status are privileges, not rights, and when you book on Priceline, you give them up. That means you can't use your elite-level upgrades to bump a Priceline ticket to business class and, technically, you're not supposed to use the elite check-in or priority boarding lines — though I've never heard of an airline stopping an elite flier from using the special lines.

Car rentals

As a Priceline customer, you have a prepaid, guaranteed car reservation for a particular class of car. That means the car-rental company must have a car available for you, of the class you requested, at the time you requested it.

If no car of the size you requested is available, it must upgrade you to the next largest model of car available.

If only smaller cars are available, it must offer the options of a partial refund or sending you to another rental company of its choice, where you will get your originally requested car at its expense.

If no cars at all are available, it must offer you a full refund or send you to another rental company and pay for your car there.

Buying Priceline's Travel Insurance

Priceline's harsh conditions make many people nervous. Travel insurance gives you peace of mind. Although Priceline occasionally makes exceptions to its strict no-refund policies, without insurance you're at Priceline's mercy.

Priceline sells very basic travel insurance, which can get you a refund on your Priceline tickets if certain things go wrong. American Home Assurance Company (AHAC), a well-known and solid insurer, provides the insurance coverage.

Priceline's insurance only covers items you bought through Priceline. So if you booked a Priceline air ticket and booked a cruise through someone else, Priceline's insurance only protects your air ticket — you're still on the hook for the cruise.

Priceline's rates for coverage are pretty reasonable, about the same as what other major insurers charge:

- ✔ For air tickets, insurance costs $15 per ticket domestic, $25 per ticket international.

- ✔ For hotel rooms, insurance costs $5 per room per night.

- ✔ For packages, insurance costs will vary depending on the destination (domestic versus international), the number of hotel-room nights, and the number of rental-car days. In order to figure out the rates, you need to add up the amounts listed earlier in this list for the air ticket per person, the amounts listed for the number of hotel nights, plus $1 per day for the rental car. (Priceline will count a three-night stay as four rental-car days, because rental-car days are based on an exact 24-hour period.)

   For example, a three-night package for two people sharing one room in Los Angeles will be $2 \times \$15$ (air), or $30, plus $3 \times \$5$ (hotel), or $15, plus $4 extra (if you include a rental car), for a total of $49. A seven-night package to London for a family of four in two rooms would be $4 \times \$25$ (air), or $100, plus $7 \times 2 \times \$5$ (hotel), or $170, for a total of $170.

Note: You can't buy insurance for just a rental car.

The insurance policy also gives you:

- ✔ Up to $1,500 in medical benefits, and money to send your injured or dead body back from a foreign country to the United States if necessary. (Cheery, isn't it?)

- ✔ Up to $500 if your baggage is damaged, lost, or stolen (and you have a police report or similar document from your airline).

- ✔ A 24-hour hotline to suggest doctors, lawyers, and ways to transfer money abroad.

Whew! You're covered

Priceline's insurance gets you a refund if you miss your trip because:

- ✔ You, a traveling companion, or an immediate family member gets injured, gets sick, or dies (and you have a doctor's note saying you can't travel).

- ✔ Your host at your destination is hospitalized or dies (for air tickets only).

- ✔ You get in a car crash on the way to the airport (and you have a police report).

✔ You're called up for jury duty or subpoenaed.

✔ The U.S. State Department tells Americans to avoid traveling to your destination.

✔ A terrorist act or natural disaster happens at your home or destination.

✔ Your airport terminal closes because of a security breach that's later reported on in the press.

Uh-oh! You're not covered

Priceline's insurance *doesn't* protect you from missing your trip because of:

✔ Health problems caused by preexisting medical conditions. In other words, if you have diabetes, go into insulin shock, and miss your trip, you *aren't* covered.

✔ Getting called up to active duty in the National Guard or Army Reserve

✔ War, "whether declared or not" (in AHAC's words)

✔ Giving birth, unless your pregnancy has "complications"

✔ Your airline, hotel, or car-rental company going bankrupt

✔ Fears about air travel caused by war or acts of terrorism

Travel Guard: The more comprehensive alternative

If you want more protection, turn to Travel Guard (www.travelguard.com), the largest travel insurer in the United States. It offers a lot more coverage than Priceline's policy, for a little more money, and it will insure tickets and rooms bought through Priceline. Travel Guard's prices vary depending on how much you paid for your trip, where you live and how old you are, but here are some examples, based on a 30-ish New Yorker we'll call "Tess the Traveler":

✔ For $19, Travel Guard will protect Tess's $250 airline ticket against an airline going bankrupt, allow her to cancel because of preexisting medical conditions, and give her up to $100 if she's delayed more than 12 hours. But it won't give her all that gruesome foreign medical and dead-body-transportation insurance.

✔ For $30 on a $450 trip, it will add in $25,000 of medical coverage, boost Tess's trip-delay coverage to $100 per day for ten days of delay, and give her up to $200 if her baggage takes more than 24 hours to show up.

✔ For $42 on a $450 trip, Tess will get even beefier coverage plus a $250 payment if she cancels just because she changed her mind.

Buy your Travel Guard coverage the same day you buy your ticket from Priceline. If you wait too long to buy insurance, you lose some coverage.

Making a claim

To claim money back from Priceline's insurance company, *immediately* send an e-mail to aigis.priceline@aig.com. Include your name and the state you live in, and describe what went wrong. You can also call the insurance company at 877-399-7765 (toll-free), or call collect from overseas at 713-267-3365.

Get official documentation for any claim you want to make. Police reports, doctors' notes, hospital admissions forms, letters from your airline saying your bags were lost — insurance companies don't like to take your word on things. When you make your claim, make sure you can back it up.

You must send in your claim less than 20 days after things go wrong, or no money for you!

The insurance company is not your friend. Insurance companies will do everything they can to avoid paying your claim. Your job is to bury them under documentation so they can't possibly refuse your claim.

Priceline, Privacy, and Security

Priceline says it's serious about your privacy. It keeps your personal data in "a single, secure database, accessible only by Priceline.com." It doesn't give your data to other companies without your permission. To read Priceline's full privacy policy, go to http://travel.priceline.com/privacypolicy/privacypolicy.asp.

Priceline keeps your e-mail address and says it'll send you e-mails about its services occasionally. It marks all its e-mails as coming from Priceline and gives you the option to unsubscribe in every e-mail. If you check the box agreeing to receive more e-mail on your Bid Review Page when you're bidding, you'll get more e-mail.

Priceline protects your credit-card number with 128-bit SSL (Secure Socket Layer) encryption, the same standard security system most major online retailers use.

Priceline and its advertisers use *cookies,* tiny bits of text saved in your Web browser, to track your movements around the site. It says it doesn't attach these cookies to any personally identifiable information, like your name or your phone number. If you'd prefer to turn your cookies off, though, Priceline will still work perfectly well. To find out how to turn your cookies off, go to http://travel.priceline.com/privacypolicy/cookies.asp.

Spamline?

Priceline doesn't give your address to spammers. But even if you use a special e-mail address only for Priceline, you'll probably get hit by spam. What's up with that?

Priceline isn't to blame here. Spammers are smart. They can guess your e-mail address without any help from Priceline, or grab your address off Priceline's e-mails as they travel through the Internet. To find out how to head off spammers, pick up *Fighting Spam For Dummies* by John R. Levine, Margaret Levine Young, and Ray Everett-Church (published by Wiley).

If you do your shopping on an unprotected wireless network, hackers can pluck your personal details out of the air before they get to the Internet. To shop safely, encrypt your home wireless network. If that sounds confusing, read *Wireless Home Networking For Dummies* by Danny Briere, Walter R. Bruce III, and Pat Hurley (published by Wiley).

Priceline's privacy policy is solid, and you don't have to worry about Priceline spreading your data around. You're in far more danger from viruses on your machine and insecurities in your home network than you are from anything Priceline may do.

When Something Goes Wrong

No matter how hard you try to make things work, things sometimes go wrong. Fortunately, you have plenty of places to turn.

Knowing who to complain to

Almost always, you should first turn to Priceline to make a complaint. They're the only people who can give you your money back. If an airline, hotel, or car-rental firm switches things on you, though, you should go to the travel supplier first.

So if Priceline gives you a perfectly good airline ticket but your airline cancels your flight and puts you on another one, turn to the airline first. Or if you arrive at a car-rental counter and it says it has no cars for you, demand to speak to a manager before you call Priceline.

Contacting Priceline

Complaining to Priceline takes some effort. You usually have to send a few e-mails or make a few phone calls before you get satisfaction. Try e-mail first (if you can), then follow up on the phone.

Via e-mail

Priceline suggests you always try to e-mail first. If you have the time — if you're not standing dazed in an airport terminal or in front of a car-rental counter — that's a good idea, because e-mailing minimizes the time you'll spend on hold and maximizes the documentation you can send. Here's how to e-mail Priceline:

1. **On Priceline's home page, click the Help link in the upper-right-hand corner.**

2. **Select the Contact Us tab.**

3. **Fill out the e-mail form shown in Figure 3-1.**

4. **Click Next.**

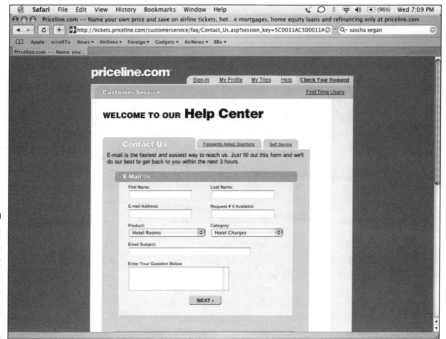

Figure 3-1:
Make your first contact with Priceline using this e-mail form.

Priceline will almost always get back to you within a few hours, though more often than not, the message will be from an unhelpful customer-service drone refusing whatever you requested. After two or three volleys of e-mails, if the customer-service person is still unhelpful, you can usually demand and receive the e-mail address of a Priceline customer-service vice president. The VPs have the power to make all things better.

Via phone

Priceline suggests you only call *after* e-mailing. That's wise, because calling Priceline takes a boatload of patience. Its phone system seems designed to infuriate people as much as possible.

Priceline's main customer-service number is 800-774-2354. Priceline will try to trap you in an endless loop, so here's the way out (as of this writing):

1. **Choose option 1, "for help with Priceline's travel-related services."**

2. **Choose option 1, "calling regarding an offer you have already submitted."**

3. **Enter your Priceline bid request number and hit the # button on your phone.**

4. **Enter your phone number and hit the # button on your phone.**

5. **Wait through about a minute of babble.**

6. **Choose option 4, "for all other requests."**

7. **Choose option 1, "for further assistance."**

   Victory! You're now on hold for a real, human operator.

Getting to an operator is only half the battle. If Priceline's first-level customer-service drone can't help you, ask for a manager — or for the direct phone number or e-mail address of a Priceline customer-service VP.

Ask and ye shall receive

When Michael G. of Cincinnati tried to turn on his faucet at the 4-star Francis Marion Hotel in Charleston, South Carolina, nothing came out. He complained to the hotel management, and they said the water would be out for several hours — but that he should ask Priceline for a one-night refund. Upon getting home, he contacted Priceline and told them the problem, and they said he'd get a refund for one night of his stay. True to their word, Priceline kicked some money back to Michael's credit card about a month later.

Complaining to the authorities

If things go wrong on your trip and Priceline doesn't take your side, you still have plenty of places to turn: your credit-card company, the Better Business Bureau, consumer advocates, journalists, and even the government.

Your credit-card company

If Priceline can't help you, your credit-card company may be able to. The Fair Credit Billing Act, a federal law, says credit-card companies must give you your money back if you don't get what you paid for.

Call your credit-card company at the phone number on the back of your card and ask for a "chargeback" of your Priceline charge. Explain what went wrong, and supply documentation and printouts or screenshots of Priceline's confirmation page if the company requests (see the nearby sidebar for information on how to take screenshots).

American Express backs its customers most strongly among the major credit-card companies, according to John Hawks, executive director of the Consumer Travel Rights Center. Visa and MasterCard are also pretty good, he says.

The Better Business Bureau

The Better Business Bureau (BBB) doesn't have any power to force Priceline, airlines, or hotels to straighten up and fly right, but most companies don't want to be on the BBB's bad side.

Generally, if you have a problem and you aren't getting anywhere with the offending company itself, you should ask the BBB to try to arrange a refund for you. Include your full name and address with your complaint, and include the offending company's name and phone number. Make your complaint polite and detailed. File a complaint with the BBB by using this online form http://complaints.bbb.org/welcome.asp.

Consumer travel advocates

If Priceline, your credit-card company, and the BBB turn you down, turn to professional journalists who like to help people fight big corporations. No, don't e-mail me. Instead, try independent ombudsman Christopher Elliott at triprights.com (http://triprights.com); e-mail him at christopher@elliott.org. Or send a snail-mail letter to the *Condé Nast Traveler* Ombudsman at Ombudsman, *Condé Nast Traveler,* 4 Times Square, New York, NY 10036.

Screenshots: Your weapon of proof

Screenshots can provide proof of the problems you're having, but in order to use them, you have to know how to take them.

If you're working in Windows, follow these steps:

1. **With the window that you'd like to take a screenshot of open and completely visible, press Alt+PrtScn.**

   Nothing happens, but don't worry.

2. **Go to Start⇨(All) Programs⇨Accessories⇨ Paint.**

3. **Choose Edit⇨Paste (or press Ctrl+V).**

4. **Choose File⇨Save to save the file on your computer.**

If you're on a Mac, follow these steps:

1. **With the window that you'd like to take a screenshot of open and completely visible, press Apple+Shift+3.**

   You'll hear a noise like a camera shutter clicking.

2. **Go to your desktop.**

3. **Look for a file called Picture 1 (or Picture 2, or Picture with any number after it).**

4. **Double-click on the Picture file with the highest number.**

   It should pop open and be your screenshot. If it is, rename it as something more useful, like "Priceline Screenshot." If it isn't, try double-clicking on the other Picture files until you find the right one, and then rename it.

Many local TV news stations and newspapers also employ consumer advocates. Try calling your local newspaper and TV news stations and asking them if they have anyone who handles consumers' problems with big businesses.

Legal advocates

Collecting money from airlines, hotels, and car-rental firms through the courts is very difficult, according to John Hawks of the Consumer Travel Rights Center (CRTC; www.mytravelrights.com). But if you're really determined, you can take companies to small-claims court to get your money back. For more legal tips, contact the CRTC at info@mytravelrights.com or 859-269-9739.

U.S. Department of Transportation

The U.S. Department of Transportation (DOT; www.dot.gov) collects complaints against airlines and summarizes them in monthly reports. It can't help you solve your individual problem, but sending your issues to the DOT is still a good idea. Its statistics end up as weapons in the hands of journalists and politicians who want to take potshots at the airlines.

Mail your complaint and supporting documents to the Department of Transportation, Aviation Consumer Protection Division, 400 Seventh St. SW, Room 4107, Washington, DC 20590. You can also call the DOT at 202-366-2220.

Chapter 4

The Basics of Bidding

. . . .

In This Chapter

▶ Bidding for flights, hotel rooms, and cars

▶ Buying vacations and mortgages

▶ Knowing how to use Priceline if you're not based in the United States

. . . .

*I*mpatient? I understand. Priceline can help you save thousands of dollars on flights, hotels, and rental cars. With Priceline, you can take trips you never dreamed of before. You can stay in plush hotels for youth-hostel prices, and you can jump on last-minute flights at prices normally reserved for early birds.

In this chapter, you get a whirlwind tour of Priceline bidding. You won't become a truly informed bidder yet — for that, you'll have to read on. But you'll be able to zip through the bidding process and maybe nab yourself a bargain.

Knowing the Two Easy Steps of Priceline Bidding

I can sum up this book in two steps. Hear that, editors? Now I don't have to write the other 359 pages!

1. **Find the lowest prices you can elsewhere on the Web.**

2. **Bid lower on Priceline.**

That first step is critically important, because Priceline doesn't steer you toward a good deal. It would be perfectly happy for you to get a *lousy* deal — that way, Priceline and its airline/hotel/rental-car partners make tons of money. But you can get some terrific rates if you shop around, and then bid lower on Priceline.

Bidding for Flights

Airline tickets were Priceline's first product, and they're still Priceline's most notorious. Priceline requires a lot of flexibility if you want to save money on airline tickets. You must agree to fly at almost any time of day, you must agree to change planes if necessary, and you must agree to plunk down your money before knowing the exact details of your flight.

In exchange, Priceline will put you on a major full-service airline and get you to your destination. How much savings that's worth is up to you. On normally-expensive routes and last-minute flights, you can save up to 40 percent over fares you find elsewhere.

Checking out the competition

Nowadays, Priceline doesn't always have the lowest fares. Airlines and other travel agencies often undercut Priceline, especially on competitive routes or when you're looking far in advance.

So smart searching is key if you intend to use Priceline for flights. At the very least, check out prices on Expedia (www.expedia.com), Orbitz (www.orbitz.com), Travelocity (www.travelocity.com), SideStep (www.sidestep.com), and a few airline sites. Use the sites' flexible-dates option if it's available. By changing your departure or arrival date by just one day, you may find much lower fares.

Priceline doesn't use low-fare airlines like Southwest and JetBlue, so if one of those airlines has a great fare, you won't find it on Priceline.

Yes, that's a lot of homework. But it's the only way to guarantee you'll get the best possible fare. Only when you've exhaustively searched the rest of the Internet can you safely turn to Priceline and ask for a lower price.

Placing a bid on a flight

Bidding and rebidding for your flight is pretty simple. Just make sure to read all the fine print and take it seriously. I take you through a flight bidding process in depth in Chapter 7. For now, here's a quick explanation of how it works:

    1. Go to Priceline's homepage, www.priceline.com, **and click on Airfare.**

2. **Enter the cities you want to leave from and arrive in, your travel dates, and how many people are traveling.**

   Along with its Name Your Own Price service, Priceline also owns a "normal" travel agency, Lowestfare.com. Priceline will show you various fares from Lowestfare.com — but those are just a smokescreen.

3. **Click on Name Your Own Price to continue bidding.**

4. **Choose the airports you want to leave from and arrive in, name your own price, and enter your name.**

   Not all of Priceline's airports are near the town you select, so you need to be smart about which airports you choose. In general, you can save 40 percent or more off last-minute or unusually high fares you find elsewhere. When calculating your bid, check out what low-season or advance-purchase fares are to your destination, and think about how much you need to save to put up with Priceline's restrictions.

   Don't just think about what you paid on some flight last year. Look and see what the prices are today.

   After you put in your details, Priceline will come back with its most important screen, the Please Review Your Request screen (shown in Figure 4-1).

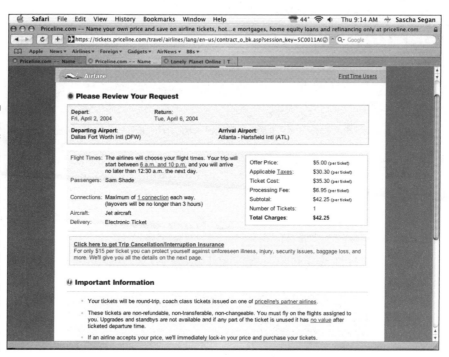

Figure 4-1: Pay lots of attention to what you're signing up for when you bid for a flight, because you can't back out after you've punched in your credit-card details.

5. **Make sure everything on the Please Review Your Request screen is correct.**

   If you make a mistake, Priceline won't fix it for you!

6. **If you're satisfied with your bid, make sure you've read all the points in the "Important Information" section, and then enter your credit-card details.**

   Now you've put your money down — you're required to accept whatever Priceline gives you.

   Priceline will accept your bid, reject your bid, or make a counteroffer where it suggests a price that would work.

If Priceline rejects your bid, you can bid again by changing some aspect of your trip — adding a possible airport, for instance, or agreeing to switch planes twice. That doesn't mean you'll *have* to switch planes twice — just that the option is open. Then you can try again. If it gives you a counteroffer, sometimes you can undercut the counteroffer by a few dollars and still win your flight.

Congratulations! You've just saved a bundle with Priceline.

Bidding for Hotels

Huge savings and few tradeoffs make bidding for hotels a no-brainer. Priceline's hotel business is booming, as thousands of travelers discover it's often possible to lie down in a plush, $200-per-night room for $60 or less.

You can't pick your exact hotel with Priceline, but you can pick its neighborhood zone and star level. For most people, that's enough. After all, as long as you're in a 4-star hotel near Times Square, it doesn't matter all that much which 4-star Times Square hotel you're in.

Figuring out the best rates

Just like with flights, you must scope out the lay of the land before you start bidding. That means checking out rates on several major travel-agency sites and hotel chains' own sites, which often (but not always) have the lowest rates of all — outside Priceline. Unlike with flights, Priceline will almost always beat everyone else's rates for hotels. But you need to see what the lowest rates are elsewhere to make sure you don't overbid.

For a full list of sites to check, turn to Chapter 20.

Bidding for your hotel

You'll be happy with your Priceline hotel room if you stay clear on two things: neighborhood zones and star levels. The zones, strictly defined with maps, show where you may get your hotel. Make sure you're comfortable with every corner of the zone you choose. If a little tail of your zone crosses a highway, remember you may get a hotel on the little tail's side of the highway.

Priceline defines star levels in terms of amenities, like whether the hotel has room service (guaranteed for 3-star hotels or higher) or a pool (guaranteed for Resort-level hotels only). Although star levels usually correspond to hotel brands — most Courtyard by Marriotts are 2½-star hotels, for instance — many brands have individual hotels in two neighboring star levels.

In Chapter 11, I cover bidding on a hotel room in more depth, but here are the basics:

1. **Go to Priceline's home page, www.priceline.com, and click on Hotels.**

2. **Enter the city you're traveling to, your check-in and check-out dates, and how many rooms you want.**

   Priceline only guarantees space for two people per room, so if you have four people, that means you need two rooms.

3. **Select the neighborhood zones where you want to stay.**

   Ignore the zone names; the maps are all that matters (see Figure 4-2). To see detailed maps of Priceline's zones, click on Area Details next to the zone name. For some suggestions of popular zones, see Chapters 21 and 22.

4. **Select the highest star level you hope to afford.**

   You may get a hotel of your selected star level or higher. If you're curious as to what the star levels mean, click on the linked star ratings, such as "4-Star Deluxe."

5. **Enter your price and the names of the people checking into each room.**

   Ignore Priceline's "suggested retail prices" (these are *not* suggested bid amounts), and base your bid on the prices you found while searching the Web.

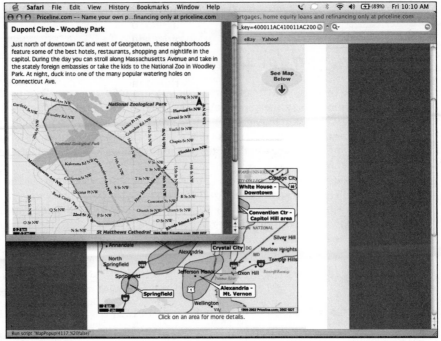

Figure 4-2:
Pay very close attention to Priceline's map of your hotel zone. You're committing to taking a hotel anywhere in the shaded area on the map.

Each room must have one person over age 21 staying in it, so if you're booking one room for Mom and Dad and one for the kids, enter one parent's name in one of the rooms, and the other parent's name in the other.

6. **If Priceline tells you that you're bidding too low, ignore it and keep going.**

7. **Pore over the Please Review Your Request screen showing details of your bid.**

   When you agree here and enter your credit-card details, you can't go back.

8. **Make sure you've read all the points under the "Important Information" section, and then enter your initials at the bottom of the screen and continue.**

9. **Enter your credit-card details and submit your bid.**

   Now you're locked in: You're committed to taking any room Priceline can find for you of your star level, in your neighborhood zone.

   Priceline will reject your bid, accept it, or make a counteroffer where it suggests a price that may work.

If Priceline accepts your bid, you have a room. Just don't tell the other folks staying at your hotel how much you paid, or they'll get awfully jealous. If Priceline rejects your bid, you can bid again by adding another neighborhood, lowering your star-level standards, or waiting 72 hours. If you add a neighborhood or lower your standards, make sure to check competing prices again, because rates in your new neighborhood may be much higher or lower than the ones in the zones you originally bid. If Priceline makes a counteroffer, you have to decide whether the counteroffer is a good deal. Priceline will often accept bids slightly less than its counteroffer.

Congratulations! You can now sleep sweetly in high-class hotels for roadside motel prices.

Bidding for Cars

Priceline's car rentals demand the least risk, but offer the least savings of its three main travel products. You know you'll get a car whose size you specify from one of five big car-rental firms (Hertz, Avis, Dollar, National, or Alamo).

Usually, you can shave at least a few dollars off other rates with Priceline. But watch out: The car-rental market is very competitive! You may find coupons, free-upgrade deals, or corporate rates elsewhere that make regular rates lower than Priceline's. As always, you have to shop around.

Shopping around for a car

Checking out rental-car rates can be even tricker than finding low airfares. Scour online travel agencies, examine rental-car companies' own Web sites looking for coupons, and even try calling the rental-car firms on the phone. Unlike with hotels and airfares, sometimes rental-car firms save their lowest rates for phone calls.

For more tips on shopping around for car-rental rates, turn to Chapter 14.

Bidding for your car

Bidding for a car is very similar to bidding for a hotel. Essentially, you tell Priceline where you want your car, how nice (or large) a car you want it to be, and how much you want to pay. Then Priceline tells you whether it agrees.

I cover bidding on cars in more detail in Chapter 14, but here are the basics:

1. **Start at Priceline's home page, www.priceline.com, and click Rental Cars.**

2. **Click a type of car, such as Mid-Size, and then click See Additional Details to see what kinds of cars and features Priceline includes in a particular car class (see Figure 4-3).**

3. **Enter the city you'll be collecting the car in, and your dates and times.**

   Don't worry about the exact times — as long as you're picking up and dropping off the car on the day you requested, you can fudge the times by a few hours down the road.

   Priceline only handles round-trip rentals, so you'll have to bring the car back to where you picked it up.

4. **Choose the location where you want to pick up your car.**

   Priceline offers hundreds of airport locations and a few downtown locations. Downtown locations can be in a pretty big swathe of a city; click Details next to the name of a downtown location to see where.

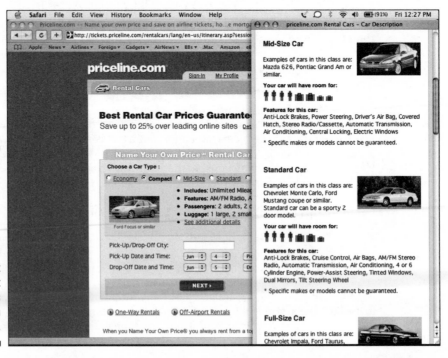

Figure 4-3: Rental-car terms like *Mid-Size* can be confusing, so Priceline lays out exactly what kinds of cars fit into each category.

An airport location may require you to take a shuttle from the terminal to the rental desk.

5. **Enter your flight information, your name and age, and the price you want to pay.**

Drivers between 21 and 24 years of age can rent cars from Priceline in most cities. Drivers who are 18 to 20 years old can also rent cars in New York City.

6. **If you get a page telling you you're bidding too low, ignore it and hold your ground.**

After you put in your details, Priceline will come back with its most important screen, the Please Review Your Request screen.

7. **Make sure everything on the Please Review Your Request screen is correct, and that you've read all the points under the "Important Information" section.**

If you make a mistake, Priceline won't fix it for you!

8. **If you're satisfied with your bid, enter your credit-card details and click Buy My Rental Car Now.**

Priceline will either tell you you've succeeded, or invite you to bid again for a different class of car. Occasionally, Priceline will offer to let you bid again immediately for the same class of car.

If you won, congratulations! Now you can afford those sky-high gas prices.

Bonus! Using bonus money

If you handed out $5 bills on the street, I bet people would like you. At least they'd be intrigued. To keep customers coming back, Priceline hands out money, too — well, almost.

Priceline's bonus-money coupons add value to your bids. If you made a successful bid at any point and told Priceline that it could send you e-mail, you may get an e-mail from Priceline days, weeks, or even months later with a bonus-money link in it. Click on the link to use your coupon.

A lot of spam is out there, and sometimes e-mail programs mistake Priceline's coupons for spam. If you have a spam-blocker, make sure to check your spam box to see if it caught a coupon. All of Priceline's coupons come from an address @production.priceline.com, and all bonus-money links start with http://www.priceline.com/ (and then they usually have a lot of other stuff in the link that specifies your exact coupon).

A $5 hotel bonus-money coupon, for example, lets you win $55 hotel rooms with a $50 bid. An individual bonus money coupon will usually only apply to one Priceline service — hotels, cars, airfares, or vacations — but Priceline sends out bonus-money coupons for each of its services from time to time.

(continued)

(continued)

To use a bonus-money coupon, don't start your bid from Priceline's home page. Instead, click on the link in the coupon. If that doesn't work, try copying and pasting the link into your Web browser.

Bid just as you normally would. But when you get to the Please Review Your Request screen (shown in the figure), make sure it includes the Add-On Bonus line you see near the bottom of that screen.

If you see Add-On Bonus, then your bonus money is in effect, and it'll buoy up your bid. If you don't see it, something may be wrong with your computer. E-mail Priceline (see Chapter 3 for more information), and it'll send you some suggestions on how to make it work.

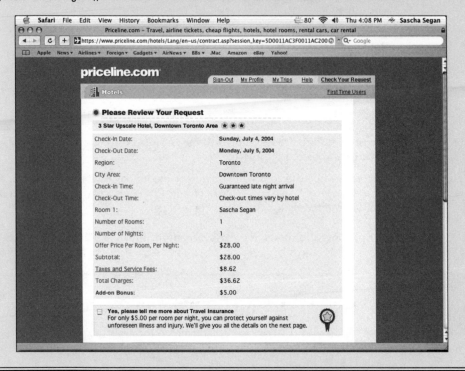

Priceline's Other Stuff

Airfares, hotels, and rental cars are Priceline's main events. But Priceline delivers discounts on mortgages and vacation packages, too. (It also sells cruises, but not at highly discounted rates.)

Buying a vacation on Priceline

Priceline's vacations include airfare, hotel rooms, and sometimes car rentals. Priceline vacations have a lot less uncertainty than you'll find in normal Priceline bidding, but Priceline's package-vacation prices are also much higher than what you'd pay if you bid for all the parts of the vacation separately.

I cover buying a vacation on Priceline in more depth in Chapter 16, but here are the basics:

1. **Go to Priceline's home page,** www.priceline.com, **and click on Vacation Packages.**

2. **Choose your departure city, your destination, your dates, how many rooms you want, and how many people are coming along.**

   Priceline shows you a list of possible hotels in your destination city, sorted by popularity. To sort the vacations by price, click on Sort By Price near the top of the screen.

3. **Comb over the details for your package.**

   You can click various links to find out more about your hotel. Scroll down to check out your flight details and to see how much adding a rental car would cost.

   Sometimes Priceline will tell you what flight you're on, but sometimes it'll leave it a mystery (see Figure 4-4). Mystery flights are almost always cheaper than known flights.

   If you book a mystery flight, you must agree to change planes if necessary, and you must agree to fly any time between 6 a.m. and 10 p.m., or any time at all for international trips.

   For last-minute packages, Priceline offers a *Playtime Guarantee,* in which it assures you of at least 44 hours (for two-night trips) or 64 hours (for three-night trips) at your destination.

4. **Enter the travelers' names for this trip.**

5. **Pore over the Your Package Summary screen to make sure you agree to all the terms.**

   Make sure you've read all the points under the "Important Information" section.

   Remember: After you put in your credit-card details, you can't cancel your trip later.

6. **If you agree to all the details, enter your initials at the bottom of the Your Package Summary form and click Next.**

7. **Enter your credit-card details and click Buy My Package Now.**

Because no bidding is involved here, you won't be rejected. After you commit to the package, you've sealed the deal. Have a great trip!

Making money with Priceline Mortgage

Priceline Mortgage is known for its low rates — but, to some extent, you get what you pay for. Well-respected Internet bank EverBank provides the initial mortgage service, though it'll probably sell your loan off to a bigger lender after you've closed. Working with a small, low-cost lender, though, means you're working with its overburdened staff, who can take ages to do the necessary paperwork.

I cover bidding for a mortgage on Priceline in greater detail in Chapter 17, but here are the basics:

1. **Go to** `www.pricelinemortgage.com`.

2. **Scroll down to Name Your Own Rate — Mortgages, and enter your details.**

    If you don't know what a 7/1 ARM is or what points are, pick up *Mortgages For Dummies* by Eric Tyson, MBA, and Ray Brown (published by Wiley).

    Priceline says it can shave up to half a percentage point over the rates you find elsewhere.

3. **Fill out a series of online forms with your financial details and the details of your home purchase.**

    If you don't have a property under contract, you'll be sent to Priceline's preapproval department.

4. **Priceline will e-mail you within six business hours (business hours are Monday through Friday, 8 a.m. to 8 p.m.) telling you whether it agrees to your terms.**

    Most of the time, rather than a flat-out agreement you'll get a counteroffer — the interest rate you requested with a few more points than you wanted, for example.

5. **If you agree to the rate, plunk down a nonrefundable $395 fee and start mailing documents back and forth to Priceline Mortgage.**

    You can back out at any time, of course — you just lose the $395 deposit. If you intend to spend hundreds of thousands of dollars on this mortgage during the next 20 years, $395 shouldn't matter too much to you.

Priceline Mortgage typically locks in your rate for 30 days. You must watch it like a hawk to make sure it makes this deadline, pursuing your loan officer on the phone, keeping copies of documents and mailing documents off on time, next-day mail. It sounds like a pain, but the rewards — thousands of dollars' worth of savings over the course of a mortgage — just may be worth it.

If You're Not in the United States

Priceline says that to use its service, you must have a U.S. credit card — but that doesn't mean non-Americans are out.

Priceline has hotel bidding sites especially for Asians and U.K. residents, and three airfare bidding sites for Asians. Canadians can use the U.S. Priceline site — they just need to be a little sneaky.

For more in-depth descriptions of Priceline's foreign sites and tactics for foreign bidders, see Chapter 18.

Using the U.S. version of Priceline outside the United States

Hundreds of non-U.S. bidders have successfully used Priceline for airline tickets, hotel rooms, and car rentals, although doing so is technically against Priceline's rules.

If you're going to try your hand at this, using an American Express card helps. Priceline usually accepts foreign American Express credit cards, but only sometimes accepts foreign Visas or MasterCards.

If you're a non-American, bid just like Americans do. Then, when it comes time to enter your credit-card details, deform your address to look more American.

For instance, try to find a two-letter state code that resembles your country code (Canadians should use California — the abbreviation is CA, same as Canada). If your country uses alphanumeric postal codes like the United Kingdom and Canada do, use the zip code 99999. And try to force your phone number into a North American format. So if your U.K. phone number is 020-71234567, type it in as 207-123-4567.

The worst thing that'll happen is that Priceline will kick back your bid saying it couldn't verify your address. Then you can try to fix your address again and resumbit your bid. Or ask for help from www.cleverbidding.com, a bulletin board devoted to Priceline U.K. bidding.

You can't use Priceline to get airline tickets *to* the United States, because all Priceline flights must start on U.S. soil.

Trying foreign Priceline sites

U.K. residents and Asians have their own Priceline sites.

U.K. residents looking for hotel rooms anywhere in the world should go to Priceline U.K. (www.priceline.co.uk). Priceline U.K. has the exact same hotel inventory as Priceline's U.S. site but charges prices in British pounds rather than U.S. dollars. Priceline U.K. does not offer Name Your Own Price airfares or car rentals.

No matter where you live, you can bid on Priceline Hong Kong (www.priceline.com.hk), Priceline Singapore (www.priceline.com.sg), or Priceline Taiwan (www.priceline.com.tw). These sites use the same hotel database as the U.S. Priceline, but charge rates in Hong Kong, Singapore, or Taiwan dollars. Priceline Hong Kong and Priceline Singapore are both in English; the Priceline Taiwan site has a button to click for an English version (otherwise, you must be able to read Chinese).

The Asian Priceline sites also let you name your own price for flights from Hong Kong or Singapore to anywhere in the world. Even if you're not Chinese, you can grab a cheap round-trip ticket from Hong Kong to Tokyo on Priceline Hong Kong, for example. Unlike the U.S. Priceline site, the Asian sites even let you demand nonstop flights on some routes.

Part II
Up, Up, and Away! Buying Plane Tickets on Priceline

The 5th Wave   By Rich Tennant

"My response to a large company-wide data crash is to notify management, back up existing data, and search Priceline.com for cheap airfare out of the country."

In this part . . .

Priceline made its name selling cheap airfares. Although it has some stiff competition nowadays, Priceline can still send you on long trips at the last minute for cheaper fares than anyone else.

In this part, you find out about the trade-offs of bidding for airline tickets on Priceline. I run you through all the other places you should check airfares *before* you place a bid on Priceline, to make sure you don't bid too high. I show you tricks to miraculously turn one bid into three or four. And I give you some comforting words about what to do if things go wrong at the airport. Pack your bags, because, at the end of this part, you'll be flying away for less.

Chapter 5

Straighten Up and Fly Right: Knowing Your Options

In This Chapter

▶ Identifying Priceline's participating airlines

▶ Deciding on airports, connections, and layovers

▶ Understanding what you can't control

▶ Knowing the best times to fly

*P*riceline's Name Your Own Price airline tickets force you to hand over a lot of control for your savings. Most importantly, you give up control over your flight times and must accept the possibility of changing planes. That turns a lot of people off from Priceline, especially because airlines nowadays often offer really low fares without Priceline's mystery factors.

But bidding for flights can still come in handy plenty of times. Priceline can get you great fares for peak-season travel to Europe or for last-minute domestic flights. The more flexible you are, the more you'll save.

In this chapter, you get comfortable with Priceline's flight offerings. I tell you what airlines you'll be flying on, as well as how much control you have over where you're going and what time you're flying. That way, you'll be able to see if Priceline is right for your trip.

Priceline's Airlines

Priceline only uses major full-service airlines. Its U.S. airlines are all big national carriers with solid safety records. Its foreign airlines are all — except for one — national-flag carriers from countries that have passed the U.S. Federal Aviation Administration's International Aviation Safety Assessment.

BWIA West Indies Airways, is the national airline of Trinidad and Tobago, which didn't meet U.S. safety standards as of April 2004. BWIA has never had a fatal accident, according to AirSafe.com. I consider it a safe airline, but if you're queasy about flying with BWIA, just don't bid Priceline for flights to Caribbean islands.

Here's a quick rundown of Priceline's airline partners:

- **American** (www.aa.com), **Continental** (www.continental.com), **Delta** (www.delta.com), **United** (www.united.com), **and US Airways** (www.usairways.com): Five of America's largest airlines, all safe and reliable with huge national and international networks.

- **Aloha** (www.alohaair.com) **and Hawaiian** (www.hawaiianair.com): Hawaii's two local airlines; they also do some business on the West Coast. Comfortable, full-service carriers.

- **Midwest Airlines** (www.midwestairlines.com): Long lauded for the best customer service in the air, it takes an unusually friendly approach to Priceline passengers, too.

- **America West** (www.americawest.com): A low-fare carrier with hubs in Phoenix and Las Vegas, it's not known for customer service, but it's safe and has plenty of flights.

- **Song** (www.flysong.com) **and Ted** (www.flyted.com): Low-fare spin-offs of Delta and United, respectively. Song has terrific seatback entertainment systems with multiple movies on most of its planes.

- **Air Canada** (www.aircanada.com): Not only does Canada's national airline run 80 percent of the flights in its home country, it sells many Priceline tickets to Europe — you usually have to connect in Toronto.

- **Aer Lingus** (www.aerlingus.com), **Air France** (www.airfrance.com), **Alitalia** (www.alitalia.com), **Austrian Airlines** (www.aua.com), **Finnair** (www.finnair.com), **Iberia** (www.iberia.com), **Icelandair** (www.icelandair.com), **Lufthansa** (www.lufthansa.com), **SAS** (www.scandinavian.net), **Swiss** (www.swiss.com), **and Virgin Atlantic** (www.virginatlantic.com): Top-notch European carriers.

- **Aerolineas Argentinas** (www.aerolineas.com), **Aeroméxico** (www.aeromexico.com), **Air Jamaica** (www.airjamaica.com), **and Varig** (www.varig.com): National carriers offering service to the Caribbean and Latin America.

- **Air New Zealand** (www.airnz.com), **ANA** (www.fly-ana.com), **Cathay Pacific** (www.cathay-usa.com), **El Al** (www.elal.com), **Japan Airlines** (www.jal.com), **Korean Air** (www.koreanair.com), **South African Airways** (www.flysaa.com), **Turkish Airlines** (www.thy.com): I can count the number of Priceline tickets I've seen to Africa, Asia, and the Middle East on one hand, but in theory, you could get a ticket on any of these airlines.

- **BWIA** (www.bwee.com): It's a safe airline from a country with low safety standards, according to the U.S. government. It only flies to Caribbean islands.

Non-Priceline airlines

Northwest, Southwest, and Alaska Airlines don't sell Name Your Own Price tickets, so you may have trouble finding low fares to Northwest's hubs of Minneapolis and Memphis, as well as to Alaska's hub in Anchorage. Southwest often undercuts Priceline with its own low fares all over the country.

Many low-fare airlines in the United States and Canada, including JetBlue, ATA, Spirit, CanJet, and JetsGo, also don't sell tickets through Priceline and may have lower fares than you can find on Priceline.

Overseas, British Airways doesn't sell Name Your Own Price tickets, but so many airlines fly to London that Priceline still has plenty of options.

Knowing Where You're Going

Priceline would be a pretty lousy deal if you couldn't control where you're going! You control where you fly with Priceline — you just give up control over *when* and *how* you get there.

Deciding on airports

Some cities, such as Phoenix, have one airport. New York has three. London has *five*. Knowing which airports to choose, and when, is key to smart bidding with Priceline.

Complicating things, Priceline often lists so-called out-of-town airports to give you more options. Figure 5-1 shows possible airports for a trip between New York City and London.

New York's three real airports are LaGuardia, Kennedy, and Newark. Islip, White Plains, and Newburgh are all distant suburban airports, a long and difficult slog from the city.

If you punch New Haven, Connecticut, into Priceline, you'll get an even wider selection of airports. New Haven airport is right in the city but offers very few flights. Hartford's Bradley airport is an easy 40-minute drive north — if you have a car. And the New York airports are 90 minutes south, but a frequent train service from New York City to New Haven exists. Alas, Priceline won't tell you any of this.

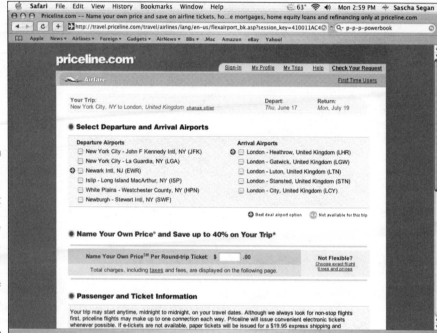

Figure 5-1:
Newburgh
airport isn't
anywhere
near New
York City,
but Priceline
gives you
the option of
flying into
there.

You have to decide which airports you find convenient. Don't trust Priceline's list of airports — do your own research by asking friends or looking at a travel Web site like www.frommers.com. A great airfare deal may not be worth it if there's no way into the city from the airport!

Priceline's favorite airports

When you select your airports during bidding, a little arrow will appear next to one departure option and one arrival option, as shown in Figure 5-2. Those airports are Priceline's "best-deal airport options." According to Priceline, at the moment you're bidding, it has more flights between those two airports than between any other pair listed.

Feel free to ignore the "best-deal airport options." They're just a suggestion, an attempt to steer you to the choices Priceline can best accommodate. Just because the airport you want doesn't have an arrow next to it doesn't mean Priceline doesn't have any flights to or from there.

Figure 5-2:
Priceline
really wants
you to
fly from
LaGuardia
to
Washington
National,
but you
don't have
to follow its
advice.

⦿ **Select Departure and Arrival Airports**

Departure Airports
☐ New York City - John F Kennedy Intl, NY (JFK)
◉ ☐ New York City - La Guardia, NY (LGA)
☐ Newark Intl, NJ (EWR)
☐ Islip - Long Island MacArthur, NY (ISP)
☐ White Plains - Westchester County, NY (HPN)
☐ Newburgh - Stewart Intl, NY (SWF)

Arrival Airports
◉ ☐ Washington - Reagan National, DC (DCA)
☐ Washington - Dulles Intl, DC (IAD)
☐ Baltimore Washington Intl, MD (BWI)

◉ Best deal airport option   N/A Not available for this trip

Going farther afield

In a few situations, you may want to go even farther afield than Priceline's air-port suggestions. For example, if you're heading to southern Ontario, flying to Buffalo or Detroit and driving across the border is often much cheaper than flying to Toronto.

The better you know your destination, the more in command of your options you'll be. Buy guidebooks. Check out online bulletin boards like the ones at www.frommers.com. The more you know about your destination, the more comfortable you'll be with Priceline.

Connecting the Dots

Priceline requires you to accept one connection on your trip. That doesn't mean you'll *have* to change planes. I've gotten plenty of nonstops on Priceline, including one from New York to Barcelona. But you must be comfortable with the idea of changing planes.

If your bid fails, Priceline will ask you if you're willing to accept a flight with *two* plane changes. You don't have to accept it, of course, but if you do, Priceline may be able to find you a lower fare.

Priceline's domestic layover rule

If your flight connects, the layover at the connecting airport can't be any longer than three hours. Priceline says 80 percent of its connections are two hours or less. A three-hour layover can be annoying, but it's manageable. Head over to an airport restaurant, get something to eat, and dig in to a book.

Unfortunately, after you get your tickets, your airline can change your schedule to whatever it wants, and you can't do anything about that. It has nothing to do with Priceline — airlines can change your schedule no matter what kind of ticket you buy.

The long road home: International layovers

Layovers can get lengthy when you're flying internationally, but at least you'll know what you're in for. As always, be prepared for the worst. Table 5-1 provides a list of Priceline's maximum and average layover times for international destinations.

Yes, this means you may be stuck in Toronto for six hours as you wait for your flight to London. Think about how much money that's worth to you.

Table 5-1	International Layover Times	
Destination	*Maximum Layover*	*Average Layover*
Africa	8 hours	3 hours
Asia	8 hours	3 hours, 54 minutes
Australia	8 hours	2 hours, 30 minutes
Caribbean	4 hours	1 hour, 30 minutes
Central/South America	5 hours	2 hours, 20 minutes
Europe	6 hours	2 hours, 20 minutes
Middle East	7 hours	3 hours, 24 minutes
South Africa	12 hours	4 hours, 30 minutes

Avoiding the scenic route

Back in the bad old days of 1999 and 2000, Priceline used to put people on truly tortured airline routings. One woman told me about a flight from Los Angeles to Houston that became a 12-hour ordeal after Priceline shunted her through Minneapolis. Fortunately, nowadays Priceline's computers are a bit more sensible. You may be sent from Los Angeles to Houston via Denver or Phoenix, but not via Minneapolis.

Stop! It's a connection!

In the airline world, there's a difference between a stop and a connection. With a *connection,* you get off one plane and onto another one. You change flight numbers, and sometimes even change airlines. With a *stop,* you may stay on the same plane or change to a different one, but your flight number doesn't change. For example, some Cathay Pacific flights from New York to Hong Kong stop in Vancouver to get more fuel and passengers. The New York passengers stay on the plane, so it isn't a connection. But stop, connection, whatever . . . it doesn't matter — they're all the same to Priceline. What matters to Priceline is how many times your plane is scheduled to touch the ground, whether you get off the plane or not.

Too-short layovers

Occasionally, Priceline will put you on a flight with an impossibly short layover. This happens most often with returning to the United States on an international flight. Because customs, immigration, and security lines take so long nowadays, a one-hour layover coming home may not cut it.

These connections are legal, so Priceline doesn't need to do anything to help you. Fortunately, if you miss your connection, the law requires your airline to put you on the next available flight to your destination.

If you get a flight with a layover of less than 45 minutes for a domestic flight or 90 minutes for an international flight, call your airline. Explain that the connection does not give you enough time to make it to your plane. The airline isn't required to do anything to help you, but it may.

Leaving on a Jet Plane?

Flying on a major airline doesn't necessarily mean you'll be on a major plane. Priceline's airlines use planes ranging all the way from super-jumbos to tiny prop planes seating fewer than 20 people. If you really dislike prop planes, you can ask Priceline to avoid them, but you may be lowering your chances of winning a flight.

Joining Priceline's jet set

Priceline always starts out by searching for flights on jet planes. Jets can be big Boeing 747 jumbos or little Embraer regional jets.

Flying on a jet plane doesn't guarantee that your plane will be new, or that it'll have an entertainment system. It just guarantees that the plane will seat 37 or more people and give you a pretty smooth ride.

Some airports, such as the airport in Page, Arizona, don't have any jet flights. To get a flight into one of those places, you'll have to accept flying on a smaller, propeller-powered plane.

Fear not the prop planes

According to AirSafe.com, propeller planes are *not* more dangerous than jet planes when flown by airlines with high safety standards. Today's prop planes range from little 19-seat commuters to models larger than some small jets.

Prop planes are slower and noisier than jets, though, and they can give a bumpier ride. In a 19-seater, you don't feel as insulated from the outside world as you do in a larger plane. Also, the bathroom doors in some 19-seaters don't fully close, so the back row can be a bit stinky.

That said, you can only get to some other small towns by flying on prop planes. And allowing Priceline to use prop planes increases your chances of getting a cheap ticket to other midsized cities, like Quebec City in Canada. (It reduces your chance of getting a nonstop flight if jet-powered nonstops exist on your route, though.)

How can you find out whether adding prop planes would improve your chances?

1. **Go to ITA Software's Flight Schedules at** `http://matrix.itasoftware.com`.

2. **Punch in your cities and dates.**

   You'll get back a list of possible flights.

3. **Look under "Warnings" for each of the flights.**

   If you see "prop plane segments" listed for many flights, you can increase your chances on Priceline by allowing prop planes.

Knowing When You'll Be Flying

Priceline sells the tickets airlines can't get rid of by other means, so Priceliners end up on a lot of crack-of-dawn flights. But you can still figure out what times you're most likely to end up flying, on some routes.

Priceline's flight times

For most domestic flights, Priceline requires you to accept a flight departing between 6 a.m. and 10 p.m., and arriving as late as half past midnight. Think about that. Airlines tend to sell Priceline a *lot* of flights departing between 6 and 7 a.m.

If your first bid fails, you can agree to look for *off-peak flights.* That means you may be put on a flight departing as early as 5 a.m. and as late as 2 a.m., arriving as late as noon the day *after* you depart.

For international flights, you must agree to leave at any time of day, period.

On some routes, you can figure out what flights you're most likely to get:

1. **Go to Priceline's home page at www.priceline.com.**

2. **Enter your departure and arrival cities and dates, and click Next.**

   For example, choose New York City, Paris, and some random dates — the dates don't matter.

3. **On the screen that appears next, scroll down and look at the flight departure times, only paying attention to flights with one stop or fewer.**

   In the case of New York and Paris, I got 18 itineraries departing New York between 5 and 11 p.m., one flight at 2:30 p.m., and one flight at 11 a.m. I can conclude that if I bid this route and these dates, I am very likely to get a flight between 5 and 11 p.m. — and I won't get a flight departing before 11 a.m.

This trick doesn't work with routes like New York–Los Angeles, where flights leave 'round the clock. But it's worth a try.

Make sure to take a *very* close look at the Please Review Your Request page you see before you put in your credit-card information (see Figure 5-3). Sometimes Priceline automatically adds the non-jet and off-peak options without asking your permission.

Best days to fly

During particularly busy periods, Priceline tries to help you by throwing a calendar of "best days to fly" on its home page.

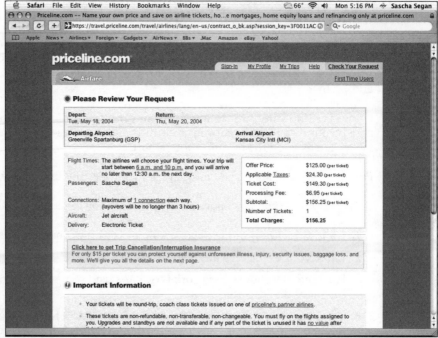

Figure 5-3:
Read this
page closely
to make
sure you'll
be flying on
a jet, if that's
important
to you.

Like its "best-deal airport options," Priceline's "best days to fly" are just helpful suggestions. They're on the level, though. Airlines don't give Priceline very many tickets to sell on peak holiday days, and when they do, they generally give Priceline the tickets just a few days before the flight.

So checking Priceline's "best days" calendar is helpful, even though the calendar isn't the last word on whether you'll be able to get a ticket.

In general, the best days to fly with Priceline are Tuesdays and Wednesdays, followed by Saturdays, Mondays, and Thursdays. Airlines charge their highest prices on Fridays and Sundays.

Understanding "Nonrefundable"

Priceline airline tickets are nonrefundable and nonchangeable, except by the sweet mercy and grace of Priceline. That means you are *not* entitled to a refund or change of dates, even if:

- ✔ You don't like the flight times or airline you got.
- ✔ One of your close family members dies.

✔ You get into a car crash on the way to the airport.

✔ You die.

✔ Your destination city falls into the sea.

Yes, I know I'm being a little extreme here, but a lot of bidders think they're entitled to exceptions when emergencies come up. You're not *entitled* to an exception. Priceline *may* help you — but if it does, treat it as a gift, not as your right. (It's not that you need to show great respect to Priceline or anything — you're just less likely to be upset if you're not expecting an exception all along.) See Chapter 8 for more on how to deal with trouble on your trip.

If you want more protection against illness, car crashes, and cities falling into the sea, consider buying travel insurance. For a rundown of travel-insurance options, see Chapter 3.

Chapter 6

Building an Airline Bid Strategy

. . . .

In This Chapter

▶ Knowing how far in advance to bid

▶ Checking competing fares

▶ Calculating the right opening bid

▶ Maximizing your bids

▶ Building a complete bid strategy

. . . .

*T*his chapter lays out all the secrets of saving money on airfares with Priceline. Here, you find out how to turn one bid into three, how to make sure you're not overbidding, and how to get the best possible flights for your price.

With a good bidding strategy, you can win big on Priceline. When fares are high everywhere else, I've seen plenty of people knock 40 to 60 percent off published rates and end up with well-timed flights on major full-service airlines. You can't beat that.

Independent analysts at Consumer WebWatch, a spin-off of *Consumer Reports,* agree with me. In a December 2003 study of major travel sites, they found Priceline gave the lowest airfares 44 percent of the time. Their savings averaged 20 percent off what they could find elsewhere, and I think they were probably bidding conservatively.

The key to smart bidding is the *bid grid,* a chart of all the bids you're going to make. Bidding for flights can be confusing, and the bid grid lays things out simply so you can't get distracted or caught up in the heat of the moment.

In this chapter, you create a perfect bid grid to take into the bidding process — and you'll be ready to save big.

Knowing When to Bid

U.S. airlines are in a fare war. That war has been going on for years now; it's the death-struggle between the full-service carriers like American and United and the low-fare carriers like JetBlue and AirTran. Every week, new skirmishes erupt: JetBlue announces a $238 fare from New York City to the Dominican Republic, or ATA Airlines lets loose with a slew of $118 round-trips from Chicago.

In this extremely competitive atmosphere, you're not going to find deals on Priceline far in advance, for routes that are frequently on sale. Priceline is a safety valve for airlines. When fares are high, the airlines fill a few seats with cheap tickets through Priceline without endangering their high fares. That may mean giving Priceline good fares at the last minute, or only giving Priceline tickets for routes that are normally expensive.

You're not going to see that $118 Chicago sale fare cut to $90 on Priceline. On the other hand, if you're flying from Houston to Seattle and can't find a fare lower than $473, it's Priceline to the rescue!

Snatching last-minute bids

Priceline spokesmen and independent watchdogs agree: The best time to use Priceline is for last-minute flights.

Major airlines have three or four main tiers of fares. The cheapest one typically requires you to buy your ticket two or three weeks in advance. Then there's a one-week-in-advance fare, a three-days-in-advance fare, and the super-high walkup fare.

If a plane still has empty seats a few days before the flight, airlines release tickets to Priceline at rates closer to the 21-day advance fare. So you're not saving much over what you would have paid if you'd bought your ticket well in advance — but you're saving a whole lot over the regular last-minute fare.

You can bid for same-day flights up until noon local time.

Giving yourself enough time

If you run out of bids, you must wait a week before you bid again. So if you're bidding on a route with normally high fares, trying to bring them down, try to start bidding five to six weeks in advance. That way, you can go through a few bidding cycles and still pick up a 21-day advance purchase fare from the airlines if Priceline doesn't pan out.

Summer fares to Europe are always expensive, and June flights rarely come on sale before late April. So one bidder on BiddingForTravel.com turned to Priceline about three months before flying and lucked out with a pair of $367 tickets from New York to London for mid-June. She knew that summer fares rarely dip below $600 after tax, so she just plugged along for a little while, bidding far enough in advance to avoid stress. ***Remember:*** Be sure to give yourself plenty of time to get the best possible price.

You can bid up to 329 days in advance for a Priceline trip, but I don't recommend it. The airline industry is a mess right now — you don't know whether your airline will go out of business in the next year (see Chapter 8 for more on airlines' financial problems). Anyway, airlines don't give Priceline many good fares that far in advance.

Checking Competing Rates

Boiled down to its essence, Priceline bidding is simple:

1. **Find the lowest rates you can elsewhere.**

2. **Bid less on Priceline.**

Finding those low rates can be a pain. Don't just bid what you think a flight is worth on Priceline. You may be missing a super-low fare elsewhere, like that $118 Chicago round-trip I mention in the "Knowing When to Bid" section earlier in this chapter. (Don't look for it — it's gone by now. But it may appear again.) Check the right sites, though, and you can bid safely.

Priceline's own fares

The best way to judge how low you should bid on Priceline is to look at Priceline's standard travel-agency fares. Other sites may have lower fares, but Priceline's rates are a good mid-range from which to judge discounts.

When you enter your arrival and departure cities on Priceline's home page, you're always funneled through Priceline's travel agency (as shown in Figure 6-1) before you get to bid.

Priceline's Name Your Own Price system may have fares between 20 and 60 percent below what you see on this screen — but so may airlines' own Web sites. That's why you need to look elsewhere before bidding.

Figure 6-1:
Looks like
$323 is the
price to beat
on this trip.

Major online travel agencies

Three online travel agencies — Expedia, Orbitz, and Travelocity — control most of the airline-ticket market in the United States. Many folks have their favorite small agency, too, like AirGorilla or OneTravel. At the very minimum, check prices on Expedia, Orbitz, and Travelocity. All three have different deals with various airlines, so all three will probably have different fares for your trip.

SideStep (www.sidestep.com), a browser plug-in that attaches like a leech to Internet Explorer, offers a more extensive selection of airlines and fares than the big three online travel agencies. Always check out SideStep after you look at the fares on Expedia, Orbitz, and Travelocity.

For more on the major online travel agencies, see Chapter 20.

Airlines' own sites

By cutting out the middlemen — in this case, travel agencies — airlines save money selling tickets. So airlines often offer really, really low fares on their own Web sites. Some low-fare airlines don't post their rates on any travel-agency Web sites, so you have to turn to the airlines' sites to get any fares at all. In any case, if you book a ticket without looking at an airline's own Web site, you have a good chance of missing the best fares.

Major airlines

Priceline's airline partners often undercut travel-agency fares with lower prices on their own Web sites. Find the lowest fare you can on a travel-agency site, then go to the airline's own Web site to compare.

For last-minute trips, most airlines release lists of e-fares on Tuesdays or Wednesdays, with super-low fares for the next weekend or two. You'll find those on the airline Web sites, too.

For a full list of major airline Web sites, go to Chapter 20.

Discount airlines

Discount airlines like Southwest, JetBlue, and Independence Air don't show up on most travel-agency sites, and Priceline doesn't book tickets on these airlines. (SideStep shows all three airlines, but the discount airlines sometimes have special sales on their own Web sites.)

Because these low-fare airlines often beat other fares — including Priceline fares! — be sure to check their Web sites for cheap tickets. For a list of low-fare airline Web sites, go to Chapter 20.

Hotwire.com

Priceline's major rival is Hotwire.com. It lets you see fares before you buy, so you can make sure never to bid higher than Hotwire's price. The site often has higher fares than you'll find on individual airline Web sites, though, so make sure to check other sites and not just rely on Hotwire.

BiddingForTravel.com

The ultimate independent Priceline watchdog, this site collects hundreds of past airline bids. Unfortunately, you can't duplicate the past bids on this site exactly, because they're too far apart and fares will have changed by the time you check the site. But you can get a good idea of how much folks are saving.

Creating a Bid Grid

After you've done some research into what the other sites are selling their tickets for, you're ready to do some smart bidding. You know what the going rates are, and you're comfortable with Priceline's most important restrictions. You're willing to fly any time between 6 a.m. and 10 p.m. (or at even weirder times for international flights), and you're willing to change planes midway if you must.

Priceline says you can only bid once per itinerary each week, but I can show you ways to get five or even ten bids per week. That way, you can start by bidding a low price and work your way up to the maximum you'd want to pay. I'll use a flight from Philadelphia to Toronto as my main example.

To help you bid confidently, you should make a bid grid. A *bid grid* is just a chart of the bids you plan to make, with all the details and prices written down. With a bid grid, you can stick to your bidding strategy even in the heat of the moment, and you'll never get lost wondering what to do next.

Choosing an airport

Start by deciding which airports in both cities you want to fly out of and into. If you're not sure, see what Frommer's Travel Guides suggests:

1. **Go to** www.frommers.com.

2. **In the Search box in the upper-left-hand corner of the screen, type in the name of a city and hit Return.**

3. **On the screen that appears, click on the main link for the city.**

   It should be at the top of the search results list and have the words *Main Destination Page* in the Type column.

4. **On the screen that appears, click Getting There under the "Planning a Trip" header.**

You don't want to check off every airport you see on Priceline. Sometimes Priceline offers airport options far from city centers, and sometimes you need to save airports for free rebids (see the "Grabbing free rebids" section later in this chapter). For now, just pick the airports you really want to fly into.

Start your bid grid by writing down your departure and arrival airports on a piece of paper, and leaving a space for your bid.

That's *too* cheap

Long ago when Priceline was young, a few airlines got really frisky and sold a whole bunch of tickets on Priceline for $1, plus taxes. A few lucky posters on BiddingForTravel.com recounted grabbing round-trip flights between Los Angeles and San Francisco or between New York and Washington, D.C., for $20 after tax!

Unfortunately, those days are over. One-dollar bids will always fail now. Although you can save plenty on Priceline, there *are* limits.

Picking a maximum bid

Putting a price tag on convenience is tough. But now's the time to try.

Priceline says you can save an average of 40 percent off other fares by using its site. BiddingForTravel.com's FAQ gives a common range of 35 to 65 percent savings. Sometimes, you can't save anything at all.

Here's what I recommend:

- ✔ **If you're bidding on a flight less than 21 days in advance,** check the sites listed earlier in the "Checking Competing Rates" section, and look for the lowest advance-purchase fare, for dates about a month in advance. In other words, if it's June 1 and you want to fly June 5, see what the fare would be for a flight in July and base your bid on that.

- ✔ **If you're bidding for a destination in *high season* (the time of year when most people are traveling to your destination, so it's when fares are highest),** base your bid on what the destination would cost in *shoulder season* (the time of year that's neither high season nor low season).

- ✔ **If you're bidding for a destination in shoulder season,** base your bid on what the destination would cost in *low season* (the time of year when the fewest number of people are traveling to your destination, so it's when fares are lowest).

- ✔ **If Hotwire.com's fare on your route is much lower than fares on other sites,** bid up to slightly below Hotwire's fare.

- ✔ **If Hotwire.com's fare is in line with fares on the other sites,** knock $100 off the lowest fare you can find, or knock $50 off fares under $200. For example, if a ticket from Philadelphia to Toronto is $250, try to pay Priceline no more than $150 to $200. Think of this last tactic as paying for convenience. Imagine that Priceline will put you on an inconvenient flight — lousy flight times and a two-hour layover. How much is that worth to you?

In my case, $100 in savings will usually get me to roll over and suffer the inconveniences involved.

The number you have now is your *maximum out-of-pocket payment*. That's not the same as your maximum bid, because bids don't include taxes.

For domestic flights, knock $40 off your maximum out-of-pocket payment per ticket to get your maximum bid.

Taxes on international flights vary widely, so to figure them out, go through a test bid with your chosen destination and dates, carrying it as far as the Please Review Your Request screen. (Turn to Chapter 7 for a step-by-step guide through a bid.) Don't worry, you won't pay any money. The Please Review Your Request screen shown in Figure 6-2 shows the taxes you'll pay, plus Priceline's $6.95-per-ticket fee. Subtract the taxes and fee from your out-of-pocket payment to get your maximum bid amount.

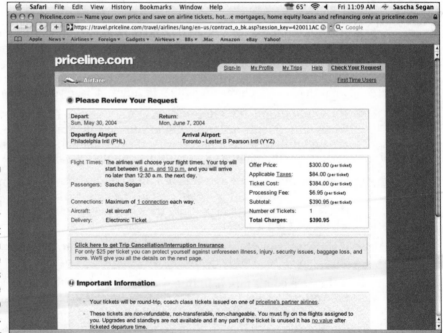

Figure 6-2:
The Please Review Your Request screen shows the taxes Priceline will add to your bid.

The pain of paper tickets

Whenever possible, Priceline will buy e-tickets. Those aren't tickets at all, just a record in the airline's computer that you're flying. Most travelers nowadays prefer e-tickets to the real thing. You can't lose them, you don't have to pay for shipping, and they give you just as many rights as paper tickets.

Airlines don't offer e-tickets on many international flights, so Priceline will tack on a $19.95 fee to send you paper tickets. Unfortunately, you can't avoid this. The fee will appear on your Please Review Your Request screen, so just factor it in when you make your bid.

In the case of the Philadelphia-Toronto example, I decided to pretend I was bidding for a last-minute ticket. The cheapest last-minute fare I found was $693 — about $610 before taxes and fees. Yikes! So I checked advance-purchase fares on various travel-agency and airline Web sites and found $250 fares for dates a month in advance. I decided to split the difference and try to pay up to $450. Because taxes and fees eat up $85 of that, my maximum bid will be $365.

Don't write any bid amounts on the grid yet. You'll do that last, when you know how many bids you have.

Grabbing free rebids

One bid is never enough. You want to turn that one bid into many. But Priceline tries to make that difficult for you. If your bid fails, you can't just raise your bid and try again. You have to change something about your bid, such as the airports, dates, or number of connections you're willing to accept.

Free rebids are new bids that fulfill Priceline's rules about changing things, but still ensure you'll get a flight you want. Free rebidding relies on adding options you can't possibly win, and then raising your bid price. You've changed something, so Priceline is happy. You've raised your price, so you have a better chance of getting a flight. But the new option you added couldn't possibly work, so you'll only get a flight with your old options — the kind of flight you actually want.

For example, you can add an airport that has no service from your originating city. You added an airport, so Priceline's happy. But because there are no flights from your originating city into the new airport, you can only win flights into the airport you first bid for, the one you really want. So the rebid is "free" — you don't have to make any real compromises, and you can raise your price.

Confused? That's okay. Read on and I clarify it.

Using ITA Software's flight search

To find free rebids, you need to use a Web site that explains when flights are on prop planes. ITA Software's flight search is a good one. You'll find it at http://matrix.itasoftware.com.

To use the schedule finder, enter in your departing and arriving airports, enter your dates, and click Go. You'll see a listing like the one shown in Figure 6-3.

Requesting impossible airports

The best kinds of free rebids are *impossible airports* (airports with no commercial airline service, airports only served by non-Priceline airlines, or airports with such limited service that there's no way to get to your destination).

If you add one of those airports to your search, you can't get a flight there. So your rebid is "free."

For example, if you're flying from Philadelphia to Toronto, Priceline suggests four Toronto-area airports: Lester Pearson, City Center, Buttonville, and Hamilton. Lester Pearson is Toronto's main airport — that's where you want to go. If you punch Philadelphia and Buttonville into ITA Software's Web site, you'll find that flying between those cities is impossible.

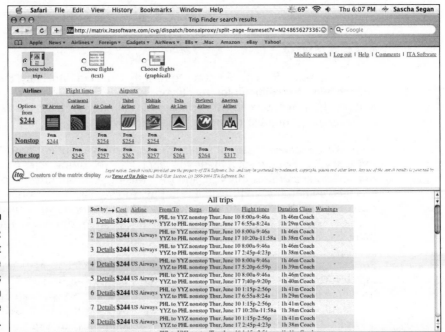

Figure 6-3:
The secret of free rebidding is hidden in lists like this one.

So if your bid to Pearson fails, you can add Buttonville and raise your price, and you're still guaranteed to only get a flight into Pearson, because there just aren't any flights to Buttonville. And that's your free rebid.

On your bid grid, you can now add another bid. Write down on a new line: ADD BUTTONVILLE.

Priceline only books flights on one airline at a time. So if you must take two airlines to get to a particular airport, you can consider that airport an impossible airport for your route.

For example, Hamilton is an impossible airport for the Philadelphia-Toronto route, because you can't get from Philadelphia to Hamilton on one airline. Priceline won't book you on a flight involving two different airlines (unless the two airlines are code-shares, and then they'd *look* like the same airline on your ticket or on a travel-agency Web site).

Returning to the Philadelphia-Toronto route, punch Philadelphia and Hamilton into ITA Software's site. In the blue box under the word *Airlines,* you'll see the only airline available is "Multiple Airlines," as shown in Figure 6-4.

That's another line for your bid grid. Write down on your piece of paper: ADD HAMILTON.

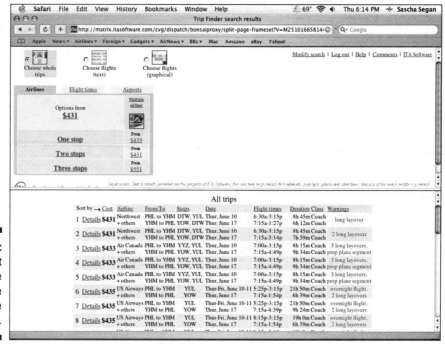

Figure 6-4:
You can't get there from here on one airline.

Using alternate cities

This trick uses a quirk in Priceline's maps to find you more bids.

Priceline lets you change cities to get a new bid. But in Priceline's world, many cities have overlapping airports. If you want to fly out of one of these shared airports, you can change your city but keep your airport, and Priceline will see it as a new bid.

For example, with the Philadelphia-Toronto flight, the city of Reading, Pennsylvania, near Philly has its own airport, but Priceline also lists Philadelphia as an airport for Reading.

So if you run out of Philly-Toronto bids, you can throw out your existing bid. Start over with a brand-new bid, and enter Reading and Toronto on Priceline's home page as your origination and destination cities.

Then, when you get to the airport selection screen (shown in Figure 6-5), don't pick Reading. Pick Philadelphia's airport only. Now you have an additional bid for Philly.

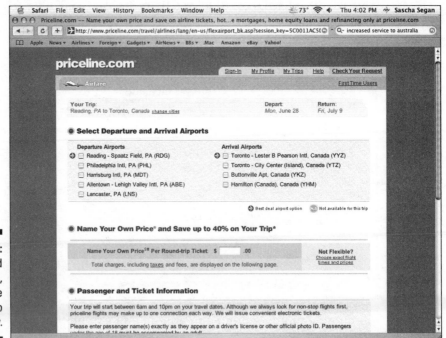

Figure 6-5:
You asked for Reading, but you're allowed to pick Philly.

Finding alternate cities takes a bit of trial and error. Go to Priceline's list of U.S. cities at www.priceline.com/travel/airlines/lang/en-us/City Codes.asp and look for other cities within 100 miles or so of your arrival or destination city. A good road atlas may help, or you can use the other cities Priceline suggests as a clue. For example, with the Philly-Toronto trip, discovering Reading shows that Harrisburg and Lancaster may also be good alternate cities (refer to Figure 6-5).

When entering bids using alternate cities, only check off the airport you actually want. Don't check off the Reading airport unless you want to fly out of Reading!

Non-jet-only airports

This strategy is a risky one.

Most of the time, Priceline defaults to searching for jet flights only. By adding an airport where no jets fly — an airport that only has prop planes — you can get a free rebid.

For example, no jets fly into Reading, Pennsylvania. So you can use Reading's airport as a free rebid if you're flying from the Philadelphia area.

It takes a true travel geek to figure out which airports have jet service and which don't. Fortunately, the moderators of BiddingForTravel.com are those kinds of geeks. If you go to BiddingForTravel.com and scroll down to the Using Alternate Airports link, you'll find lists of major cities with non-jet-only airports nearby. Click on your major city, and you'll get a preliminary list of the non-jet cities you can use as free rebids.

BiddingForTravel's moderators warn that those lists may not have been updated very recently, though, so if you decide to use this trick, post a question in BiddingForTravel's "Questions Specifically Related to Alternate Airports" section asking if the airport you're about to use is really still non-jet-only.

If you plan to use this trick, you *must* pay very close attention to your Please Review Your Request screen. Next to Aircraft Type, it *must* say Jet Aircraft Only. *If it says anything else, don't use this trick.* Abort!

Two-connection-only airports

This strategy is also a risky one.

Priceline always asks your permission before you book a flight with two connections. If you don't give Priceline that permission and select an airport that only offers two-connection flights, that airport becomes a free rebid.

To discover whether an airport only has two-connection service, punch your potential free rebid airports into the ITA flight search (see the "Using ITA Software's flight search" section earlier in this chapter). If *all* the routes you get back involve two connections (in other words, three flight numbers), you can use the airports you chose as a free rebid.

In the case of Philly-Toronto, the Toronto City Center airport requires either two connections or multiple airlines. So you can safely add Toronto City Center as long as Priceline is only searching for flights with one connection.

If you plan to use this trick, you *must* pay very close attention to your Please Review Your Request screen. Next to Connections, it *must* say Maximum of 1 Connection Each Way, as shown in Figure 6-6. *If it says anything else, don't use this trick.*

Figure 6-6:
If your review screen says this, you can use two-connection airports as free rebids.

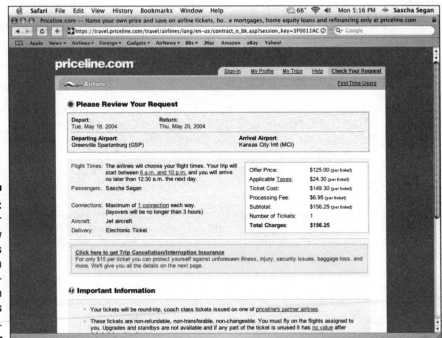

Putting it all together

Okay, so you now have a bid grid that looks like this:

Philadelphia	Toronto	<blank>
ADD BUTTONVILLE	<blank>	
ADD HAMILTON	<blank>	
NEW BID FROM READING		
Philadelphia	Toronto	<blank>

Put the Buttonville and Hamilton free rebids down at the bottom again, so you have six bids. (You could turn it into nine bids by doing another new bid using Lancaster as the origination city.) Take your maximum bid and put it in the blank right-hand space in the bottom column. Then work backward, filling in smaller bids. Because my maximum bid here is $365, I work back by increments of $30 to ensure a nice big spread of possible fares:

Philadelphia	Toronto	$215
ADD BUTTONVILLE	$245	
ADD HAMILTON	$275	
NEW BID FROM READING		
Philadelphia	Toronto	$305
ADD BUTTONVILLE	$335	
ADD HAMILTON	$365	

Now you have a great bid strategy. Time to go put it into action — and to get your flight for as little money as possible.

Chapter 7

Bidding On and Winning a Flight

. . . .

In This Chapter

▶ Making your first bid

▶ Responding to counteroffers

▶ Submitting rebids

▶ Understanding Priceline's ticketing options

▶ Boarding with a Priceline ticket

. . . .

*B*idding is the fun, exciting, nerve-wracking part of Priceline travel. It's a little like playing a video game, a little like playing blackjack in Vegas, and a little like bartering for a carpet in Istanbul. Along the way, you'll feel a lot of pressure to raise your bid big-time, or to walk away discouraged. Don't. Priceline bidding involves a lot in the way of smoke and mirrors, but yes, there actually is an airline ticket behind Door #3.

In this chapter, I take you step-by-step through winning and losing bids for airfare. You'll see all the ways Priceline tries to get you to bid higher, and which of its so-called warnings to ignore. With any luck at all, you'll come out of this with an airfare that will cause your friends' jaws to drop in amazement.

If you haven't read Chapter 6, I recommend heading back there now and finding out about creating a *bid grid,* a bidding strategy that can maximize your bids and help you save as much money as possible. Having a strategy in front of you helps you stay calm as Priceline subtly encourages you to bid higher and higher, and it helps you keep track of the bids you've already made.

Bonus!

Sometimes Priceline sends e-coupons called *bonus money* to frequent customers. These coupons arrive in your e-mail box and contain a link that will add a small amount to your bids, usually $5 to $25. To start a bid with a bonus-money coupon, click on the link in the coupon — don't go to Priceline's home page. For more on bonus money, see Chapter 4.

Beginning to Name Your Own Price

You don't need to bid for an actual ticket to play with Priceline's bidding process. Priceline only makes you put in your credit-card details at the very end, and until then, you can abort any time.

So as you're just starting to figure out how to bid, try a bunch of fake bids. Punch various locations into Priceline's system and see what happens. Grow comfortable with Priceline asking you to raise your bid, and get accustomed to reading Priceline's fine print. Then, when Priceline asks for your credit-card number, don't enter it. Close everything and start all over again.

Start any bid — whether you intend to follow through with it or not — on Priceline's home page (www.priceline.com), shown in Figure 7-1. On the home page:

1. **Select the Airfare radio button near the top of the large orange box on the right-hand side of the page.**

2. **In the Departure City field, enter the *departure city* (the city you're leaving from) for your first bid.**

   Enter U.S. cities with their state name — for example, either "Atlanta, GA" or "Atlanta, Georgia." Enter foreign cities with their country name — for example, "Paris, France." If you don't know a city's state or country, don't worry — Priceline will offer you a list of possibilities when you click Next.

3. **In the Arrival City field, enter the *arrival city* (the city you're traveling to) for your first bid.**

4. **From the Departure Date drop-down lists, select your departure date.**

Figure 7-1:
Start all your
bidding on
the Priceline
home page.

5. **From the Return Date drop-down lists, select your return date.**

Priceline only books round-trip tickets. If you want to use Priceline for a one-way trip, you can use the first half of the ticket but not the second half. See Chapter 2 for more information.

6. **From the Number of Tickets drop-down list, select the number of tickets you want to purchase.**

Children under age 2 who will sit in your lap don't count, but all other children do.

If you're bringing a 1-year-old, bring along some proof your child is under age 2.

7. **Click Next.**

A screen appears listing fares from Priceline's ordinary travel agency, Lowestfare.com, as shown in Figure 7-2. *Note:* This is *not* the place to name your price.

Figure 7-2:
Fares from
Priceline's
normal
travel
agency.
Move on
by, nothing
here to see.

8. **Take a look at the fares here, say "Mm-hmm," and click the Name Your Own Price and Save Up to 40% link.**

   You can save a lot more than 40 percent, but Priceline doesn't want to get your hopes up.

TIP

Church groups and theater troupes: Buying tickets for group travel

Priceline only accepts bids of up to eight tickets. If you have a group larger than that, you can break them up into two separate bids. But remember, you have no guarantee that your two bids will end up with the same flights! If you're unwilling to risk having to make two trips to and from airports, call the airlines that serve your route instead and ask if they have large-group rates.

Making Your First Bid

After you've named your departure and return cities, your dates of travel, and the number of tickets you need, you're ready to start bidding (see Figure 7-3 for a look at the screen where you'll place your first bid). This part of the process is when my heart starts pounding, and it doesn't stop until I've won a ticket. Don't worry about the sense of excitement you get here — and don't let it stop you or change your bidding strategy. Priceline's job is to convince you to overbid. My job is to tell you that your strategy is just fine.

To make your first bid, follow these steps:

1. **In the Select Departure and Arrival Airports section, check the appropriate boxes next to the departure and arrival airports you'd prefer.**

   The more airports you check, the better your chances are. Only check airports you really want to end up with, of course.

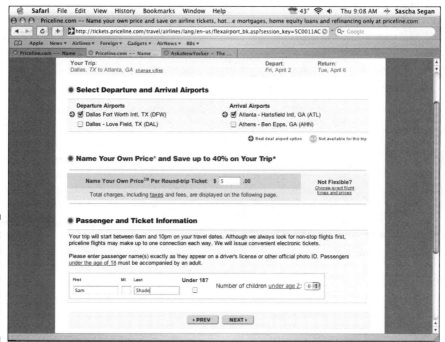

Figure 7-3:
Here's where the magic happens, on the bidding screen.

Expert bidders can increase their number of bids by leaving certain airports *unchecked* and adding them later. These airports are called *free rebids*. Not every city has free rebids, and figuring out which airports are free rebids is a little tricky. Check out Chapter 6 if you're intrigued.

2. **In the Name Your Own Price and Save Up to 40% section, enter your bid amount in the Name Your Own Price Per Round-Trip Ticket field.**

   Curious about how much to bid? Priceline says you can save an average of 40 percent off retail fares. For more-specific details, see Chapter 6.

3. **In the Passenger and Ticket Information section, enter the first and last names of each passenger (middle initials are optional).**

   Although Figure 7-3 shows a bidding screen for one ticket, you'll always see enough spaces on the bidding screen to enter as many passengers as you picked on the home page.

4. **If any passenger is under 18, check the box next to the passenger's name.**

   Each Priceline trip must have at least one adult; children can't fly alone through Priceline. Why? Because some airlines refuse to book unaccompanied minors on the last plane of the day — and Priceline very well may put you on the last plane of the day.

5. **If you're flying with children, use the Number of Children Under Age 2 drop-down list to select the number.**

   Each adult can only have one baby on his or her lap. (And besides, who would want to have to hold more than one — especially when they start crying?)

   Air-safety experts strongly advise against holding babies in your lap on flights. Yes, booking a seat for every child is more expensive. But when turbulence hits, a baby is safest strapped into an FAA-approved car seat. Most car seats nowadays come with a sticker on them that says "This restraint certified for use in motor vehicles and aircraft." As long as you have that sticker, airlines are legally required to install it — and your safely swaddled bundle of joy — in an airplane seat that you've paid for.

6. **Click Next.**

   The We Want You to Get Your Tickets screen (shown in Figure 7-4) appears. If you don't see this screen, jump to the "Check, Check, and Check Again" section in this chapter.

   Priceline wants you to get your tickets. But Priceline also wants to please the airlines. So it'll almost always try to get you to raise your bid by showing the vast gap between your bid and the lowest "official" price it could find.

   Ignore this page completely. It's just propaganda — it means nothing.

7. **Click Next and get on with your bidding.**

Figure 7-4:
Yes, you
know your
bid is low.
That's okay.

Check, Check, and Check Again

After making your first bid (and after you tell Priceline that, yes, you really do want to place such a low bid — see the preceding section), you'll get the Please Review Your Request screen (shown in Figure 7-5). Go over this page very closely. Treat it like a love letter or, if you're feeling morose, a will. This is your last chance to make sure your bid is correct. Be sure to check the following:

- **The departure and arrival dates:** Are they the right months? The right days of the week?

- **The departure and arrival airports:** Are you comfortable with all of them?

- **Your offer price:** Make sure you didn't enter any extra zeroes ($150 and not $1,500, for example).

Still nervous? Priceline will let you buy trip insurance here for $15 per ticket ($25 per ticket for an international flight). The insurance protects you if you or an immediate family member gets too sick to take the trip, if you get in a car accident on the way to the airport, or if the airport is shut down because of a security problem.

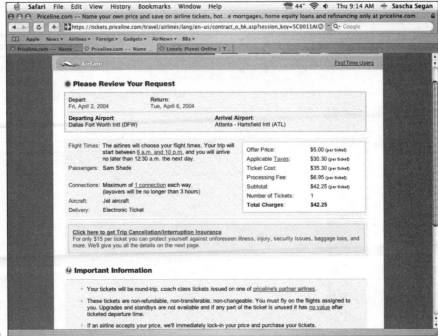

Figure 7-5:
The Please
Review Your
Request
screen is
your last
chance
to make
changes
or correct
mistakes.

Priceline's trip insurance doesn't protect you if you've made mistakes in your bid, or if you're just plain afraid to fly because of a war or terrorist incident that doesn't actually shut down airports or cause the government to issue travel warnings. For all the details, see Chapter 3.

If you want to buy the insurance, follow these steps:

1. **Click the link that says Click Here to Get Trip Cancellation/Interruption Insurance.**

2. **On the following page, scroll down all the way and enter your initials in the Initial Here field.**

3. **Click Next, which will bring you back to the bid-review page.**

4. **Check the details of your bid again!**

If all the information on the bid-review page looks correct, it's time to complete your bid:

1. **Print out the Please Review Your Request page.**

   If something goes wrong with your ticket, you can use this page to show you know what you agreed to.

2. **Scroll down, read the "Important Information" section, and enter your initials in the Initial Here field.**

   Enter at least your first and last initials; the middle initial is optional.

3. **Click Next.**

4. **On the following page, enter your credit-card information.**

   Priceline offers to keep your personal information in a *secure profile*, which means you won't have to re-enter your credit-card details every time you bid, and you'll be able to look up your past bids more easily.

   Setting up a secure profile gives you one big bonus: You get coupons in the mail for *bonus money,* special links that add value to future hotel or airfare bids. That's a compelling reason to sign up.

   But because signing up for *anything* these days usually results in more spam, I suggest you sign up with a free Yahoo! or Hotmail address that isn't your main e-mail address. Then check that free mailbox every once in a while to see if you have a coupon.

5. **If you don't want to set up a profile, ignore all the stuff under Register Now and SAVE!**

   If you do want to set up a profile, fill out the information under Register Now and SAVE!

   You'll have a bunch of options for passwords to use with Priceline — your first car, the city you were born in, that sort of thing. One of those options is "your preferred Internet password." Don't give Priceline the password you use to log on to the Internet or download your e-mail. Not that I don't trust Priceline or anything, but not spreading these things around is a good idea.

6. **Click Buy My Tickets Now.**

   Cross your fingers — this is the moment of truth!

Spamline

Priceline's privacy policy says it doesn't give your e-mail address to third parties. But there's clearly a leak somewhere in the system, because I get spam sent to the e-mail address I use exclusively for Priceline. I also get spam to the addresses I use for other online shopping services, so this problem isn't only Priceline's problem.

My suggestion: Don't use your real, personal e-mail address when bidding on Priceline. Instead, use a special address that you use only for shopping online. If you're on AOL, you can create a new screen name just for shopping. Otherwise, open a free Web-based e-mail account through sites like Yahoo! (http://mail.yahoo.com) or MSN (www.hotmail.com).

Oh, No! A Counteroffer!

When you submit your bid, one of four things will happen:

- ✔ **Your bid will be successful.** If your bid is successful, congratulations! Jump to the "You Won! Now What?" section, later in this chapter.

- ✔ **Your bid will be nowhere near successful.** If this is the case, you'll be presented with the Rebid Screen. Flip to the "Bidding Again and Again" section, later in this chapter.

- ✔ **Priceline's computers will be jammed.** If this happens, you'll get a page telling you to check back in 15 minutes or so. It'll have a bid request number on it, in the form 123-456-789-10. Write down that number; you may need it later. Now wait until you get an e-mail from Priceline saying it has information for you. (Or you can keep the window open and check back in a few minutes. Or click through the Check My Request link on Priceline's home page.) Click on the link in the e-mail, and you'll find out whether your bid succeeded or failed.

  If you signed up for a secure profile and used a throwaway e-mail address, Priceline's alert e-mails will appear in that mailbox, not in your regular mailbox. Also, if you use a spam filter, it may trap Priceline's e-mails, so make sure to check your spam mailbox to see if anything from Priceline was dumped in there.

- ✔ **Priceline will make a counteroffer.** If Priceline thinks your bid is okay but you need a nudge, you'll see the screen shown in Figure 7-6, indicating it would like to make a *counteroffer*.

Knowing whether to take the counteroffer

Counteroffers are good news — they mean Priceline has tickets on the route you want, just not at the price you want. A counteroffer may require that you change airports or accept multiple connections, too.

Priceline will usually accept bids below its counteroffer, so if the counteroffer isn't spectacular, just keep bidding. A bid below the counteroffer will often just result in a higher counteroffer, but you can usually get your ticket by bidding up to the counteroffer through normal means.

I say "often" and "usually" because nothing's certain with Priceline, so if the counteroffer looks really good to you, and you're dying of suspense, take it.

If you decide to take a counteroffer, *print out the counteroffer page* before agreeing. That way, you have a printed record of what you agreed to in case something goes wrong.

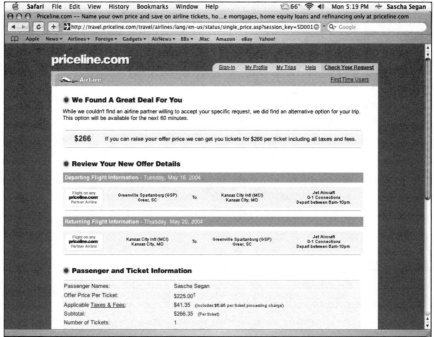

Figure 7-6:
Priceline
sometimes
comes back
to you with a
counteroffer.

Using counteroffers to discover nonstop flights

If you're willing to pay extra to guarantee nonstop flights, you can figure out whether a flight is nonstop from the counteroffer page. Doing so is a little tricky, but it's the only way to guarantee nonstop flights with Priceline. Here's how to figure out if the counteroffer flight is nonstop:

1. **Write down the amount Priceline shows for taxes and fees under Passenger and Ticket Information on the counteroffer screen.**

2. **Subtract $11.95 from the taxes and fees.**

3. **Go to** www.faa.gov/arp/PFC/reports/airports.xls.

   This page is an Excel spreadsheet listing extra fees added to tickets by individual airports. *Note:* If the page doesn't open, see the tip following this numbered list.

4. **Look up both your arrival and departure airports in Column F of the Excel spreadsheet.**

   If an airport isn't listed, there's no fee.

5. **Add the fees for your arrival and departure airports together.**

6. **Subtract the total airport fees (from Step 5) from the amount you got in Step 2.**

   Anything left? If you hit zero, your flight is almost certainly a nonstop. Otherwise, it will have a stop.

If the math looks too complicated, Sheryl Mexic from BiddingForTravel.com offers a rule of thumb: If the taxes and fees are under $20, the flight is *probably* nonstop. Exceptions do exist, though, and doing the math yourself is more reliable.

If you continue bidding, you have no guarantee that you'll get a nonstop flight. To accept a counteroffer, click on the link under the counteroffer. To make a new bid, click Continue to Name Your Own Price.

Bidding Again and Again

So your bid failed. That's okay. It's all part of the strategy, right? Now's the time to rebid — time to start inching your way toward a real airline ticket.

In order to rebid, Priceline requires you to change something other than the price. That can mean adding a possible airport, allowing for prop planes, or accepting off-peak flights. Figure 7-7 shows your options for rebidding.

Clicking these options doesn't mean you'll get an off-peak flight or one on a prop plane. It just means there's a chance you'll get those kinds of flights. More importantly, it lets you raise your bid, so you have better chances of getting any flight at all.

Off-peak? We don't think so

Jennifer H. of New York City took a gamble that paid off when she checked the Off-Peak Flights option for a flight from Philadelphia to San Francisco. After raising her initial bid of $125 to $133, she nabbed a ticket with very same flight times: outbound at 7 p.m., back in at 1:25 p.m.

Her luck continued when she got to the airport on her way home from San Francisco. Although she was booked on a connecting flight, United let her stand by for an earlier nonstop to Philadelphia, and she got home hours earlier than planned.

Adding airports

Adding airports and raising your bid is the best way to increase your chances on your next bid.

The best airports to add are *impossible airports,* otherwise known as *free rebids.* In Figure 7-7, for instance, I'm trying to fly from Philadelphia to Toronto. One of the other airport options for Toronto is Buttonville. There are no flights from Philadelphia to Buttonville. (To understand how to figure that out, see Chapter 6.)

So if I click Buttonville and increase my bid, my rebid is "free." There's no chance of my getting a flight to Buttonville, because there aren't any. I will get a flight from Philadelphia to Toronto just like I want.

Of course, if there are other airports you're okay with adding, but that you just didn't prefer, you can add them while rebidding. For example, if you live halfway between Philadelphia and Newark, you may want to add Newark.

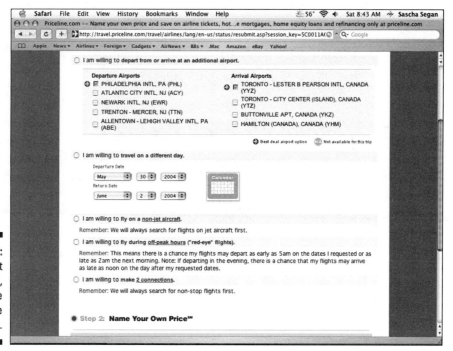

Figure 7-7:
If you want to rebid, choose one of these options.

Before you add Newark or another airport with flights to your destination, check the prevailing fares from that airport using the sites in Chapter 20. If fares are much lower there than at the airport you first bid, you won't want to raise your bid.

Always add airports one at a time. That way you maximize the number of bids you have. If your next bid fails, you can add another airport.

Allowing prop planes

Priceline almost always starts out by searching only for flights on jet planes. If you allow Priceline to search for flights on prop planes, you can increase your bid.

Adding prop planes may slightly increase your chance of getting a flight with a connection rather than a nonstop, but generally it's a safe way to increase your chances.

In the case of my Philadelphia-Toronto flight, the vast majority of flights are on jet planes. Some are nonstop; some involve changing planes in Boston or Montreal. But a few itineraries on United Air Lines require taking a prop plane to New York City and making a connection there. Allowing prop planes gives me access to those flights. More importantly, it lets me raise my bid, so I have a better chance of getting all those other flights, too.

Accepting off-peak flights

Off-peak flights leave between 10 p.m. and 5 a.m., and arrive as late as noon the next day. They can throw a real crimp into your plans for a short-term trip.

If you're willing to take a late-night or early morning flight, though, you can add this option. Checking flight schedules on a site like `http://matrix.itasoftware.com` will show you what you're getting into. To see how many off-peak flights there are on your route:

1. **Go to** `http://matrix.itasoftware.com`, **enter your flight details, and click Go.**

2. **On the top half of the screen that appears, click on Flight Times.**

3. **Click Midnight–6 a.m.**

   That will show you all the flights that leave before 6 a.m. on your route.

4. **Now click on either of the 6 p.m.–Midnight links.**

   Scroll down and look for flights that leave after 10 p.m.

With the Philadelphia-Toronto route, we find there are some Continental flights that leave as early as 5:14 a.m. and a few US Airways flights that leave as late as 10:20 p.m., but nothing that gets into Toronto past midnight. That doesn't look so bad, now does it?

Before you add the off-peak option, check on travel-agency and airline sites to make sure fares for late-night flights aren't much lower than fares for daytime flights. If fares are much lower, you may not want to raise your bid when you add this option. But if they're the same as or higher than daytime flights, you'll want to raise your bid.

Raising your bid

The real goal of all of this adding and clicking, of course, is to be able to raise your bid. If you read Chapter 6 and created a bid grid, you know how much to raise your bid by. If you're working without a strategy, though, you'll have to choose an amount by the seat of your pants.

Don't get carried away and bid more than you can spend — or bid more than you can find elsewhere!

Starting a new bid

If you've run out of options to add to your bid, you can use some sneaky tricks to nab a few more bids. Throw away your existing bid and start a brand-new one using a different origination or destination city that's very nearby your desired city. (For instance, use Reading if you want to fly from Philadelphia.) Then when the airport-selection screen comes up, pick only the airports you want.

If you ask for a flight from Reading to Toronto, for example, Philadelphia comes up as an airport for Reading. So you can check only the Philadelphia airport, and you'll only get flights from Philadelphia.

For detailed instructions on how to do this, see Chapter 6.

Waiting a week

If you've totally run out of possibilities, you can always wait a week. Priceline will let you bid again after exactly seven days. So if you placed your final bid Sunday at 10 a.m., you'll be able to bid again the next Sunday at 10 a.m.

You Won! Now What?

Hopefully, all that research and bidding will pay off, and you'll win a ticket. Congratulations! You just saved big bucks with Priceline.

When you win a ticket, you'll see the screen shown in Figure 7-8.

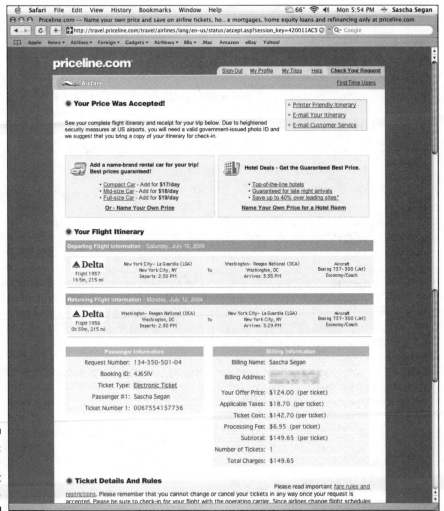

Figure 7-8:
Great news!
You've got
a ticket.

The first thing you want to do is print out this itinerary. Heck, print two copies and keep one in a safe place. You need to take one copy to the airport (see "Boarding your plane," later in this chapter).

Now look under the Passenger Information header at Ticket Type:

✔ If you got e-tickets, this page is the only printed confirmation you'll ever get of your trip. (Feel like printing it out again? Be my guest.)

✔ If you got paper tickets, they'll arrive by Express Mail to your credit-card billing address within four days.

You probably won't ever need the ticket number or airline confirmation number, but the Priceline request number on this page is worth keeping track of. If you have a problem with your ticket, that's the number you need to use to get Priceline to pay attention.

Before you fly

Now you have your tickets, call your airline and try to request seats. Priceline doesn't assign seats, and if you ask in advance you may be able to get better seats than if you just get your seats assigned at the airport.

If you need special meals (on flights where airlines serve food), now's the time to ask for that, too.

If you're flying internationally, make sure your passport will still be valid when you're traveling. Then go to `http://travel.state.gov/travel_warnings.html` and find out whether you'll need a visa for your destination. Getting a visa usually involves calling a foreign embassy or consulate and filling out some forms.

Although a few countries, such as Canada, Mexico, and the Bahamas, will accept an original U.S. birth certificate and driver's license instead of a passport, the U.S. State Department strongly recommends using a passport whenever you leave the United States. So go get that passport. You can find out how to get a passport at `http://travel.state.gov/passport_services.html`. Even tiny babies need passports to travel now!

A day or two before your flight, call your airline again. Make sure the plane is still scheduled to fly.

Annoyingly, airlines have the legal right to change their schedules however they want, even bumping you onto a different flight without compensation, as long as they do it at least a day before you fly. That has nothing to do with Priceline — I've been switched around on tickets bought through Expedia and even on tickets bought through the airlines themselves. Does that sound unjust? You bet it is. Take it up with your representatives in Congress. For now, remember to check with the airline a day or two before you fly.

Boarding your plane

Except for a few things, your Priceline ticket is just like everyone else's. You check in at the same counter, have the same rights if you're bumped or your flight is delayed, and get the same priority in seating. The only things you can't do are the following:

- ✔ You can't change your flight times or dates.

- ✔ You can't get frequent-flier miles.

- ✔ You can't upgrade your ticket to business or first class.

- ✔ Unless you're on United, you can't stand by for earlier flights on your day of travel.

- ✔ You're not *supposed* to be able to use special check-in or boarding lanes if you're an elite frequent flier. But that rule isn't usually enforced.

Bring your Priceline confirmation page or paper ticket to the airport. When you check in, show your paper ticket or just hand over your driver's license to the ticket agent. It's time to fly!

Chapter 8

Dealing with Air-Travel Problems

. . . .

In This Chapter

▶ Fixing mistakes with airline tickets

▶ Finding reservations that have gone missing

▶ Dealing with an airline that goes bankrupt or on strike

▶ Coping with lousy airline customer service

▶ Handling flight delays and cancellations

. . . .

*N*owadays, flying is tough. Several major airlines teeter on the brink of bankruptcy, and sometimes it seems like their staffs are totally unconcerned with the welfare of the passengers. Flight delays and cancellations crop up for no apparent reason at all, and security lines stretch for what feels like miles.

Fortunately, as a Priceline ticket holder, you have rights. You don't have as many rights as you should, but you have the same rights as any other traveler. In this chapter, I tell you how to fix mistakes, how to deal with airline errors, and how to make sure you get what you deserve when something goes wrong in the air.

If you're really worried you won't be able to take a Priceline trip, consider buying travel insurance. (See Chapter 3 for the pros and cons of Priceline's insurance policy.) Insurance protects you against missing your trip because you're ill, because you get into a car crash on the way to the airport, or for a bunch of other reasons. (Unfortunately, most insurance doesn't protect you if your airline goes bankrupt.)

I Made a Mistake!

Priceline is a lot harsher with fixing airline-ticket mistakes than with fixing hotel-reservation problems.

If you made a gross, obvious error — like entering $5,000 instead of $500, or Paris, Texas, instead of Paris, France, Priceline *may* allow you to cancel your ticket for a $75 to $100 penalty.

But if you were trying some sort of intricate bidding strategy and slipped up, forget about it. Priceline also usually turns a deaf ear to pleas of illness, pregnancy, or even being called up to active duty with the military.

If you think you may have to cancel your trip and can't afford to lose the cost of the ticket, buy travel insurance. To see what travel insurance protects you against, turn to Chapter 3.

To Priceline's credit, most other travel agencies and airlines nowadays are almost as heartless. Highly discounted tickets all come with $75 to $200 change fees, and airlines stand firm on imposing those fees in as many circumstances as possible.

But, hey, asking for help never hurts. If you made a major mistake, e-mail Priceline's customer service with your successful bid request number (it looks like 123-456-789-10 and it's under "Passenger Information" on your winning bid page) and tell them how you screwed up. You may be able to get away by paying a penalty less than the price of your ticket.

Get in touch with Priceline the minute you discover something's wrong. The longer you wait, the more skeptical Priceline will be about your troubles.

I Didn't Hear Back from Priceline!

Sometimes Priceline's computers get jammed up. If you bid for a ticket and haven't heard back from Priceline in about an hour:

1. **Go to Priceline's home page (`www.priceline.com`).**

2. **Click Check Your Request, in the upper-right-hand corner.**

3. **Click Airline Tickets.**

4. **Enter your Ticket Request Number (it looks like 123-456-789-10, and should have appeared on the page telling you to wait after you placed your bid) and the e-mail address you gave Priceline.**

   If you don't have your Ticket Request Number, click Click Here If You Don't Have Your Number. Priceline will try to find your request based on your e-mail address and credit-card number.

   You should now see your bid results. If you don't, or if Priceline can't find your request, *don't place another bid.* E-mail Priceline's customer service instead and explain that your bid seems to have vanished.

5. Only place another bid when you have written confirmation from Priceline that your first bid did not succeed.

I've seen plenty of instances where it looks like a bid vanished, only for the results to crop up days later. In the meantime, bidders have won tickets on a later bid, and they ended up stuck with extra tickets they couldn't use.

If you have an e-mail from Priceline assuring you that your first bid is dead, you can use that e-mail as leverage in case that bid comes back to life.

I Didn't Get What I Asked For!

Priceline can be confusing. In the heat of bidding, you can easily click on options you don't really want. If you didn't look closely enough at the Please Review Your Request screen or the counteroffer screen before you agreed to buy a ticket, you can't do anything about it. You *did* agree to the terms — you just may not have *meant* to do so.

If Priceline really does give you a ticket you didn't agree to, though, e-mail its customer-service department immediately (see Chapter 3 for information on contacting Priceline). Include in your e-mail:

- ✔ Your bid number (it looks like 123-456-789-10).
- ✔ What went wrong.
- ✔ An offer to fax the printout you made of the Please Review Your Request screen showing you didn't agree to whatever Priceline gave you.

Priceline will almost always make things right if it screwed up. If it doesn't make things right, and the error was truly Priceline's, turn to your credit-card company (see Chapter 3 for more information).

Something's Wrong with My Airline!

It's a difficult time to be a big, traditional airline. JetBlue, Southwest, Frontier, and the like are winning away travelers, forcing the behemoths of the air to cut prices, eliminate unpopular routes, and sometimes go out of business altogether. The rights of travelers who are trapped in the middle of this business ballyhoo are limited — but they do have *some* rights.

Buying your ticket through Priceline doesn't change your rights — you're in the same boat as the CEO who bought his $2,000 first-class ticket direct through the airline.

Priceline's travel insurance does *not* protect you from an airline strike or bankruptcy. Insurance from Travel Guard (see Chapter 3) protects you from *some* strikes and bankruptcies. For lists of the strikes and bankruptcies Travel Guard *doesn't* protect you from, go to www.travelguard.com and click on Travel Guard Alerts (for bankruptcies) and Airline Strike List (for strikes).

When your airline eliminates your route

Desperate to save money, airlines are hacking away at their route lists left and right. That may leave you in the lurch if you have a ticket to Toronto and, one day, your airline decides to stop flying there.

Good news! Your airline is required by law to get you to your destination, or to give you a full refund. Priceline won't help you, but your airline will. Get in touch with your airline by calling the airline's customer-service number (see Table 8-1) and explain that, as a ticketed passenger, it must get you to your destination.

Table 8-1	Airline Customer-Service Numbers
Airline	*Phone Number*
Air Canada	888-247-2262
Aloha Airlines	800-367-5250
America West Airlines	800-235-9292
American Airlines	800-433-7300
Continental Airlines	800-525-0280
Delta Air Lines	800-221-1212
Hawaiian Airlines	800-367-5320
Icelandair	800-223-5500
KLM	800-374-7747
Lufthansa	800-645-3880
Midwest Airlines	800-452-2022
Northwest Airlines	800-374-7747
Swiss International Air Lines	877-359-7947
United Air Lines	800-241-6522
US Airways	800-428-4322

When your airline goes on strike

Cost-cutting measures have made many airline employees' lives miserable. So there's a chance they'll strike, making *your* life miserable. Don't blame the airline employees — they're just trying to make sure their kids have health insurance. You'd do the same if you were them.

Annoyingly, airlines aren't required to get you to your destination (or even help you at all), if their employees go on strike. That little bit of consumer-unfriendliness is written into ticket contracts, and the government cheerfully lets it happen. (Have a problem? Take it up with Congress.)

Priceline won't help you, so don't bother calling. But even though the airlines aren't required to help you, they usually will. They don't want the bad press that goes with telling thousands of fliers to stay home. Usually, your airline will book you on another airline's flight with similar times.

Call your airline's customer-service number (refer to Table 8-1) and ask to be rebooked. Have your ticket number handy, and don't mention Priceline. (The very mention of Priceline tends to turn customer service agents rigid and grumpy.) Good luck!

When your airline goes bankrupt

In the upside-down world of the airline business, bankruptcies are frequent, and bankruptcy doesn't mean an airline has stopped flying. Continental Airlines has gone bankrupt twice. United and Air Canada are bankrupt right now, and they have hundreds of planes in the air.

What travelers fear isn't bankruptcy but liquidation. *Bankruptcy,* otherwise known as Chapter 11, is when a company goes to a court for help managing its debts. The court supervises the company's operations and gives the company power to break contracts and cut costs (for instance, by firing unionized employees, or by canceling unprofitable routes). If a bankrupt company can't cut enough costs or make enough new money to keep running, it enters Chapter 7, or *liquidation.* That's the traveler's disaster, when an airline stops flying and a court sells off the airline's routes, planes, and gates to cover its bad debts.

If you're holding tickets on an airline that stops flying, you'll probably be protected by law. I'm saying "probably" because the relevant parts of the laws that protect you — the Aviation and Transportation Security Act and the Century of Aviation Reauthorization Act — expire on November 19, 2004. With any luck, Congress will extend those laws.

If the laws are still in effect, you'll be able to get a standby ticket for your cities and times on another U.S.-based airline for no more than $25, as long as:

- ✔ You find another airline flying the exact same route as your original ticket.
- ✔ You contact that airline within 60 days of your original airline's liquidation.

Remember: This is a *standby* ticket. You don't get a guaranteed ticket to your destination. But it's better than nothing.

If the laws expire and nothing replaces them, you're totally unprotected. In the past, some airlines have offered discounted fares to travelers holding worthless tickets. Keep an eye on the news.

Priceline has no obligation to refund your money or find you alternate transportation if your airline liquidates.

My Flight Is Delayed or Cancelled!

If your flight is delayed or cancelled, you have the same rights as any other traveler. For a full rundown, see Chapter 3.

Dealing with delays

If weather, airport congestion, or air-traffic control caused your delay, you're pretty much stuck waiting. Then again, so is everybody else at your airport. Head down to the airport bookstore and pick up a good read.

If the delay only affects your one plane — for example, it's caused by mechanical failure, lack of crew, or a late plane flying in from somewhere else — go to the gate agent and ask to be confirmed on the next available flight. You may have to wait until your delay becomes "major" in the airline's eyes — and that length of time depends on the gate agent's mood.

Coping with cancellations

The moment you hear your flight is cancelled, there's going to be a mad rush to the ticket counter or to the airline's customer-service counter to get new tickets.

Really cheap sleeps at the airport

In severe weather situations, there's often no room at the local inns. First, ask an airline employee if you can get a cot or access to the first-class lounge. Hey, you may get lucky. If that doesn't pan out, get to an Internet kiosk and punch up www.sleepinginairports.net, a brilliant guide to where and how to lay your head in airports from Anchorage to Zanzibar.

By all means, rush. But the moment you get to the line, whip out your cellphone and your Priceline confirmation sheet.

Using your cellphone, call your airline's customer-service number (from Table 8-1) and explain that your flight was cancelled and you'd like to be put on another flight. If you're lucky, you'll get your new confirmation number before you reach the customer-service counter.

Being confirmed on your airline's next flight to your destination where seats are available is your legal right.

If your airline has no other flights to your destination that day, forget about the cellphone and go to the customer-service counter. If another airline's flight to your destination has room, you can usually get a ticket to take to the second airline's customer-service counter and get on its flight.

If there's no way out of the airport at all — say, because a blizzard has cancelled hundreds of flights — you may be able to get a hotel voucher at the customer-service counter. You don't have any legal right to get a free hotel room because of a weather delay, but airlines don't want you to hate them, so they sometimes give in.

At the very least, ask about *distressed-passenger rates* at nearby hotels (these are just lower rates for people like you, who are unexpectedly stuck in the airport overnight). As always, elite status and a good rapport with gate agents can pay off big-time here.

If you don't get anywhere with the airline, try calling the American Society of Travel Agents' (ASTA) 24-hour toll-free referral line at 800-965-2782. It can recommend a travel agent in the area where you're waylaid who may be able to tell you which local hotels offer distressed-passenger rates.

If a mechanical or crew problem keeps you in the airport overnight, you generally *do* have the right to a free hotel room. Check your airline's Contract of Carriage document (see Chapter 3).

I Got Bumped!

Getting bumped can be a lot of fun — *if* you're doing it on purpose. (See Chapter 2 for how to get bumped, get free tickets, and still get to your destination.)

The tantalizing promise of free tickets usually empties enough seats for airlines not to have to bump anyone against his or her will. But involuntary bumpings still happen from time to time.

As a Priceline customer, you have the same rights as any other traveler. You won't be the first one to get bumped, unless you would have been for some other reason (like, you checked in really late). Generally, an airline will bump latecomers first (unless the latecomers are flying on super-expensive business tickets).

To avoid being bumped, always be at your gate at least 30 minutes before departure for domestic flights, and an hour before departure for international flights. That means showing up at the airport an hour before flying for domestic flights, and at least 90 minutes before flying for international flights — to allow yourself time to check in and make your way to the gate.

Each airline has a different policy on what you'll get if it bumps you. Before you fly, read your airline's policy. If you're really paranoid, print it out and bring it with you. To find out how to get copies of those policies, see Chapter 3.

You have additional legal rights if:

✔ You're flying on a U.S. carrier.

✔ Your plane has more than 60 seats.

✔ Your airline can't get you to your destination within an hour of your original arrival time.

If the carrier can put you on a plane in one or two hours, it must compensate you for the cost of your one-way fare, up to $200. If the wait lasts longer than two hours (four hours for international travel), you're entitled to twice the value of your one-way ticket, up to $400. (If these amounts seem low, it's because they haven't been changed since 1978.)

After you've agreed to the airline's compensation, the airline must issue your free ticket, cash, or check *immediately*. If it doesn't, forget the deal and ask the airline to refund your original ticket on the spot.

Part III

Nabbing a Hotel Room with Priceline

The 5th Wave   By Rich Tennant

"St. Bronx?! St. Bronx?! Why couldn't you have used Priceline.com
when booking us on one of the lesser known Caribbean islands?"

In this part . . .

After you book a hotel room through Priceline, you'll be addicted. There's just something undeniably attractive about shacking up in a $300 hotel room for $60, living like a mogul on a student budget. I know one traveling businessman who saved $12,000 in 18 months by using Priceline for hotels — maybe you won't save *quite* that much, but I think you'll still be pretty impressed.

This part cuts through many of the mysteries of Priceline hotel bidding. You discover what Priceline's star levels mean, when to trust its hotel zones, and how to turn 2 bids into 5 (or 10, or 15). Finally, because life doesn't always go as planned, I tell you what to do in case something goes wrong when you try to check in. Sleep tight — and sleep cheap!

Chapter 9

Taking Control of Your Hotel Options

*P*eople like to be in control when they're spending their hard-earned cash. Priceline demands you give up some control over your hotel stay to save money, and that makes a lot of people nervous. In this chapter, I tell you what you can control when you're bidding on Priceline, and where you're just going to have to throw up your hands.

Don't worry — Priceline is pretty trustworthy, and you don't have to give up much control to net big savings. For thousands of happy bidders over the past five years, that trade-off has made sense. I think it'll make sense for you, too.

Understanding Priceline's Hotels

Almost everywhere in the United States, Canada, Europe, the Caribbean, Mexico, and Asia (including Australia), you'll find Priceline hotels. More than 10,000 hotels around the world sell rooms through Priceline. The list includes hotels in major cities like New York, Chicago, London, and Hong Kong. And even if you're wandering through towns as remote as Tok, Alaska, and Dillon, Montana, you'll find Priceline hotels there.

For a list of every city in the world where Priceline has hotels, go to http://travel.priceline.com/hotels/Lang/en-us/city_list.asp?c=US&r=US.

Priceline considers Australia to be part of Asia. Yes, I know Australia is its own continent. But if you're looking for Australia, pick Asia on Priceline's menus.

If Priceline's hotels were people, they'd be a pretty diverse group. If they were at a party, they'd span a wider range of types than any high-school reunion. In the following sections, I show you around.

U.S. and Canadian hotels

The vast majority of the hotels at Priceline's party are in the United States and Canada. Priceline uses hotels all over the spectrum of quality in the United States and Canada, from roadside motels to luxury hotels where rooms regularly go for $400 a night to non-Priceliners.

Major labels

Over here, you see guys in suits. Hundreds of them. Some of them are in polyester and some of them wear Armani, sure, but these guys all look like decent businessmen. In fact, you could swear you've done business with them before.

All the major chains in the United States and Canada participate with Priceline. Marriott brings its JW Marriott, Marriott, Renaissance, Courtyard, Residence Inn, Fairfield Inn, TownePlace Suites, and SpringHill Suites hotels. Starwood delivers Sheraton, Westin, W, and Four Points. Hyatt and Hilton are in the crowd, too. You may not know Cendant's name, but you certainly know his face: He's the owner of Super 8, Wingate Inn, Howard Johnson, Travelodge, Ramada, Days Inn, and others. Smaller chains like Baymont Inns, Adam's Mark, and Red Lion help out travelers to the American heartland, and Fairmont, Sandman, and Delta represent Canada.

Oddball independents

What a strange bunch! Milling around the buffet in Priceline's ballroom, you see a completely mismatched group of people. A few look nervous — they're clean and honest, but wearing T-shirts and torn jeans. A couple of guys from Hawaii wear leis and sandals. Some guys look like artists and writers, real creative types. And is that? — yes it is! — one of the wealthiest people you've ever seen.

Depending on the star level you're bidding, an independent hotel may be a roadside motel or a hip hangout for the cultural elite. At the high end, Priceline sells rooms at Las Vegas's opulent Venetian and at charming, historic hotels like the Kimpton boutique chain. At the low end, you'll get older hotels with very basic accommodations.

Priceline's fishiest hotels

They call it "guppy love." In San Francisco, Seattle, Denver, Chicago, Salt Lake City, New Orleans, and Washington, D.C., the Kimpton Group's Monaco hotels will give you a pet goldfish for the duration of your stay. Trained Hotel Monaco staff will care for your finny friend — all you have to do is love the little guy. Other quirky independent hotels on Priceline include Chicago's music-themed House of Blues and the Napa River Inn, a historic boutique hotel in Northern California's wine country.

Don't worry about getting the seedy motel down the street with the bars on the windows. Even at the bottom of its range, Priceline only signs up motels that can compete with your average Motel 6 or Super 8.

European hotels

Speaking a polyglot of languages, a bunch of European businessmen have begun to mingle with the Americans. Some of them look a lot like the U.S. crew, but some of them wear distinctly foreign garb.

Almost all of Priceline's European hotels come from the Continent's major chains — brands like Libertel, Mercure, Movenpick, Novotel, Sofitel, and Sol Melia.

Priceline focuses on 3- and 4-star hotels in Europe. A small number of 2-star hotels (in London, for instance) are included, but you'll find very few true bargains here. If you're looking for the absolute cheapest decent place to stay in a European city, B&Bs (bed-and-breakfasts), *pensiones* (small, often family-run hotels with basic amenities), or *hostals* (the Spanish word for *pensione*) will beat Priceline almost every time.

Even 4-star European hotels may not have air-conditioning in all the rooms, and may not have rooms with king- or queen-size beds. Rooms in European hotels also tend to be smaller than rooms in U.S. hotels. That's not Priceline's fault — it's just the way things are in Europe.

I don't use Priceline much for hotels in Europe. I like to stay in cozy B&Bs or budget hotels with personality. Most of Priceline's hotels are too big and bland for my taste.

No, that isn't French humor

Yes, there is a Paris Hilton. There are three Hilton hotels in Paris. The one next to the Eiffel Tower shares its name with the famous heiress and TV personality. Unfortunately, I've never seen anyone nab the Paris Hilton on Priceline (she's not a discount kind of girl).

Caribbean and Mexican hotels

Olé! There's a party going on in this corner of the room, and you're invited. The vast majority of Priceline hotels in Mexico and the Caribbean are beach resorts. Although a few non-resort hotels (several in Mexico City, and a few in Old San Juan) are included, most travelers using Priceline in the Caribbean are headed to the beach.

Priceline doesn't let you bid for all-inclusive resorts; these aren't Club Med–, Beaches-, or Sandals-type places. Instead, Priceline's Caribbean and Mexican resorts are big hotels with good beachfront access.

Sheraton, Hilton, Wyndham, Marriott, Hyatt, and Intercontinental all sell resort rooms through Priceline.

Asian and Australian hotels

This snooty crew is loaded with bling-bling. Chatting away on their cellphones, checking their Rolex watches, this small clot of Chinese, Japanese, Malaysian, Thai, and Australian business folk isn't afraid to show off.

Priceline doesn't have many hotels in Asia and Australia, but the ones it has are among the best. Priceline specializes in delivering 4- and 5-star hotels in Asia and Australia.

A bit of grade inflation is going on. An Asian 5-star hotel is like a good 4-star in the United States. An Asian 4-star is like a standard 4-star in the United States.

Most of Priceline's Asian hotels are standard-issue business hotels like Marriotts, Sheratons, Le Meridien Hotels, and Swissotels. A few are really luxurious, though, like the Langham Hotel in Hong Kong and the Shangri-La in Bangkok.

Choosing a Hotel

If specific hotel names don't matter much to you, and you think all rooms in a hotel are pretty much the same, then you'll do fine with Priceline. Does it really matter to you whether you get the Marriott or the Westin in downtown Chicago? Priceline lets you specify the neighborhood zone your hotel will be in, its quality, and (of course) the price you want to pay.

On the other hand, if you need a special kind of room (a family room, for instance) or demand to stay in one hotel in particular, stay away from Priceline. Choosing your specific room and your specific hotel are the two things you can't do when you're saving this much money.

What you control

Priceline lets you pick three key aspects of your hotel stay: your hotel's quality, roughly where your hotel will be, and the price of your room. If you pay attention to Priceline's maps and to the tips on sites like BiddingForTravel.com, you can usually narrow the list of hotels you may get to a dozen or fewer.

Price

Name your price. Priceline will beg, implore, and inveigle you to raise your bid on practically every screen, but you still control how much you pay.

Never bid more than you feel comfortable with — and try not to get caught up in the excitement of bidding. You can save 40 to 60 percent over retail rates with Priceline, but you have to bid intelligently.

City

Priceline has hotels in hundreds of U.S. cities and dozens of Canadian cities. It also sells rooms in a slew of European cities, some major Caribbean and Mexican destinations, and a few Asian hot spots.

If the city you pick has zones (see the following section), some of the zones may be in nearby suburbs, not in the city itself. It's up to you to keep an eye on the map and choose your zones intelligently.

Zone

Priceline divides most cities up into groups of neighborhoods, or *zones*. By picking a zone, you can nail down your hotel to a specific part of the city.

Requesting early or late check-in

It's 6 a.m., and you just got off a grueling red-eye flight. When you stumble into your hotel, the desk clerk just frowns and points to a sign that reads, "Check-in 3 p.m."

Or it's 11 p.m., and you just got off the worst flight of your life. You sat between a screaming baby and a passenger with the Ebola virus, and all you want to do is sleep. Will there be a room at your inn?

Priceline guarantees all rooms for late arrival, but hotels often ignore that guarantee. If you're planning to arrive after 8 p.m., call your hotel the morning of your arrival and tell the staff when you're showing up. Most of the time, that will ensure you'll have a room to collapse in.

Occasionally, rapacious hotel managers may decide to stick you in the worst room of the house or, worse, walk you to another hotel nearby. (*Walking* is when a hotel sells more rooms than it has available and spills you over to another hotel.) Stand firm: You have a confirmed reservation. (See Chapter 12 for more on walking and what to do when hotel clerks turn evil.)

And what if you arrive early? Unfortunately, you don't have a leg to stand on. Be nice, and you may get into your room early. Otherwise, you can almost always leave your luggage with the staff (for a small tip) while you explore the city you've landed in.

Don't trust the zone names. Priceline's zones always come with maps, and the maps always tell the truth. A "city center" zone may include areas outside the city center, and a zone named for a city may include chunks of a suburb. Check the map and make sure you really want to stay in that zone.

Star level

Priceline uses eight star levels to rate hotels, based on their room quality and amenities: 1-star, 2-star, 2½-star, 3-star, Boutique, 4-star, Resort, and 5-star. (In Chapter 10, I explain exactly what those star levels mean.) Priceline's star levels are fairly reliable, and they give you pretty good control over the quality of hotel you get.

What you can't control

There's no such thing as a free lunch. Because you're saving money on Priceline, you have to make a few trade-offs. I, for one, think they're well worth it — and so do thousands of other happy bidders.

Hotels gone wild!

Even if you *don't* book through Priceline, you may still get stuck in a room you don't want. The Hyatt Regency Jersey City once stuck my wife and me in a room with two double beds on our anniversary weekend; I booked that room directly through Hyatt and requested one king- or queen-size bed.

The Ramada in New Orleans's Garden District once put me in a hideous smoking room that smelled like something had died in there. I booked that one through Expedia.

Priceline is just more up front about what it doesn't guarantee.

Exact hotel

There is no way to guarantee a specific hotel with Priceline. If you're not comfortable with this, stop here. I don't care if BiddingForTravel.com says that everyone in the past six months has gotten the same hotel. When you bid, things may change.

If you're not comfortable with every hotel of the right star level in your zone, don't bid.

Scared yet? Don't worry. Enjoying Priceline is all about managing your expectations. If you expect to get a Hyatt, you'll be annoyed when you get a Hilton. But if you expect what Priceline promises — a 4-star hotel in the right zone — you'll be satisfied whether you get a Hyatt, a Hilton, or for that matter a Sheraton or a Kimpton.

Number of beds

Priceline guarantees that every room will sleep two adults. That's it. You can't guarantee that you'll get two beds (or that you'll get one bed). You certainly can't guarantee space for a third person. If you're bringing kids and don't want them to sleep with you, bid for more than one room.

That said, 95 percent of the time in the United States and Canada, you'll be able to request a queen-size bed, king-size bed, or two double beds when you check into your hotel. And unless you're staying in New York, San Francisco, or downtown Chicago, you'll probably be able to get a cot or a rollaway bed into your room for a small fee. Some hotels on Priceline even provide suites. You just can't *guarantee* any of these things.

Priceline bargain goes up in smoke

One woman learned what Priceline *doesn't* guarantee the hard way. Bidding $60 for a 2½-star hotel in Bakersfield, California, she was initially thrilled to see that she'd been bumped up to a 3-star room at the local Red Lion. But that hotel was full, so the management dumped her in a stinky, smoky room when she wanted a peaceful, smoke-free place to sleep. To top it off, the furnishings looked tired, and the shower had trouble summoning hot water.

Sleazy fees

Don't blame Priceline if you see a slew of "surcharges" tacked on to your hotel bill when you check out. No matter how you book your room, most hotels nowadays will add a slew of dubious fees to your bill. For example, you may be charged a resort fee for use of the pool, a fee for use of your room safe, or even an energy surcharge for use of the lights!

You can usually get the energy surcharge taken off if you scream bloody murder about it, but the resort fees are virtually unassailable.

Just rest assured that everyone's paying these irritating fees, not just Priceline customers.

Smoking versus nonsmoking

This issue is a thorny one. Priceline doesn't guarantee smoking or nonsmoking rooms. Once again, you'll be able to get the kind of room you want about 90 percent of the time if you request it upon check-in. But if you have a medical condition that requires you to stay in a nonsmoking room, don't use Priceline.

Chapter 10

Bidding Smarter for Hotels

. . . .

. . . .

*E*very page you read in this chapter will save you money. Priceline's hotel partners count on bidders' cluelessness to make big bucks. This chapter gives you the clues, so you can get what you want for the lowest possible price.

The key to smart bidding is the *bid grid,* a chart of all the bids you plan to make. Building a good bid grid requires lots of homework, and it can be tedious. Persevere. The more work you do now, the better a hotel you'll get and the more you'll save.

If all this seems like too much for you, take a break. Get inspiration from BiddingForTravel.com, where successful bidders post their victories every day.

And even if you don't want to slog through a bid grid, at least read the sections of this chapter on Priceline's star levels and zones. That way, you'll know what you're bidding for.

You're a Star! Understanding Priceline's Star Levels

You can't select a specific hotel with Priceline, but you can select your hotel's star rating. Priceline quizzes hotel chains about the amenities available at their hotels and rates each property accordingly — so one Courtyard by Marriott may be 2 stars while another may be 2½ stars.

Priceline rates hotels from 1 to 5 stars, plus two oddball ratings, Resort and Boutique.

Priceline can upgrade any bid to a higher star level. So if you bid for a 3-star hotel, you may get a Boutique-level hotel or a 4-star hotel instead.

Priceline's star ratings

Priceline rates hotels according to eight quality levels, from humble 1-star motels all the way up to 5-star luxury palaces. (Resort- and Boutique-level hotels don't have stars, but they still fit into the system.) You can do a pretty good job of pinpointing the kind of hotel you want using Priceline's star system, whether you're looking for something cheap, simple, and clean or you want a classy, romantic getaway in the middle of a big city. In the following sections, I explain everything you need to know about Priceline's star levels so you can find the hotel that's right for you.

1-star hotels

Many bidders avoid 1-star hotels, many of which are low-end motels out by highways (see Figure 10-1 for an example). You'll find only the most basic of furnishings in a 1-star hotel, and although Priceline swears they're clean, bidders have had mixed results.

Figure 10-1: Clean and basic, this Baymont Inn is a 1-star hotel.

Sunrise design is a signature mark of Baymont Inns, Inc.

> ## Mis-rated hotels
>
> Everyone hates mis-rated hotels. Typically, they're once-decent hotels that have back-slided, or rogue hotels belonging to generally high-quality chains. If you get a filthy room or find yourself at a 3-star with no restaurant, contact Priceline's customer service immediately. Priceline will rarely admit its error, but you may get your money back and find, mysteriously, that the hotel has been kicked down by a star when you bid the next time.

Priceline says 1-star hotels are "generally low-rise hotels located near major attractions, convenient intersections, or major interstates. Furnishings are basic, clean, and in good condition. Restaurants are either on-site or close-by." Each room must have the following:

✔ Color TV

✔ Telephone

✔ Private bathroom (*all* Priceline rooms have private bathrooms)

Popular 1-star chains in the United States and Canada include Baymont Inn, Comfort Inn, Days Inn, Econo Lodge, Howard Johnson, Ramada Limited, Rodeway Inn, Sleep Inn, Super 8, Travelodge, and Wellesley Inn.

Although there are 1-star hotels in Europe, Asia, and the Caribbean, I've never seen anyone win one.

2-star hotels

Two-star hotels are a bit of a crap shoot. You may get a spic-and-span suite in a hotel with free parking, free local phone calls, and free muffins in the morning. But you may also get a room in a run-down former 3-star hotel slowly sliding toward oblivion.

Checking the hotel lists on BiddingForTravel.com lessens your risk — although it can't guarantee that you'll get a hotel on its list, it can tell you whether other bidders have gotten a lemon recently.

Priceline says 2-star hotels in the United States and Canada are "generally located near major attractions, intersections, and casual dining restaurants. Some hotels may offer limited restaurant service within the hotel." Each room must have the following:

✔ Color TV with premium channels

✔ Telephone

✔ Radio alarm clock

Popular 2-star chains in the United States and Canada include Baymont Inn, Best Western, Candlewood Suites, Clarion, Comfort Inn, Days Inn, Fairfield Inn, Four Points Sheraton, Hampton Inn, Holiday Inn, Holiday Inn Express, Homestead Inn, Homestead Village, Howard Johnson, La Quinta, Microtel, Quality Inn, Ramada, Red Lion, SpringHill Suites, TownePlace Suites, and Wellesley Inn & Suites.

Very few 2-star hotels are available in Europe and the Caribbean. Priceline calls them "basic but functional." I call them motels. European 2-star chains include Libertel and Comfort Inn. Successful bids are few and far between, and in Europe you'll probably have more success finding a local B&B through other means. Forget about bidding for 2-star hotels in Asia.

2½-star hotels

A sweet spot for value, 2½-star hotels often have free parking, free phone calls, and big rooms with mini-kitchens, like the Hawthorn Suites in Figure 10-2.

Figure 10-2: For a chance at a kitchen, bid for a 2½-star hotel like this Hawthorn Suites.

Two-and-a-half-star hotels just don't have the level of service and polish that you'd expect from a higher-class place — room service, for instance, is rare at this level. Priceline says 2½-star hotels "are well appointed and often feature amenities for the business traveler. While hotel services may be somewhat limited, 24-hour Front Desk and daily housekeeping services are provided. Hotels usually feature a restaurant for breakfast." Each room must have the following:

- ✔ TV with premium channels
- ✔ Telephone
- ✔ Radio alarm clock
- ✔ Iron and ironing board
- ✔ Hairdryer

The hotel must also have a business center and a 24-hour reception desk.

Big names on the 2½-star circuit include AmeriSuites, Country Inn and Suites, literally *hundreds* of Courtyard by Marriott hotels, Doubletree Club, Hampton Inn, Hilton Garden Inn, Holiday Inn, Ramada Plaza, Residence Inn, Staybridge Suites, Summerfield Suites, Wellesley Inn & Suites, Wingate Inn, and Wyndham Garden.

You can't bid for 2½-star hotels outside North America.

3-star hotels

Now we're talking *hotels.* With 3-star hotels, you start to see room service, gyms, and locations closer to city centers.

Some smart bidders actually prefer 2½-star hotels over 3-star hotels. Many 2½-star hotels offer free parking, free phone calls, and rooms with sofa beds. In a 3-star hotel, you'll probably be charged for parking and gouged for phone calls, plus your room may be tiny. But you'll be in a hotel atmosphere, as opposed to the glorified motels you get at lower star levels.

Each room in a 3-star hotel must have the following:

- ✔ TV with premium channels
- ✔ Telephone
- ✔ Radio alarm clock
- ✔ Iron and ironing board
- ✔ Hairdryer

Baby, you can park my car

Priceline doesn't handle parking charges, which can be fearsome at many 3-star and better hotels. Most San Francisco hotels, for example, charge at least $30 for (mandatory) valet parking. If you're staying in a city center, you may be able to park your car on the street or in a nearby public lot. If you're staying out in the sticks or at a resort, you may just have to pay. If savings are more important than luxury, most 2-star and 2½-star hotels offer free parking. (Just hope you don't get automatically upgraded to a 3-star on your 2½-star bid.)

The hotel must also have the following:

- ✔ A business center
- ✔ A 24-hour reception desk
- ✔ A restaurant
- ✔ Room service (but not necessarily 24-hour!)

Three-star chains in the United States and Canada include Adam's Mark, Club Quarters, Crowne Plaza, Doubletree, Embassy Suites, Four Points, Hilton, Holiday Inn, Hyatt, Marriott, Omni, Park Plaza, Radisson, Red Lion, Renaissance, Sheraton, and Wyndham.

Three-star hotels in Europe include some Mercure, Golden Tulip, Melia Confort, Thistle, and Holiday Inn properties. Three-star hotels available through Priceline are very rare in Asia; Hong Kong's Novotel Century Harbourview is one example.

Boutique-level hotels

Boutique-level hotels are cozy, historic, and sometimes a little funky. Usually independent or run by small chains, they often have more personality than the big-name 3-star and 4-star hotels.

If you're looking for a big room or two beds, bid for 4-star (or higher) hotels rather than Boutique-level hotels. Some Boutique-level hotels have very small rooms that only fit one bed for two people. Bidding 3-star hotels doesn't save you, because any 3-star hotel bid can be upgraded by Priceline to Boutique level.

Boutique-level hotel rooms must have the following:

- ✔ TV with premium channels
- ✔ Telephone
- ✔ Radio alarm clock
- ✔ Iron and ironing board
- ✔ Hairdryer

The hotel must also have the following:

- ✔ A business center
- ✔ A 24-hour reception desk
- ✔ A restaurant

The best example of a Boutique-level chain is the Kimpton Group (www.kimptongroup.com). Its hotels include the Hotel Monaco in San Francisco and the Hotel Burnham in Chicago.

Outside the continental United States, only the San Juan, Puerto Rico, zone offers Boutique-level bidding. Expect San Juan Boutique-level hotels to be historic resort properties.

4-star hotels

If you want to be assured of comfort, just bid a 4-star hotel. Four-star properties like Boston's Langham Hotel, shown in Figure 10-3, are solid, upscale, maybe even luxurious; they're the kinds of places where you really feel like you're on vacation, or like you're ready to close that big deal. Four-star hotels are where you'll find the biggest percentage savings with Priceline — this is the level where you'll get $240-per-night hotels for $90 per night. Just prepare to be socked with parking charges if you're taking a car.

According to Priceline, 4-star hotels "are the world's deluxe hotels, offering premium-level service and amenities for the most discriminating traveler. These hotels typically offer appointments, bathrobes, minibars and comprehensive business services."

Each room in a 4-star hotel must have the following:

- ✔ TV with premium channels
- ✔ Telephone
- ✔ Radio alarm clock
- ✔ Iron and ironing board
- ✔ Hairdryer

Figure 10-3:
Boston's
4-star
Langham
Hotel has an
award-
winning
restaurant.

The hotel must also have the following:

- A business center
- A 24-hour reception desk
- A restaurant
- Room service (but not necessarily 24-hour!)
- Bellman
- Concierge
- Gym

In the United States and Canada, that means chains like Embassy Suites, Hilton, Hyatt, Loews, Marriott, Omni, Renaissance, Sheraton, W, Westin, and Wyndham.

In Europe, 4-star chains include Melia, Sofitel, Sheraton, Thistle, Hilton, and Radisson. And there are plenty of 4-star hotels in Asia, with chains like Novotel and Regal.

Resort-level hotels

If you absolutely need a pool (and don't need to be near a city center), pick a resort. It's the only way to guarantee a pool.

According to Priceline, resort hotels "offer a spa or fitness facility, one or more pools, and multiple food and beverage choices. All Priceline.com resorts reflect the area and the season with recreational options such as water sports, tennis, snow skiing, or golf. Those resorts in coastal areas will feature beachfront access."

In Priceline's system, resorts have 4½ stars — so a 3-star or 4-star bid may get upgraded to a resort.

Each room in a Resort-level hotel must have the following:

- ✔ TV with premium channels
- ✔ Telephone
- ✔ Radio alarm clock
- ✔ Iron and ironing board
- ✔ Hairdryer

The hotel must also have the following:

- ✔ A business center
- ✔ A 24-hour reception desk
- ✔ A restaurant
- ✔ Room service (but not necessarily 24-hour!)
- ✔ Bellman
- ✔ Concierge
- ✔ Gym or spa
- ✔ A pool!

Resort-level hotels have one big downside: Many charge resort fees of $10 a day or so on top of whatever you're paying Priceline. You can't do anything about this, and you should be ready to pay these fees if you're bidding in a zone that features resorts.

Priceline resorts include hotels like the Fountainebleu Hilton Resort in Miami Beach, Florida, and the Hilton Palm Springs Resort in Palm Springs, California.

A galaxy of star levels: Figuring out the different systems

What do travel Web sites and first-grade teachers have in common? They both love to give out lots of gold stars. Expedia, Travelocity, the American Automobile Association (AAA), Hotwire, and Priceline all rate hotels on their Web sites. The problem is, their ratings don't match.

USA Today travel writer David Grossman compared nine different star rating systems and found many of them vary by a star or so. The Hilton Chicago is a 4-star hotel on Priceline but a 3-star on Travelocity. The Sheraton at Fisherman's Wharf in San Francisco, meanwhile, is a 4-star on Expedia but a 3-star on Priceline.

Grossman found Expedia to be the most liberal of the rating services. Because it's now owned by the same folks as Hotwire, expect Hotwire to be a bit more generous than Priceline, too. Travelocity was the strictest.

When you're looking for 4-star hotels to try to figure out what Priceline offers, turn first to the Priceline watchdog bulletin boards, BiddingFor Travel.com and BetterBidding.com.

Priceline owns Travelweb.com, so you can also turn to Travelweb to find out how Priceline rates a hotel. Travelweb has one flaw: It rates all Priceline 2½-star hotels as 3 stars.

Whatever you do, don't trust Hotwire's hotel rating system. Yeah, I know it's tempting, because Hotwire usually offers the second-lowest rates you can find, so you'll really want to compare Hotwire to Priceline. But you can safely assume that there's a good chance what Hotwire calls a 4-star hotel, Priceline calls a 3-star hotel.

5-star hotels

Five-star hotels are, simply, the ultimate. You'll pay a lot for these places, even with Priceline. But you'll get fluffy bathrobes, celebrity chefs, and attentive service that makes *you* feel like a star.

Each room in a 5-star must have the following:

- ✔ TV with premium channels
- ✔ Telephone
- ✔ Radio alarm clock
- ✔ Iron and ironing board
- ✔ Hairdryer
- ✔ Bathrobes
- ✔ Twice-daily maid service
- ✔ High-quality linens and bath amenities

The hotel must also have the following:

- A business center
- A 24-hour reception desk
- A restaurant
- "Extended-hour" room service
- Bellman
- Concierge
- Fitness center

There are only a handful of 5-star hotels in the United States and Canada. The Venetian in Las Vegas and the Waldorf Towers in New York are two good examples. You'll find more in Europe and Asia, where the top-notch hotel in any given large city will probably be 5 stars.

Stars in your eyes: Figuring out which level is right for you

How many stars will make you happy? I've got a handy-dandy guide to your preferred star level based on the kind of traveler you are:

Who are you?	Star level
Hard-core budget traveler	A 1-star hotel is fine. Sure, the walls may be caving in. But you've stayed in a mud hut in India. It's all about saving money.
Traveling salesman	Go for the 2-star hotel. You can usually keep costs under $40 a night this way, and because you'll have your own car, the free parking means a lot.
Family vacation	Time for a 2½-star hotel. The gamble here is that you may get a suite hotel, with extra room for the kids.
Average Joe (or Jane)	Start with a 4-star, and work down to a 3-star. These are your run-of-the-mill, pretty nice hotels.
Amphibian	Shoot for a 4-star or a Resort-level hotel if you need a pool. Four-star hotels don't always have pools, but most of them do. All Resort-level hotels have pools or a beach.
Once-in-a-lifetime tripper	For those special honeymoon moments, try to avoid using Priceline. If you must use Priceline, never bid below 4 stars. You don't want any letdowns on this trip.

There's No Place Like Zone

You know *what* kind of hotel you want. Now you need to pick *where*. Priceline divides most major metropolitan areas into *zones* (neighborhoods or collections of neighborhoods). When you bid for a hotel, you can restrict your search to a particular zone, ensuring you won't get stuck out in the boonies.

Whether you actually want to bid for a hotel in a particular zone or not, knowing all the zones in a metro area is critical to smart bidding. That's because you can use unwanted zones to get *free rebids* — extra bids in the zones you actually want. (See the "Finding free rebids" section later in this chapter for an explanation of free rebids.)

The more you know about the city you're staying in, the better you'll be at picking the right zone. In Chapters 21 and 22, I list some popular hotel zones. But comparing Priceline's zone maps to the maps in a good guidebook, such as the *For Dummies* travel guides or Frommer's (both published by Wiley), is definitely the best way to go.

Don't pay any attention to zone names. Always look at the maps instead. Priceline's City Center zone in Vienna, Austria, for instance, includes areas outside the innermost ring road that defines the center of the city. The zone is marked correctly on the map, though.

Understanding zone maps

Zone maps all work the same way. They have a main map covering an entire metro area, and then little maps showing the exact locations of zones.

Take a look at a sample zone map for some practice:

1. **Go to Priceline's home page,** www.priceline.com.

2. **Select the Hotels radio button below Find Your Next Travel Deal.**

   A screen appears listing popular cities for bidding hotels.

   If you don't see a list of United States cities, click on the U.S. link above the list of city names.

3. **Select the Boston radio button below Choose a City.**

4. **From the Check-In Date drop-down lists, pick a random date about a month from now.**

5. **From the Check-Out Date drop-down lists, pick a date a few days later than the one you just entered.**

6. **Click Next.**

   You're now looking at the main zone map screen for Boston (shown in Figure 10-4). Looks blobby, doesn't it? Boston's eight zones are scattered all over the metro area, from the heart of downtown to leafy suburbs miles away.

7. **Click on the words Area Details next to the Cambridge check box near the top of the page.**

   A window (shown in Figure 10-5) should appear showing the exact dimensions of the Cambridge zone. You may want to print out this window and compare it to a map of Boston or information about Boston in a guidebook.

The map, not the zone name, is what matters. The Cambridge zone doesn't contain all of Cambridge, and it contains a small part of Boston that isn't Cambridge, on the other side of the Charles River.

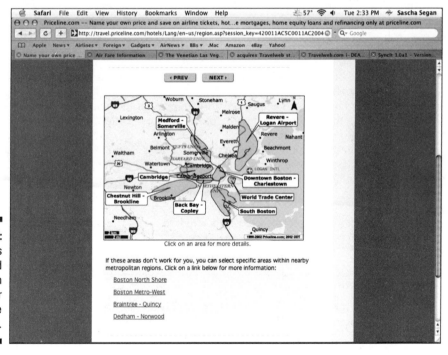

Figure 10-4:
The zones around Boston stretch far into the suburbs.

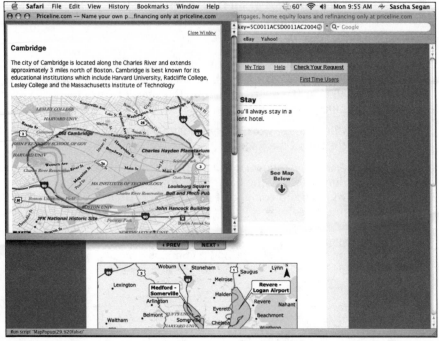

Figure 10-5:
The zone map, not the zone name, shows where you'll get your hotel.

Get acquainted with all the zones you think you may like. If you're heading to a city, that means looking at the detailed maps of the most central zones. If you're heading to a specific suburb, eyeball the nearest suburban zone, which may sprawl well past your exact destination.

Just because a hotel is in an airport zone doesn't mean it has an airport shuttle or transportation to the airport. Boston's Revere-Logan Airport zone, for instance, stretches way up Route 1 north of the airport. If you absolutely need a complimentary airport shuttle, Priceline isn't for you.

When you've picked the zones you like, write them down on a sheet of paper. You'll need that list later.

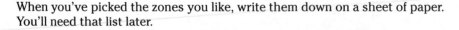

The big, bad international zones

In some cities outside the United States, Priceline's zones are so large as to be useless. Take Barcelona. Both of the zones there include vast, unattractive industrial areas far from the city center. The "central" Brussels zone, as well, stretches far south of the city center. *Remember:* If you're not prepared to get a hotel *anywhere* in your zone, don't bid for that zone.

Oh, no! No zones!

Many smaller towns and cities don't have any zones at all. In those cases, all Priceline guarantees you is a hotel within the city limits. Many of those hotels may be out by highways or shopping malls. They may be miles from downtown. If you won't have your own car, you should stay away from zoneless cities.

No free rebids exist in zoneless cities. If your bid fails, you can switch bidders (see the "Switching bidders" section later in this chapter), lower the quality level of the hotel you're willing to accept, or wait 72 hours and bid again.

Finding free rebids

What's better than a discount? Something free! Normally, if your first bid is rejected, Priceline demands that you add a zone or wait 72 hours before bidding again. If you don't particularly want any other zones, that puts you in a pretty tight spot.

That's where free rebids come in handy. You can find free rebids in the form of zones that you can add where you have no chance of getting a hotel in that zone, because hotels of your quality level aren't offered there.

For instance, as of this writing, Boston's Medford-Somerville zone only had 1- to 2½-star hotels. So if you're bidding for a 4-star hotel in Downtown Boston, you can add Medford-Somerville and safely get another bid. Because there are no 4-star hotels in Medford-Somerville, you can't get a hotel there. Pow! Free rebid.

Priceline loves to change zone maps and star levels. By the time you read this, there may be 4-star hotels in Medford-Somerville. Or the Medford-Somerville zone may not even exist. But the general strategy here will still hold.

To find potential free rebids, start at the main zone map screen (still using Boston):

1. **Click the first check box under Improve Your Chances.**

   Make sure none of the other check boxes below it are clicked.

2. **Click Next.**

   You see the screen in Figure 10-6.

3. **On a piece of paper (you can use the same one you used to write down the zones you liked), write down the zone name and the highest star level that appears (as shown in Figure 10-6).**

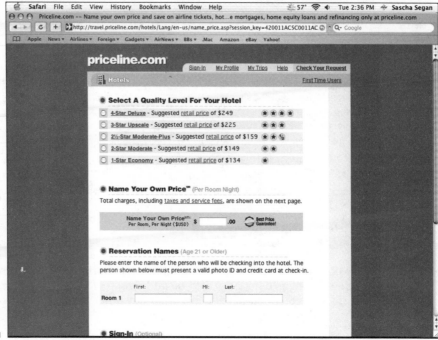

Figure 10-6:
Boston's
Back Bay–
Copley zone
offers 1-star
through
4-star
hotels.

In this case, you'd write, "Back Bay–Copley, 4 stars."

Resort-level hotels count as 4½ stars, and Boutique-level hotels count as 3½ stars.

4. **Click the Back button on your Web browser.**

5. **Uncheck the check box under Improve Your Chances.**

6. **Check the next box down from the one you just checked.**

7. **Head back to Step 2, and repeat until you have a list that looks like this:**

Back Bay–Copley	4 stars
Cambridge	4 stars
Chestnut Hill–Brookline	2½ stars
Downtown Boston	4 stars
Medford–Somerville	2½ stars
Revere–Logan Airport	4 stars
South Boston	2½ stars
World Trade Center	4 stars

Great news! Looks like plenty of free rebids for high-class hotels are here. If you're looking for 3- or 4-star hotels, you can add the Chestnut Hill, Medford, and South Boston zones without fear, because they don't offer any 3- or 4-star hotels. That gives you four free chances to bid where you once had one.

Deciding How Much to Bid

You know what star level you want, and what zones you want. Now you need to figure out how much to bid.

Priceline won't tell you if you're bidding too much, because that's how it and its hotel partners make money. Priceline often complains (wrongly) that you're bidding too little; always ignore Priceline's complaints. Instead, turn to competitors and to the hotels themselves. Shop around. Find the best rates. Then make sure to bid lower on Priceline.

Knowing which hotels to check

To get the right rates, you have to check the right hotels. That's where BiddingForTravel.com's Hotel Lists come in. They're online lists of hotels people have won with Priceline in the past. To find the list for your zone:

1. **Go to** www.biddingfortravel.com.

2. **Scroll down below the Hotels header until you see a link covering the area you're bidding.**

3. **Click on that link.**

   You should get a list of successful bids with a link to a hotel list at the top.

4. **Click on the link for the hotel list.**

BiddingForTravel.com's lists aren't comprehensive. You may end up winning a hotel that's not on its list!

Pick a few hotels off the list that are in the right zone and star level for you and see what its rates are for your travel dates, using the Web sites listed in the next few sections. If you feel up to it, you can check *all* the hotels in your zone and star level!

Travel agencies

You should always check around the major travel agencies to make sure nobody has a specially negotiated rate that may trump whatever you were intending to bid. Check these sites before bidding:

- **Expedia** (www.expedia.com)
- **Travelocity** (www.travelocity.com)
- **Orbitz** (www.orbitz.com)
- **Hotels.com** (www.hotels.com)
- **Travelweb** (www.travelweb.com; owned by Priceline and shown in Figure 10-7)
- **Hotel Reservation Service** (www.hrs.de; for European hotels)
- **Venere.com** (www.venere.com; for European hotels)
- **Asia Travel** (www.asiatravel.com; for Asian hotels)

Write down the best rates you get. Ignore AAA and government rates, unless you're eligible for them — you want the best rate that you, yourself, can actually book. You don't want to overbid!

Figure 10-7: Check hotel rates at Travelweb, a hotel site owned by Priceline.

Hotel sites

Hotel chains' sites provide the most reliable arbiter of what Priceline's rates will be. If rates are low on a hotel's own site, they'll probably be low on Priceline.

For a list of hotel Web-site addresses, go to `www.biddingfortravel.com`. Scroll down to the Hotels–General section. Click on Websites for Checking Hotel Rates, and then click on Website Addresses — MUST READ FOR FIRST-TIME USERS.

Scroll down on that list and you'll find dozens of links to hotel chains' Web sites, each of which lets you check prices.

You can also turn to Chapter 20 for a list of hotel-chain Web sites.

Hotwire.com

Hotwire.com is a lot like Priceline: You don't know exactly what hotel you're getting, and you must choose by zones. But Hotwire tells you the prices of your hotels in advance, so you can use Hotwire as a benchmark for very discounted hotels. Note that the price Hotwire initially displays does not include taxes and fees.

Hotwire's zones aren't exactly the same as Priceline's. If you want to use Hotwire to complement Priceline, use the same diligence with Hotwire as you would with Priceline, checking Hotwire's zone boundaries and making sure it's not charging above what the hotels are charging on their own sites.

Hotwire is usually a bit more generous than Priceline when it comes to star levels. A 4-star hotel on Hotwire may be a 3-star hotel on Priceline.

BiddingForTravel.com and BetterBidding.com

Sheryl Mexic, the owner of BiddingForTravel.com, *hates* it when people do this, but here goes: You can use past bids on BiddingForTravel.com (and its competitor, BetterBidding.com) to gauge what you should bid in the future.

Sheryl warns that hotels change their Priceline rates all the time. They also frequently add and remove rooms and hotels from the system. And the posts you see on BiddingForTravel.com may be overbids. So you can't use BiddingForTravel.com as a crutch because you're too lazy to check rates in other places.

TIP

An entertaining read

Especially for 2-star hotels, you can often find really low rates in the Entertainment Book, a coupon book offering hundreds of two-for-one and percentage discounts for hotels and restaurants across the United States and Canada.

Entertainment Books for most metro areas cost $25 to $45, and the coupons last a year. Check it out at www.entertainment.com.

She's right. But if a dozen people are getting a particular hotel for $37, you still have a pretty good chance of getting it for $37. To see what other people have won, follow the instructions in "Knowing which hotels to check" earlier in this chapter — but instead of going to the hotel list, keep scrolling down to look at BiddingForTravel.com's list of past bids.

Picking a maximum bid

If you're not a nitpicker, and you've found your exact preferred dates and zones on BiddingForTravel.com or BetterBidding.com, you can just set your maximum bid at what others have been paying. If you have a whole bunch of bids available, set your maximum bid higher and put the rate others have been paying somewhere in the middle of your list of bids. That tactic isn't foolproof, but it's a decent rule of thumb.

Otherwise, if Hotwire's rates are lower than everyone else's, set your maximum bid at $5 or $10 below Hotwire's price.

If you want to pay less than Hotwire or can't find the right data on Bidding ForTravel.com, you have to decide how much you're willing to pay for convenience. After analyzing more than 200 successful bids, I found the following average savings over the best rates available on hotels' own Web sites:

- **For hotels under $69:** 34 percent
- **For hotels between $70 and $99:** 48 percent
- **For hotels over $100:** 55 percent

TIP

If you only have one or two bids, bid a little higher than the average. If you have plenty of bids available (because of free rebids, or because you're bidding far in advance), start lower than the average and work your way up.

Peeking behind the curtain

Hotels never talk about how they determine their Priceline rates, but I got a glimpse behind the curtain when an internal document from the Utell hotel booking service popped up on the chain's public Web site. The document said:

✔ Hotels should have three Priceline rates.

✔ Their lowest Priceline rate should be lower than shoppers can find anywhere else. But there should also be two higher rates.

✔ Priceline will charge the highest rate your bid qualifies for.

So you may get the same hotel with two different bid amounts — you'd just be paying two different Priceline rates.

If a hotel is in high demand or a convention is in town, you may have to bid much higher than the average to succeed.

You'll pay about 10 to 15 percent more than you bid, because of taxes and fees. Don't worry — Priceline will tell you the total amount you pay before you enter your credit-card number.

Making a Bid Grid

This is it. The moment you've been waiting for: smart bidding.

You know what zones you want, what star levels you want, and what your maximum bid will be. Take out a fresh piece of paper, and write yourself a strategy. You'll stick to this strategy, so you don't get confused or anxious in the heat of bidding.

A simple bid grid

Make three columns. Start by writing down your ideal zones and star level in the first two. Leave the third column blank. Here's an example:

Back Bay and Downtown   4 stars   <blank>

Now list all your possible free rebids (for more information, see "Finding free rebids," earlier in this chapter), with the word *ADD* in front of them:

Back Bay and Downtown	4 stars	<blank>
ADD Chestnut Hill	4 stars	<blank>
ADD Medford	4 stars	<blank>
ADD South Boston	4 stars	<blank>

Now fill in the bottom of the third column with your maximum bid (for more details, see "Deciding How Much to Bid," earlier in this chapter), and work down by $10 increments if your maximum bid is over $80, or by $5 increments if it's less than $80:

Back Bay and Downtown	4 stars	$55
ADD Chestnut Hill	4 stars	$60
ADD Medford	4 stars	$65
ADD South Boston	4 stars	$70

Now you know what your four bids will be. Let's turn that into eight bids.

Switching bidders

Traveling in twos means twice the bidding possibilities. If you switch the name a hotel room is registered under, Priceline sees your bid as completely new. You can even use the same credit card to bid. (Using a new credit card *without* changing names doesn't get you a new bid, so put away that handful of plastic.)

If you have another person over the age of 21 coming with you, copy your bid grid over again. With the bid grid in the preceding section, for example, using two bidders turns four bids into eight. You can now start bidding at $35, work up by fives, and still get to $70 before running out of bids.

You must start a completely new bid when switching bidders. That means going back to Priceline's home page and re-entering all your information as if you had never bid before.

Lowering your standards

Want to lower your star level or add a non-free zone? Remember to research those options from scratch. Your pretty-darn-good bid for a 4-star hotel may be a wild overbid for a 3-star hotel. Similarly, your good bid for a downtown zone may be a wild overbid for a suburb. And if you drop down a star level in quality, some of your previous "free" rebid zones will probably no longer be free.

If you're starting over with a new star level or new non-free area, make a blank line and write *NEW BID:*

Back Bay plus Downtown	4 stars	$55
ADD Chestnut Hill	4 stars	$60
ADD Medford	4 stars	$65
ADD South Boston	4 stars	$70
NEW BID		
Cambridge	4 stars	$45
ADD Chestnut Hill	4 stars	$50
ADD Medford	4 stars	$55
ADD South Boston	4 stars	$60
ADD Back Bay	4 stars	$65
ADD Downtown	4 stars	$70

Hey, what's with the Back Bay and Downtown additions at the end? Notice that in the first four bids, you already bid $70 for Back Bay and Downtown. So you know there are no 4-star hotels in those zones for $70 or less. That makes Back Bay and Downtown free rebid zones for $70 or less, so you can use them to pump up the value of your Cambridge bid.

If you had two people bidding, you'd now have 16 possible bids to try. That could take a while!

By the end of the process, you should have a grid with anywhere from 2 to 20 bids. That's a lot of bids, requiring a lot of patience and a lot of flexibility. But now you have control: You know what you're going to pay for a hotel of a certain quality, where you want it. And you're prepared to pay as little as you can. That's worth the work!

Chapter 11

Bidding On and Winning a Hotel Room

. . . .

In This Chapter

▶ Deciding when to bid

▶ Making your first bid

▶ Responding to counteroffers

▶ Submitting rebids

▶ Checking in to your hotel

. . . .

A little mystery (but not too much) adds thrill to life. Bidding on Priceline for hotels involves a little mystery, but fortunately, not too much. After all, you control the neighborhood your hotel will be in, and you control the quality of your hotel. Which hotel you'll get, of course, is the mystery.

In this chapter, I take you step-by-step through a Priceline hotel bid. I show you all the ways Priceline tries to get you to bid more, and which of its warnings to ignore. You'll be able to save at least 40 percent off the lowest hotel rates you find anywhere else.

If you haven't already read Chapter 10, I strongly suggest you do so. The strategies in Chapter 10 give you more bids, let you squeeze prices lower than you thought possible, and explain how Priceline defines neighborhoods and levels of hotel quality, giving you a real sense of control over your bidding experience.

Figuring Out When to Bid

Priceline lets you bid up to 11 months before you check in, but that doesn't mean booking far in advance is the best idea. Many hotels only give rooms to Priceline at the last minute, especially if a convention or a major tourist event is in town.

Bidding far in advance doesn't hurt, of course. You can bid every 72 hours if you feel like it, but if you're a few months out, try bidding once a week. Make sure to recheck non-Priceline hotel rates each time you bid — rates may go down with time, depending on whether hotels are booking as many rooms as they expected to. Don't start really raising your bid until you get close to the time you *must* book your room.

Priceline guru Sheryl Mexic suggests you always book a cancelable backup hotel. That means booking a room through a hotel's own Web site, using the lowest rate that lets you cancel with no penalty. That way, you can bid on Priceline without fear — even if Priceline never pans out, at least you have somewhere to stay. Cancelable backups should be decent places with low rates. Comfort Inns, Days Inns, Baymont Inns, and Motel 6s make great cancelable backups. Just make sure that you really can cancel the room before you book it.

Need a room right now? Priceline lets you bid in some zones up to 6 p.m. of the day you check in. For the widest selection of absolute-last-minute rooms, book a day in advance.

Last-minute savings

Some hotels don't release rooms to Priceline until the last minute. Allan D. of Bellingham, Washington, sussed that out, and now he saves big bucks staying near Sea-Tac airport when he has early-morning flights. "Rather than get up at 3 a.m. and leave from home, I often drive to SeaTac and stay at an airport hotel. I've found that if I wait until a week or so before my flight, I can get these hotels at a significantly reduced rate through Priceline. My last three stays have been at the Marriott ($45), the Hilton ($40), and the Coast Gateway ($35)," he says.

Beginning to Name Your Own Price

Before you start bidding, poke around the Internet to find the lowest hotel rates on other online services. (For tips on where to look, see Chapters 10 and 20.) Then head to Priceline's home page (www.priceline.com), where you can start bidding:

1. **Click on Hotels under Find Your Next Travel Deal.**

   A screen appears listing popular cities for hotel bidding, as shown in Figure 11-1.

2. **If you're bidding for a hotel outside the United States, click the appropriate area under Choose a City.**

   For instance, click the Europe link if you want to bid for a hotel in Europe.

   For hotels on the Canadian side of Niagara Falls, choose Canada. For hotels in Puerto Rico and the U.S. Virgin Islands, choose Caribbean. For hotels in Australia, choose Asia.

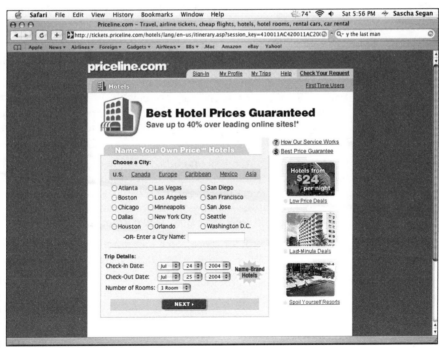

Figure 11-1:
Start your bidding here.

3. **If you see the name of the city you want, click the radio button for that city. Otherwise:**

   - **For U.S. and Canadian cities,** enter the name of the city you're bidding for in the Enter a City Name field.

   - **For European cities,** choose your city from the Choose a City drop-down list. If your city isn't in the drop-down list, you can't get it through Priceline.

   - **For Caribbean, Mexican, and Asian cities (including cities in Australia),** the radio buttons are all you get. If you don't see the name of your city or island, you can't bid for it through Priceline — but you may be able to get it through Priceline Hong Kong. See Chapter 18 for more information.

4. **From the Check-In Date drop-down lists, select the date you plan to check in.**

   Most hotels let you check in around 3 p.m.

5. **From the Check-Out Date drop-down lists, select the date you plan to leave the hotel.**

   Most hotels will want you to check out around noon, though you can usually push that to as late as 4 p.m. if you're a member of the hotel's frequent-guest program.

6. **From the Number of Rooms drop-down list, choose the number of rooms you want, up to four.**

   You can only bid for up to four rooms with Priceline. Multiply that by two people per room, and you're stuck if you have a group larger than eight. If you need more than four rooms, call hotels directly and ask them if they have group rates.

   Priceline only guarantees one bed, fitting two people. Although most hotels will give you a two-bed room or roll in a cot, you're taking a risk. Generally, you won't have a problem fitting three or even four people in a suburban hotel — but *never* try to fit more than two people into a Priceline room in New York City or San Francisco.

   When in doubt, ask for more rooms. ***Remember:*** You can probably get two Priceline rooms for the price of one room booked the usual way!

7. **Click Next.**

   Now you'll either see a screen showing the neighborhood zones where you can choose your hotel, or, if there are no zones, a list of nearby towns. To continue with your bid, see "Making Your First Bid," later in this chapter.

He saved $12,000 with Priceline!

Mark R., a Canadian consultant, isn't even supposed to be able to use Priceline. (For his slick way around Priceline's anti-Canadian policies, see Chapter 18.) But he saved an amazing $12,000 in 15 months with Priceline. He uses Priceline for all his business trips, paying an average of $47.42 per night for 2½-star and 3-star hotels in the northern United States and Canada. For three months starting at the end of September 2003, he practically lived at the 2½-star Les Suites hotel in Ottawa, Canada. "It was like having an apartment, right on the Byward Market nightclub and restaurant district," he told me.

Making Your First Bid

Everything before this was mere preparation. Now you enter the nitty-gritty of your bid — the neighborhood and the star level of the hotel you want, and the price you're willing to pay. Details matter here, so try to pay extra-close attention to what you're punching in at this phase of the process.

At any point before you enter your credit-card number, you can always walk away and come back when you're feeling fresher.

Choosing zones and star levels

After you've picked your city, it's time to tell Priceline what kind of hotel you want. You can choose a *zone* (a neighborhood or group of neighborhoods), and a *star level* (a level of quality for your hotel). So it's certainly possible to say, "I only want fancy, downtown hotels," or "I need a cheap motel out by the highway so I don't have to drive into town."

To become a true master of the zones, read Chapter 10, which details the precise difference between various zones and star levels. Or jump to Chapters 21 and 22 for lists of popular U.S. and international zones.

You can practice bidding by entering tiny amounts that Priceline has no chance of accepting. Priceline rejects all bids under $15 (unless your bid includes bonus money), so feel free to try Priceline's system by making all the $1 bids you want.

Figure 11-2 shows the zone-selection screen. Spend some time here exploring and choosing the zones you want. (If you read Chapter 10 and have a bid grid, you can just click on the zones for the first bid on your grid.)

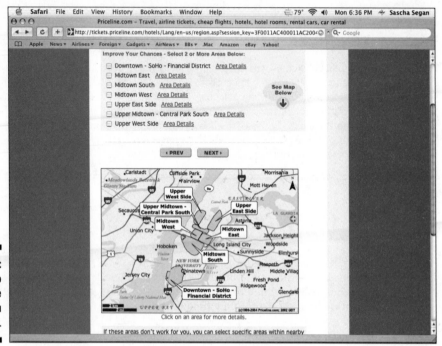

Ignore the names of the zones, which are often misleading. Instead, pay attention to the zone maps. To get a detailed map of a zone, click on Area Details next to the name of that zone. Priceline guarantees you'll get a hotel in the area marked on the map.

1. **Select the check boxes next to the zones you want.**

2. **Click Next.**

   For your first bid, only pick zones you actually want to stay in. If you only like one zone, pick only that zone.

   Some smaller towns don't have any zones. In those cases, you'll see Figure 11-3 instead of a zone map. By selecting a town name on this screen, you agree to stay anywhere within the town limits. You can pick multiple towns if you like, by checking the boxes next to the town names. When you're done picking your towns, click Next.

   You're now at the page where you choose the quality level of your hotel, shown in Figure 11-4. Go to Chapter 10 if you want to know what all these star levels mean.

   If you don't want to read Chapter 10, click on one of the quality levels (such as "2-Star Moderate") to find out what you'll get at that level of quality.

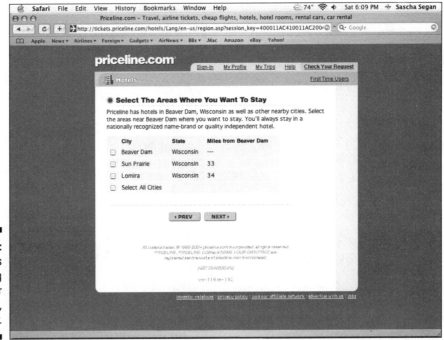

Figure 11-3:
This town's
not big
enough for
two zones,
pardner.

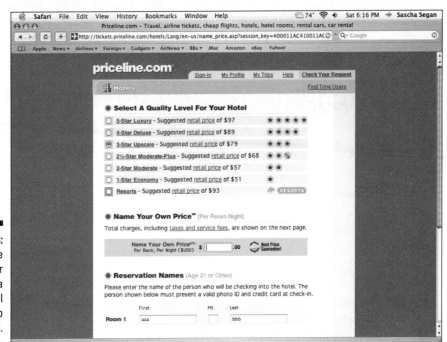

Figure 11-4:
Decide
whether
you want a
classy hotel
or a cheap
motel.

3. **Click the radio button next to the *lowest* star level you're willing to accept.**

   You can get any hotel of that star level or higher. So if you click 1-star, you may also receive a 2- or 3-star hotel.

   Resort-level hotels appears below 1-star on the screen, but Resort-level hotels are really above 4-star in quality. Go figure. If you pick Resort, you'll only get a Resort-level hotel or a 5-star hotel.

   If you're a nervous first-time bidder who wants a nice hotel, stick to 4-star establishments or Resort-level hotels.

Placing your bid

You've taken a look at the Priceline roulette wheel, and decided on 7-Red — or, in this case, a star level and zone. It's time to put your chips on the table and take a spin.

Ignore Priceline's "suggested retail prices." They have no relationship to reality at all — they're only there to get you to bid higher than you would otherwise.

1. **In the box next to Name Your Own Price, enter the amount of your first bid. No matter how many rooms or nights you're bidding for, this should be the amount you're paying for one room, for one night.**

   Priceline will add taxes and fees of at least $10 or so per night to your bid. You'll see the final amount you pay before you enter your credit-card details.

2. **Under Reservation Names, enter the first and last names of the person who will be responsible for each room.**

   Everyone entered here must be over 21. So if you have six kids and you're bidding for four rooms, just enter your own name four times (once in each room), because you're responsible for all four rooms.

3. **Click Next.**

4. **You may get a page titled We Want You to Get Your Hotel Room, where Priceline complains your bid is too low; if you do, ignore it and click Next.**

   You'll get the Please Review Your Request screen, which I walk you through in the next section.

Check, check, and check again

After making your first bid, you'll get the Please Review Your Request screen (shown in Figure 11-5). Go over this page very closely. Print it out, and go over it on paper. This is your last chance to make sure your bid is correct. Make sure to check:

- ✔ **The star level:** Will you be comfortable in a hotel of that quality? If you don't know what the star level means, read Chapter 10.

- ✔ **Your check-in and check-out dates:** Are they the right days of the week? The right months? The right year?

- ✔ **Your zones (listed here as City Areas):** Will you be okay with getting a hotel in any of these zones?

- ✔ **Your offer price:** Make sure you didn't enter any extra zeroes and bid $500 when you meant $50.

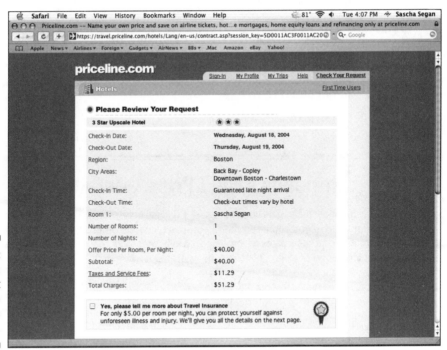

Figure 11-5: This screen is your last chance to get things right.

Still nervous? Priceline will let you buy trip insurance here, for $5 per room, per night. The insurance protects you if you or an immediate family member gets too sick to take the trip, if you get in a car accident on the way to the airport, or if the airport is shut down because of a security problem.

Priceline's trip insurance doesn't protect you if you've made mistakes in your bid, or if you're just plain afraid to fly because of a war or terrorist incident that doesn't actually shut down airports or cause the government to issue travel warnings. For full details, see Chapter 3.

I'd only buy the trip insurance for hotels if I were spending $200 or more, and I thought there was a chance I couldn't take the trip. You can decide on your own comfort level, but I think paying $5 for insurance on one night in a $40 room is unnecessary.

If you want to buy the insurance, follow these steps:

1. **Click on the check box next to Yes, Please Tell Me More about Travel Insurance.**

2. **Scroll all the way down, reading the "Important Information" section, and, in the Initial Here box, enter your initials.**

3. **Click Next.**

4. **On the following page, scroll all the way down and enter your initials in the Initial Here box.**

5. **Click Next.**

Priceline's Best Price Guarantee

Priceline is so confident it can give you the best rates, it guarantees it. If you find a regular rate for the same room on the same dates on any other Web site after you win a Priceline bid (no AAA, no military, no government, and no corporate rates allowed), Priceline will refund you the difference. To get the refund, you must e-mail Priceline at hotel_accept@production.priceline.com within 48 hours of winning your bid, and before you check in to your hotel. Include your

Priceline hotel request number and details of how you found the other rate — a screenshot of the Web page with the other, lower rate would be great.

Smart bidders should never have to use this guarantee. Priceline saves you up to 60 percent over other Web sites' rates. If all you're getting is a price that matches others' rates, you're wasting Priceline's power.

If you *don't* want travel insurance:

1. **Scroll down, reading the "Important Information" section, and enter your initials in the Initial Here box.**

2. **Click Next.**

Whether or not you chose insurance, you'll now see a page where you enter your credit-card information.

1. **Enter your credit-card details into the appropriate fields.**

   Priceline offers to keep your personal information in a secure profile. That means you won't have to reenter your credit-card details every time you bid, and you'll be able to look up your past bids more easily.

   Signing up for a profile also lets you get special bonus-money coupons through e-mail, which can add value to future Priceline bids. For a few words on using bonus money, see Chapter 4.

   For example, a $5 Priceline bonus-money coupon may turn a $50 bid into $55 — you pay $50, but the hotel will act as if you bid $5 more.

2. **If you don't want to set up a profile, ignore all the stuff under Register Now and SAVE!**

   If you do want to set up a profile, fill out the information under Register Now and SAVE!

3. **To reduce the spam you receive and avoid getting bonus money, *uncheck* the box next to Yes! I Would Like to Receive Exclusive Promotions, Coupons, and Discounts.**

4. **Click Buy My Hotel Room Now.**

Cross your fingers — this is the moment of truth!

Oh No, a Counteroffer!

When you submit your bid, one of four things will happen:

> ✔ **Your bid will be successful.** Great! If your bid is successful, print out the confirmation page you receive and jump to "I Won! Now What?" later in this chapter.

✔ **Your bid will be nowhere near successful.** If your bid is way too low, you'll see the rebid screen. Jump to "Bidding Again and Again," later in this chapter, and try again.

✔ **Priceline's computers will be jammed.** When this happens, you'll get a page telling you to check back in 15 minutes or so. Close your Priceline window and wait until you get an e-mail from Priceline (sometimes it takes up to an hour or two). Click on the link in the e-mail, and you'll find out whether your bid succeeded or not. Or, you can check your request later (if you have your request number) by clicking on the Check My Request link on the top right-hand corner of Priceline's home page.

✔ **Priceline will make a counteroffer.** Sometimes Priceline comes back and proposes a price that will let you "try the same request again right now," as shown in Figure 11-6. Congratulations! You've forced Priceline to show its hand. In the case of Figure 11-6, it doesn't have any rooms at $40, but it has some at $52.

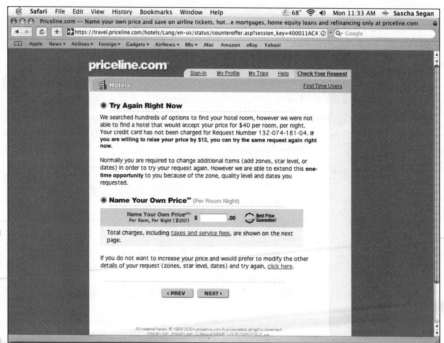

Figure 11-6: Bidding $40 won't do, so Priceline suggests $52.

If you think Priceline's counteroffer is great, go ahead and take it. In this case, I was bidding for a 4-star hotel in Miami's Coral Gables area, where the cheapest rate I could find otherwise was $199. Paying only $52 netted a 70 percent savings — pretty amazing!

To accept the counteroffer, enter your new amount in the Name Your Own Price field and click Next. You'll be back at the Please Review Your Request screen, ready to commit your hard-earned cash.

Priceline will almost always accept less than its counteroffer. If you have several bid possibilities left, ignore the counteroffer. Write down the bid request number, go back to Priceline's home page, and start a completely new bid. Use the details of the next bid you would have made.

As you bid higher, you may get higher counteroffers. This is perfectly normal. Don't worry. If you end up bidding higher than your first counteroffer, go back to your original bid and accept the counteroffer:

1. **Go to Priceline's home page (**www.priceline.com**).**

2. **Click on Check Your Request in the upper-right-hand corner of the page.**

3. **Click the Hotels icon.**

4. **Enter your original Priceline bid request number — the one that got the counteroffer — and your e-mail address.**

5. **Accept the counteroffer by increasing your bid by as much as Priceline recommends.**

6. **Click Next.**

   You'll return to the Please Review Your Request screen, hopefully headed for success this time.

You usually won't save much by underbidding a counteroffer. The hotel that Priceline offered me at $52 I got at $46. But if you have plenty of time and plenty of rebidding possibilities, playing around may be worth it.

Bidding Again and Again

Don't worry if your first bid fails. It's all part of the plan. By rebidding, you work your way up to Priceline's price, ensuring that you pay as little as possible for your hotel.

I *want* my first bid to fail. That way, I know I didn't overbid. When I increase my bid by $5 or $10 and it succeeds, I know I paid close to the minimum possible price to win a hotel. That's smart bidding.

In order to rebid, you must change something other than the price. Figure 11-7 shows Priceline's rebid screen. If you read Chapter 10 and made a bid grid, you're golden. Check the options from the next bid on your grid, enter the price from the next bid, and click Next.

If you don't have a bid grid and don't want to read Chapter 10, here's a quick rundown of what you can change:

✔ **The bidder:** The first rebid you should make (if you don't have a bid grid) isn't on the rebid form at all. If you're traveling with a friend, throw away your original bid and start a new one under your friend's name. You can even use your own credit card! Priceline sees a new name as creating an entirely new bid, so you can submit the exact same bid as you did before, just with a slightly higher price.

✔ **The zone:** You can add another neighborhood. Before you do:

  • Check to see if Priceline offers hotels of your star level in your zone. (To find out how, see Chapter 10.) If it doesn't, the zone is a *free rebid*. You have no chance of getting a hotel in that zone, so you can increase your bid and you'll still get a hotel in your original, favorite zone.

  • If your new zone isn't a free rebid, click on the Details link next to the neighborhood you're considering adding. Do you really want to stay there?

  • Go back and check non-Priceline rates for hotels in your new zone, using BiddingForTravel's Hotel Lists and online travel agencies. (See Chapters 10 and 20.) If the rates are much lower in your new zone, you may want to *lower* your bid, not raise it.

✔ **The star level:** You can lower the quality of the hotel you're looking for. But before you do so, go back and check non-Priceline rates for hotels at your new star level. If the non-Priceline rates at your new star level are much lower than the hotels you were previously looking for, don't raise your bid!

✔ **The dates:** You can change your check-in or check-out dates. If you're just poking around to find cheap dates to stay somewhere, sure, give it a try. But most people I know have specific dates in mind when they're booking a hotel!

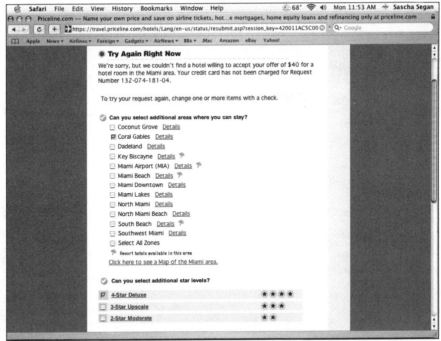

Figure 11-7:
If at first
you don't
succeed,
bid, bid
again!

Finally, scroll down and increase your bid price if you think it's smart. Priceline *always* says "you should consider a price above your original offer" — so if you don't feel like increasing your price, don't. Click Next.

You'll probably see another We Want You To Get Your Hotel Room screen. Hold the line, and don't change your bid. Click Next.

You will now see another Please Review Your Request screen (refer to Figure 11-5). Go over this screen with loving care. Computer bugs can alter bids, so make sure your dates, city areas/zones, and bid amounts are all correct. Scroll down, enter your initials in the Initial Here box, and click Buy My Hotel Room Now.

As the shampoo bottle says, lather, rinse, and repeat. And repeat, and repeat, and repeat. Depending on how many options you change, you could bid twice or a dozen times. Even if bidding starts to wear you down, persevere. Think of all the money you're saving.

If you run out of bids, you can start all over again in 72 hours.

I Won! Now What?

Congratulations. The hard part is over. You have a place to stay, and you've paid less than you ever dreamed possible. Now you just need to check in and enjoy your room.

Print out your bid acceptance page (shown in Figure 11-8) and take it to the hotel with you. Sometimes hotel computers misplace or misspell reservations. Your bid acceptance page is proof you have a confirmed room. If you're really worried, call the hotel before you show up and make sure its staff knows you're coming.

If things go wrong at your hotel, don't worry. Just bring this book and turn to Chapter 12, where all your problems will (hopefully) be solved.

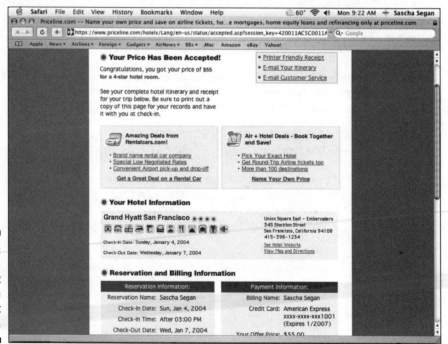

Figure 11-8:
You won! Now print out this page and take it to the hotel.

Staying on a hotel's good side

Many hotels hate Priceline, and there are plenty of reports of hotel clerks treating Priceline guests with disdain. You can't do anything about that, but you can do a few things to make your check-in experience easier.

✔ **If you want a nonsmoking room, two double beds, or anything else in particular, call the hotel's main reservation line a week or two before you get to the hotel.** Say you have a reservation, give your name, the hotel name, and the dates, and say you want to add a few preferences to the reservation. Tell them your hotel chain frequent-guest number, if you have one (see "Upgrades and bonuses" later in this chapter). Don't mention Priceline. Sometimes the reservation person will make a note in his computer that will give you a better chance of getting what you want.

✔ **Check in close to your hotel's earliest possible check-in time.** To find out what that is, call your hotel or check the hotel's Web site. For most hotels, 4 p.m. is a great time to check in.

✔ **Use a hotel frequent-guest card when you check in, if possible.** Frequent-guest program members get privileges that often override any Priceline stigma.

✔ **If you're going to check in after 8 p.m., call your hotel directly on the morning before you arrive and tell the staff when you're showing up.** That way, they'll make sure to hold a room for you. Although Priceline guarantees that you'll get some sort of room even if you don't call, it may be the worst room in the house — or a room at a sister hotel down the block — if you don't call to reconfirm.

✔ **When you get to your hotel, don't mention Priceline or hand over anything that says Priceline on it.** Just say you have a reservation and you'd like to check in. Give the hotel desk clerk a credit card for incidentals (room service, phone calls, that sort of stuff), and mention any preferences you have, such as a nonsmoking room or a king-size bed.

✔ **Be polite, be sweet, and understand your lack of rights here.** You don't have a right to a nonsmoking room or to two beds. Your ability to get what you want depends on how much the clerk likes you (and what rooms are available). Be likeable.

✔ **If a clerk doesn't have the kind of room you want, ask if one will be available if you drop off your bags and check in later.** Sometimes, rooms open up later in the afternoon that weren't available earlier in the day.

Upgrades and bonuses

When you bid on Priceline, you supposedly give up the ability to get frequent-guest points or the bonuses you get by belonging to a hotel chain's frequent-guest program. But that's not always the case. So it pays to sign up for a hotel chain's frequent-guest program as soon as you win your bid. You can sign up on the hotel chain's Web site, which is always free.

Present your spanking-new (or spanking-old) hotel frequent-guest card when you check in. Although you won't get any points for your room, you'll probably get points for charging room service or making phone calls. And you very well may get moved to a club level, or you may get a free newspaper in the morning. You're also less likely to get stuck in the dreaded *Priceline room* (the worst room in the house), if you're a member of the frequent-guest program.

If your hotel has a club level or suites, you can sometimes upgrade your room with charisma, luck, or cold hard cash. At check-in, ask if you can be moved to a higher class of room. Friendly hotels have moved many Priceline travelers into club rooms or suites for $20 to $50 per night extra, and sometimes even for free. Unfriendly hotels will just say no, so you have nothing to lose.

1 want more!

Some Priceline rates are so great that you just have to extend them. Priceline sometimes lets you extend a stay after you've won a bid, to up to 21 nights total! There's no guarantee here — Priceline needs to get your hotel to agree, and that depends on the hotel's individual policies.

To extend your stay:

1. **Make sure to ask before you check in, and no more than 30 days after your bid was accepted.**

2. **From Priceline's home page, click on Help near the top of the screen.**

3. **In the Top Questions For drop-down list, select Hotel Rooms.**

4. **Click on Can I Add Nights to My Accepted Hotel Reservation?**

5. **Click the Click Here link near the bottom of the page of text.**

6. **Enter your Priceline hotel request number and e-mail address, and click Next.**

7. **Enter the number of days you'd like to add, and click Next.**

   Priceline will get back to you within 24 hours telling you whether you can extend your stay.

Priceline can't add rooms to a hotel stay, or extend stays won more than 30 days ago. But many bidders have been able to add rooms by calling their hotels directly. Call your hotel at the number on your bid-acceptance page and ask for the reservation desk. Explain that you'd like to add rooms or nights to your reservation, and ask *very politely* if you can get them at the same rate you have now.

Chapter 12

Solving Common Hotel Problems

. . . .

In This Chapter

▶ Fixing bidding mistakes

▶ Dealing with low-quality hotels

▶ Solving reservation and billing problems

▶ Avoiding getting stuck in an undesirable room

. . . .

*P*riceline has come a long way since the dark days of 2000, when its lousy customer service got it kicked out of the Connecticut Better Business Bureau. Dealing with Priceline's voice-mail system and its often unhelpful staff can still be a chore, but persistent folks usually get satisfaction after a few phone calls. Priceline is back in the BBB's good graces, too.

The key to dealing with Priceline problems is to know the site's rules. Priceline has little patience for people who want refunds just because they changed their minds. But it'll gladly help you out if you can show that a hotel broke Priceline's rules. And if you made a genuine mistake while bidding, you'll find Priceline to be pretty forgiving — as long as you don't make the same mistake again.

Whether your 3-year-old clicks Buy This Hotel Room by accident, your computer explodes and loses your confirmation number, or you have trouble checking into a hotel, Priceline's official answer for everything is to call or e-mail its customer-service department. But that's easier said than done. Priceline's automatic answer to most e-mails is "no," and its customer-service phone line makes you jump through flaming hoops of voice-mail menus before you get to an operator. (For the full details on how to get in touch with Priceline, head to Chapter 3.)

So, now that I've got Priceline's official recommendation out of the way, in this chapter I show you what you should *really* do when things go wrong.

If you're really worried you won't be able to take a Priceline trip, consider buying travel insurance. (See Chapter 3 for the pros and cons of Priceline's insurance policy.) Insurance protects you against missing your trip because you're ill, because you get into a car crash on the way to the airport, and for a bunch of other reasons.

I Made a Mistake!

Everybody makes mistakes. Bleary-eyed after a hard night of bidding, you may type "500" instead of "50" and spend way more than you planned. It's also pretty easy to enter "June 5" when you mean "May 5."

Try not to bid when you're tired or when you're distracted by other things, such as work, small children, cooking dinner, or bidding on eBay.

Don't panic if you get a screwed-up reservation. E-mail Priceline's customer service with your successful bid request number (it looks like 123-456-789-10 and it's on the top of your winning bid page), and tell them how you screwed up. Priceline will usually allow you a one-time exception and cancel the bid so you can start over. (Usually, it'll make you win another bid before it cancels your earlier one, but you should always ask *before* making that second bid.) Make sure to get things right this time!

Persistence pays off

When his vacation plans went wrong, Kevin H. of Council Bluffs, Iowa, grabbed onto Priceline's leg like a pit bull, and he didn't give up until he got what he wanted. Kevin booked a vacation package to New York City with a room in the New York Hilton and Towers. (Priceline's packages let you pick a specific hotel, not just a zone and star level.) A month before his trip, Priceline sent him a note saying the Hilton was full, and he would have to stay in the Waldorf-Astoria, which has smaller rooms than the Hilton. When he complained to Hilton, the hotel sent him back to Priceline. After ten phone calls over a two-week period, Kevin finally got to a Priceline vice president, who moved his family back into the Hilton and Towers — Kevin's hotel of choice.

Dealing with Priceline's customer service can be a contest of wills. If you're convinced you're in the right, keep plugging away; you'll eventually get satisfaction.

Priceline's one-time exceptions aren't really one-time. It'll probably allow you one screwup every couple of months. Just don't rely too much on Priceline's generosity, though.

Get in touch with Priceline the minute you discover something's wrong. Priceline may require you to resubmit your bid with your fixed price or dates before it gives you a refund. Although it's pretty forgiving about mistakes, it's less forgiving if it thinks you're just trying to get out of a reservation late because your travel plans changed.

No Reservation?

Ever forget your keys? Everyone's a little forgetful sometimes, and that includes hotels. When Priceline's computers don't quite connect to a hotel's reservation system, you can show up at a hotel only to find it has no idea who you are. Fortunately, this is a very rare problem.

To make sure the hotel will be expecting you:

1. **Confirm your reservation the morning before you arrive.**

   Call the hotel's main reservation number, and say you're just double-checking your reservation. If the hotel says it can't find your reservation, provide the hotel confirmation number from your winning bid page (it's different from the Priceline request number). If the hotel *still* can't find your reservation, it's time to call Priceline at 800-774-2354. (Refer to Chapter 3 for a guide through Priceline's voice-mail menus.)

2. **Print out your winning bid page and bring it with you to the hotel.**

3. **Check in as early as possible.**

   If you have trouble at the front desk, you'll be able to call the hotel's central offices and Priceline. Although Priceline's customer-service line is open 24 hours, many managers and decisionmakers vanish after 5 p.m.

This Isn't the Room I Bargained For

Not all hotels play fair, alas. Some places misrepresent themselves to Priceline. They tell Priceline they're in a particular neighborhood when they aren't, or that they're clean and tidy when they aren't, or that they treat Priceline customers decently when they don't. Here's what to do if your room feels more like a prison than like a palace.

Hurricane Priceline

One Priceliner smelled a rat when he won a room at the Grand Cayman Marriott resort on Priceline. Two years of hurricanes had totally eroded the beach next to this once-proud resort, and the hotel's managers confirmed it had no beachfront access. Resort hotels in beachy areas must have access to the water, so this savvy traveler fired off an e-mail to Priceline. Three phone calls and two e-mails later, Priceline agreed to refund his money.

Dealing with heinous hotels

Heinous hotels are the bane of Priceline bidders. They poison entire zones. So what qualifies a hotel as heinous? It may be given more stars than it's worth; it may not really be in the zone it's supposed to be in; or it may be just plain lousy.

Mis-rated hotels

The first thing you should do when you see a low-quality room is to turn to Chapter 10 in this book. Run down the list of required amenities in the star level that you bid. If any amenities are missing, you'll probably get a refund.

Three-star hotels without room service, restaurants, or business centers, as well as coastal resorts without beach access, qualify you for a refund.

Priceline doesn't guarantee you a smoking or nonsmoking room. It only guarantees you'll be able to fit two adults in the room, and it doesn't guarantee you'll get the size of beds you prefer. It doesn't guarantee a hotel will have parking or an airport shuttle. It doesn't guarantee a hotel will have a pool, unless it's a Resort-level hotel.

Priceline won't move you to another hotel if your room is mis-rated. Instead, it'll offer you a refund. Stay in your mis-rated hotel and (if you can) take photos of exactly what's wrong with it. When you get home, write a detailed e-mail to Priceline. Give Priceline your bid number, the dates of your stay, and the hotel you stayed in, and explain specifically which amenities the hotel lacked. Priceline will probably contact the hotel, too, so be prepared for an argument. Keep bugging Priceline — it may take five or more e-mails and phone calls before it resolves your problem. Eventually, you'll get your money back.

Mis-zoned hotels

Very, very rarely, a hotel chain will give incorrect location information to Priceline. And if this happens, you may end up with a *mis-zoned hotel* — a hotel that's outside of the zone it claims to be in.

If you think your hotel is mis-zoned, print out Priceline's map for the zone you won. Then go to Expedia (www.expedia.com), look up your hotel, and print out Expedia's map. Compare the two. Is the hotel actually in Priceline's zone?

Zone names mean nothing. The maps mean everything.

You're entitled to a full refund on mis-zoned hotels, but getting that refund out of Priceline is a pain. Usually, the first customer-service person you e-mail or speak to will claim that you're lying. Offer to fax Priceline the two maps. Demand to speak to a manager or vice president. If your hotel is really outside its zone, you'll eventually get your money back, though it may take a few calls.

Just plain lousy hotels

These hotels have all the amenities Priceline requires — they're just shabby. They may have tiny rooms, dingy carpets, and rock-hard beds. Tired linens share space with worn-out towels, and there's almost always a mysterious stain somewhere in the room that you don't want to think about.

Keeping an eye on the "Hotel Misratings and Quality Issues" forum on BiddingForTravel.com helps you avoid bidding zones with shabby hotels. When you're stuck in a low-quality room, though, all you can do is make the best of it.

When you get home, make sure to send an e-mail to Priceline about your lousy hotel. Include specific problems — and pictures, if you have a camera with you on your trip. Priceline probably won't refund your money, but it may downgrade the hotel so future bidders don't get burned.

Only a tiny percentage of Priceline bids end up in low-quality hotels. And you have almost as much of a chance of booking these lemons *without* Priceline, because most of Priceline's shabby hotels are rogue agents in chains with generally good reputations.

Avoiding the "Priceline room"

For years, Priceliners bid in fear of the Hilton New York, which locals call by its old name of the New York Hilton and Towers. That hotel shoehorned Priceline customers into *Priceline rooms,* tiny closets in corners by stairwells that desk clerks told one poster to BiddingForTravel.com were "undesirable and unbookable." Hilton seems to have changed its tune in the past year or two, but I still get reports of Priceliners occasionally getting stuck in rooms nobody else wants.

Priceline won't help you in these situations, but you can minimize your chance of getting stuck in a Priceline room by following these tips:

✔ **Try to check in during the late afternoon.** If you check in late at night, the more desirable rooms may already be taken.

✔ **Always check in using your frequent-guest card.** Membership in a frequent-guest program usually overrides the Priceline stigma.

✔ **Never, ever mention Priceline or the rate you paid at check-in.**

✔ **When you check in, politely ask for a room away from the elevator and stairwell.** Often, that's enough to move you away from the default Priceline room.

✔ **Politely ask for a room upgrade.** You just may get one.

✔ **If your room isn't satisfactory, grab your bags, return to the front desk, and complain.** Most hotels would rather move you than deal with your dissatisfaction. If the desk clerk won't help, ask to speak to a manager.

✔ **If you're stuck in a lousy room, take pictures of the room.** When you get home, post your experience on BiddingForTravel.com and send an e-mail to Priceline. If your room lacked amenities that Priceline promises at a certain star level, point those out, and offer to send along the pictures. If you keep bugging Priceline, you just may get a partial refund — or bonus money for a future stay.

What's This Charge?

Sometimes hotels and Priceline cross wires, and sometimes hotels are just sleazy. In any case, sometimes you'll end up getting charged more than you should be. Fortunately, there are ways to undo erroneous charges.

Fixing double charges

Check your credit-card statement closely after you win a bid with Priceline or stay at a Priceline hotel. Your card should have at most two charges on it: one from Priceline for your reservation, dated when you made your bid (see Figure 12-1), and a much smaller one for any additional fees the hotel charges, dated when you checked out (see Figure 12-2). If you see two charges, the hotel charge is equal to or higher than the Priceline charge, and the hotel charge is more than your amenities actually cost, you've been double-charged.

Figure 12-1:
Your credit-
card bill
should
show one
charge from
Priceline.

New Activity continued		Amount $
09/30/03	PRICELINE HOTEL 800-657-9168 CT	194.79
	NO REFUNDS	
	ROC No. 0069957469	
Total of New Activity		

Figure 12-2:
After you
check out of
the hotel,
your credit-
card state-
ment should
show a small
charge from
the hotel
for extra
fees, room
service,
and such.

New Activity continued		Amount $
11/10/03	MILLENIUM HILTON NEW YORK NY	60.71
	Arrival Date Departure Date	
	11/09/03 11/10/03	
	00000000	
11/20/03	Periodic FINANCE CHARGE	
Total of New Activity		

As far as I can tell, charges beyond these two expected ones are always glitches — they're not malicious. Priceline's computers aren't perfect, and they occasionally register two bids where one should be. Hotels use dozens of different computer systems, some of which don't match up with Priceline's all that well.

If you think you've been charged incorrectly, complain to the company that made the inappropriate charge (either the hotel or Priceline). If the hotel charged you, call the hotel's main reservation line and explain the problem. Tell the representative that:

✓ You had a prepaid Priceline reservation.

✓ The hotel charged for an extra room that you did not reserve.

✓ The hotel must remove the charge.

If the double charge comes from Priceline, first fill out the form at `http://tickets.priceline.com/customerservice/email/hotel/emailanswer.asp`. You can also call Priceline at 800-774-2354. Have your Priceline request number ready (it looks like 123-456-789-10, and it appears at the top of your winning bid page).

If you didn't print out your winning bid page, you can still get it if you have the e-mail from Priceline, or you can use the Check Your Request link on Priceline's home page to get it.

See Chapter 3 for help getting through Priceline's voice-mail menus and reaching an actual human being.

Fixing sleazy hotel charges

Hotel owners often slap sleazy extra charges onto your bill, things that should be included in the room rate. The three that Priceliners most often see are a $10 to $15 resort fee for use of a hotel's spa and pool, a $1 to $2 fee for use of your room's safe, and a $3 to $6 energy surcharge that has no reasonable explanation at all.

I won't even touch on hotels' insane valet-parking fees and sky-high rates for phone calls. Many hotels even charge for calls to toll-free numbers. (Never, ever make a call from a hotel phone; use your own cellphone or the pay phone in the hotel's lobby instead.) If parking fees bother you, look for a lot nearby.

These sleazy fees aren't Priceline's problem. Everybody, no matter how they booked their rooms, ends up paying these charges.

You can't do anything about resort fees, so don't try. Whether you can get other charges removed depends on your persuasive powers, whether you're an elite member of the hotel's frequent-guest program, and what kind of mood the desk clerk is in.

I've had plenty of luck getting energy surcharges and safe surcharges removed when I've complained. I tell desk clerks that the surcharge wasn't in the room rate I agreed to, and they'd usually rather knock off the energy surcharge than argue.

Getting Walked

Hotels *overbook* (sell more rooms than they have). If the hotel is already full when you show up with your guaranteed, prepaid reservation, you may end up getting *walked* (sent to another hotel down the street with empty rooms).

Walking the plank?

One man I spoke to arrived at San Francisco's Cathedral Hill Hotel for his 35-year high-school reunion with high hopes. Then the hotel staff told him all the rooms were full and sent him across the street to the La Quinta Inn — which told him all *its* rooms were full and offered to send him to a hotel in the Tenderloin, one of San Francisco's shadiest areas.

After two hours of bickering, he got the Cathedral Hill Hotel to give him a room. He e-mailed Priceline when he got home, and it offered him a one-night refund for his troubles.

This sleazy practice has nothing to do with Priceline. I've been walked on reservations booked through a hotel's own Web site. And I've found no evidence that a Priceline bid will get you walked more often than any other kind of reservation.

If you do get walked, demand special treatment. If a hotel employee gives you guff about Priceline, explain that the hotel is breaking its contract with Priceline by moving you to another building. You should get free, round-trip transportation to the other hotel, and maybe a room upgrade or a free breakfast. Get the first and last name of the employee deciding to walk you — you'll need it later.

If you're walked to a lower class of hotel, call Priceline when you get home from your trip. (Check BiddingForTravel's hotel lists to see what Priceline rates your new hotel.) Provide your bid number, the dates of your stay, and all the details of your experience, including the name of the employee who decided to walk you. If you ask, you may get a partial refund or at least a coupon for future Priceline bids.

Part IV

Hot Wheels: Renting a Car through Priceline

The 5th Wave   By Rich Tennant

In this part . . .

Are you driven to save? Want to save when you drive? Priceline doesn't sell gas anymore (though it used to!), but it can still find you a great deal on a rental car. Just like with flights and hotel rooms, getting a rental car you're happy with depends on understanding Priceline's forest of options and definitions — in this case, its 11 car types.

In this part, you get to take Priceline's car types for a test-drive, decide which one you want to drive away with, and bargain the salesman down to a good price. Just in case they give you trouble, I'm right behind you with tips for dealing with those smart-aleck car guys. In this part, you shift your savings into high gear.

Chapter 13

Driving within Priceline's Lanes

. . . .

. . . .

*I*n this chapter, you find out exactly what kind of car you'll get when you pick out a vehicle on Priceline. I let you know where you can pick up your car, what's included with a Priceline rental, and what's extra.

The most important factor in Priceline rentals is Priceline's slightly oddball definitions of car categories. Picking the right car class can make the difference between zipping away happy with your choice and standing around frustrated, wondering what to do with your luggage.

Otherwise, using Priceline for rental cars doesn't have too many tradeoffs. But the two big ones are, indeed, big — guaranteeing a four-door car is tough, and you can't guarantee your rental desk will be in your airport terminal.

You'll save much less with Priceline rentals than you will with Priceline hotels. Typically, you'll only be able to shave off a few dollars a day. If you're booking your car for several days, though, those few dollars can add up to significant savings.

As always, deciding whether the trade-offs are worth the savings you can net by bidding for cars is up to you.

Priceline's Rental-Car Partners

Priceline works with five of the biggest rental-car agencies in the United States: Alamo, Avis, Budget, Hertz, and National. Service and price-wise, they span the range of the industry. Hertz tied with Avis for best car-rental company in a 2003 survey by research firm J.D. Power and Associates. National rated in the middle, and Alamo and Budget rated below the industry average — but Alamo and Budget are usually cheaper than Hertz and Avis.

Several big rental-car firms *don't* participate with Priceline, and that's one of the reasons you need to shop around. Dollar, Enterprise, Advantage, and Thrifty don't participate with Priceline, and they all (especially Thrifty) often have great rates.

You have a pretty even chance of getting any of Priceline's partners, except in a few circumstances:

- ✔ **You want a pickup truck.** Budget is the only one of Priceline's partners that rents pickup trucks.

- ✔ **You're under 25 years old.** Drivers under 25 will usually get cars from Budget.

Picking Up and Returning Your Car

Priceline only sells round-trip car rentals. That means you must pick up and return your car to the exact same location. Fortunately, Priceline's partners have hundreds of locations throughout the United States. To see all of Priceline's rental-car cities, go to http://tickets.priceline.com/rentalcars/lang/en-us/city_list.asp. The list doesn't reveal which cities only let you rent cars at the airport and which let you rent cars elsewhere. To discover whether your city has a downtown rental option, you must start bidding (but stop before you pick a price).

If you rent from an airport, you must return your car to that same airport. If you rent from a downtown location, you must return it to that same downtown location.

Airport locations

Priceline lets you rent cars at most major U.S. airports.

Some of Priceline's partners are in airport terminals; you can pick up your car by going to a counter in the arrivals hall, before you leave your terminal. Others are outside the airport, so you need to take a free shuttle bus from the terminal to the car-rental company's office. You can't possibly guess or predict whether you'll get an in-terminal car-rental firm or whether you'll have to ride the bus.

Other locations

Sometimes picking up your car downtown is more convenient than picking it up at the airport. Priceline offers *some* downtown locations. (Sometimes it calls downtown locations *suburban locations,* just to confuse you.)

Priceline won't tell you exactly where your car-rental firm will be before you win your bid, but it'll show you a circle on a map; the car-rental office must be within the circle. Unfortunately, no comprehensive list of cities where Priceline offers downtown rentals is available. You just have to start bidding and choose your city, and you'll see whether a downtown option appears before you put in your price.

A few of the cities where Priceline *does* allow people to pick up and return cars downtown are:

- Chicago
- Disney World (Downtown Disney)
- Los Angeles
- Miami Beach
- New Orleans
- Philadelphia
- Washington, D.C.

Priceline *doesn't* let you rent downtown in:

- Denver
- Detroit
- Honolulu
- Houston
- Las Vegas
- New York City
- Portland, Oregon
- San Diego
- San Juan
- Seattle

Bidding with Class

Choose your car class carefully — it's the most important factor in bidding on Priceline. Although "normal" renters often get free upgrades, Priceliners don't — so pick a car you'll be comfortable in.

Priceline offers 11 car classes, from tiny little subcompacts up to SUVs. For examples of cars in each class, see Table 13-1. Priceline doesn't guarantee any specific model, but it does guarantee a few things about each class of car.

Table 13-1			Sample Car Models			
Car Type	Priceline	Alamo	Avis	Budget	Hertz	National
Economy	Chevrolet Metro	Chevrolet Aveo	Chevrolet Metro	Hyundai Accent	Hyundai Accent	Chevrolet Metro
Compact	Ford Escort, Ford Focus	Chevrolet Cavalier	Chevrolet Cavalier	Ford Focus	Ford Focus	Chevrolet Cavalier
Mid-size	Mazda 626, Pontiac Grand Am	Oldsmobile Alero	Oldsmobile Alero	Hyundai Sonata	Mazda 6	Pontiac Grand Am
Standard (may be two-door)	Chevrolet Monte Carlo, Ford Mustang	Chevrolet Impala	Chevrolet Monte Carlo	Ford Taurus	Ford Taurus	Buick Regal
Full-size (always four-door)	Chevrolet Impala, Ford Taurus, Buick Regal	Chevrolet Impala	Buick Century	Ford Taurus	Ford Taurus	Buick Regal
Premium	Pontiac Bonneville, Ford Crown Victoria, Buick LeSabre	Pontiac Bonneville	Buick LeSabre	Mercury Grand Marquis	Mercury Grand Marquis	Buick LeSabre
Luxury Park	Lincoln Town Car, Cadillac Sedan DeVille	Buick Park Avenue	Cadillac Sedan DeVille	Lincoln Town Car	Lincoln Town Car	Buick Avenue

Car Type	Priceline	Alamo	Avis	Budget	Hertz	National
Convertible	Chevrolet Cavalier, Ford Mustang	Chrysler Sebring	Chevrolet Camaro	Ford Mustang	Ford Mustang	Chevrolet Camaro
Minivan	Chevrolet Venture, Ford Windstar	Chevrolet Venture	Chevrolet Venture	Ford Windstar	Ford Freestar	Pontiac Montana
SUV	Chevrolet Blazer, Ford Explorer	Chevrolet Blazer	Chevrolet Blazer	Ford Escape, Ford Explorer	Ford Escape, Ford Explorer	Chevrolet Blazer
Pickup	Ford Ranger	N/A	N/A	Ford Ranger	N/A	N/A

Economy cars

Economy cars are the tiniest of the tiny, the munchkins of the road. They'll fit four adults (or two adults and three skinny kids with two small bags in the trunk. Economy cars on Priceline will also have:

- ✔ Airbags
- ✔ AM/FM radio
- ✔ Automatic transmission
- ✔ Air-conditioning

Compact cars

Compact cars are normal, ordinary-sized small cars, the kinds of cars young people typically buy. They'll fit four adults, with three bags in the trunk. Compact cars will have everything economy cars have, plus:

- ✔ Power steering
- ✔ Tinted windows
- ✔ Dual mirrors

Mid-size cars

Choosing mid-size gives you a reasonable, comfortable car about the size of your average taxicab. Watch out, though, if you have a family: Mid-size cars may have either two or four doors. Mid-size cars include the following:

- Anti-lock brakes
- AM/FM radio with cassette
- Power steering
- Automatic transmission
- Air-conditioning
- Central locking
- Electric windows
- Covered hatch
- Driver's-side airbag

Full-size cars

Now we're getting big and busy. If you want a comfortable, four-door vehicle to tote around the kids or Grandma Ethel, rent a full-size car. You'll get a four-door with plenty of trunk space and a nice, big back seat. Full-size cars include everything mid-size cars have, plus:

- Cruise control
- Power locks and windows
- Tinted windows
- Dual mirrors
- Tilt steering wheel

Standard cars

Standard cars are pretty similar to full-size cars, except that full-size guarantees you a four-door, and standard cars may have two doors. Standard cars also feature:

- ✔ Antilock brakes
- ✔ Cruise control
- ✔ AM/FM radio
- ✔ Power steering
- ✔ Automatic transmission
- ✔ Air-conditioning
- ✔ Tinted windows
- ✔ Dual mirrors
- ✔ Tilt steering wheel
- ✔ Airbags

Premium cars

Premium and luxury cars (see the following section) are pretty similar. Both classes guarantee you a comfortable four-door that can seat five adults without a problem. Premium cars also include everything standard cars have, plus:

- ✔ Power locks and windows
- ✔ AM/FM radio with cassette player
- ✔ Delay wipers

Luxury cars

These big ol' land sharks come with lots of amenities and have the most interior room of anything that isn't a minivan. Luxury cars also feature:

- ✔ Antilock brakes
- ✔ Cruise control
- ✔ AM/FM radio with cassette player
- ✔ Leather interior
- ✔ Power driver's seat
- ✔ Tire-inflation monitor
- ✔ Dual climate zones

- ✔ Power steering
- ✔ Automatic transmission
- ✔ Air-conditioning
- ✔ Central locking
- ✔ Tinted windows
- ✔ Dual mirrors
- ✔ Tilt steering wheel
- ✔ Airbags
- ✔ Power locks and windows
- ✔ Delay wipers
- ✔ 6-cylinder supercharged engine

Convertibles

Ah, to ride with the wind in your hair! Convertibles aren't available everywhere (don't try to get one in Anchorage), but where they are available, you'll probably get a two-door that seats four with a tiny trunk. Convertibles will also have all the amenities standard cars have, plus:

- ✔ Power top
- ✔ Power door locks

Minivans

If you have a big brood, rent a minivan. Priceline says minivans will seat seven passengers, with room in the back for a few big suitcases. Minivans also feature:

- ✔ AM/FM radio
- ✔ Power steering
- ✔ Automatic transmission
- ✔ Air-conditioning
- ✔ Tinted windows
- ✔ Dual mirrors

- ✔ Airbags
- ✔ Power locks and windows
- ✔ Delay wipers

SUVs

Not all sport-utility vehicles (SUVs) have four-wheel drive. If you want to rent a vehicle that will go off-road, one that can ford rivers, or one that needs snow chains, do *not* rent through Priceline. Priceline's SUVs will get you high off the road, and they'll seat five with plenty of room for luggage, but they won't necessarily get you into the wilderness.

SUVs have all the amenities minivans have, plus:

- ✔ Tilt steering wheel
- ✔ Cassette player

Pickup trucks

Priceline only rents Ford Ranger pickups through Budget Rent A Car. As of this writing, none of Priceline's other partners offered pickup trucks. So if you want a truck, check Budget's lowest rates and underbid them.

Pickup trucks booked through Priceline offer:

- ✔ Secured 6-foot trunk (this is why you're renting the truck, right?)
- ✔ Air-conditioning
- ✔ AM/FM radio with cassette player
- ✔ Automatic transmission
- ✔ Dual airbags
- ✔ Rear antilock brakes
- ✔ Power steering
- ✔ Power brakes
- ✔ Dual mirrors
- ✔ Rear sliding window
- ✔ Closed cab

> ## Four-door fever
>
> If you absolutely need a four-door car on Priceline, you must select the full-size, luxury, or premium category. One renter I spoke to discovered this the hard way when he rented a mid-size car and assumed it had four doors. Not only did his car have two doors, he couldn't fit all his suitcases in the trunk. He got what he paid for — but he should have read the fine print.

What's Included — and What Isn't

As a Priceline renter, you're guaranteed a car. That's about it. Car-rental firms are famous for nickel-and-diming people, and they nickel-and-dime Priceline renters worst of all.

Priceline *will* guarantee:

- ✔ **You'll get the car you asked for, or a car of a higher class.** This is more controversial than it looks, because car-rental employees can be very sleazy (see Chapter 14 for more information).
- ✔ **You won't be charged for mileage.**
- ✔ **You'll be able to pick up your car up to 24 hours late.**

Priceline will *not* guarantee:

- ✔ **Free upgrades:** Even if they're offered to everyone else, the rental-car folks may not offer them to you.
- ✔ **A smoking or nonsmoking car**
- ✔ **An in-car CD player**
- ✔ **Hand controls for disabled drivers**
- ✔ **Child seats:** This is lousy, I know. Child seats are mandated by law, yet Priceline will not guarantee one will be available at your rental location. That said, I haven't heard of any situations where they *weren't* available. Bring your own child seat if you can.

The following items will cost extra:

✔ **Child seats:** See Table 13-2 for various rental firms' prices.

✔ **Additional drivers:** Sometimes your spouse can drive for free. Read your rental contract closely. Sometimes rental-company employees will lie about the contents of the contract to get you to pay an extra-driver fee.

✔ **Gas:** You're in the same boat as everyone else here — return the car with a full tank, or pay your car-rental firm's incredibly inflated gas prices.

✔ **Insurance:** This is, of course, a nightmare. Always avoid buying car-rental firms' insanely overpriced insurance if at all possible. You may have car-rental insurance from the credit card you booked your car with, from your own private car-insurance policy, or from your homeowner's insurance policy (see Chapter 2 for more information).

Table 13-2	Car-Rental Companies' Extra Charges				
Item	*Alamo*	*Avis*	*Budget*	*Hertz*	*National*
Additional driver	$7/day	$25/rental	Varies	$7/day	Varies
Child seat	$8/day	$8/day	$7/day	$8/day	$8/day

Chapter 14

Bidding On and Winning a Rental Car

. . . .

In This Chapter

▶ Knowing when to bid

▶ Finding the right car for you

▶ Determining the competing rates

▶ Bidding and rebidding

▶ Getting an upgrade on your car

▶ Picking up your car

. . . .

*G*as prices are going crazy. As of this writing, most of the United States is paying at least $2 per gallon at the pump, with some poor folks forking out $2.60 for premium petrol. What's a driver to do? Beat the high gas prices by shaving a few bucks off your car rental, of course.

Rental cars aren't as expensive as hotels or airfares, and Priceliners see slimmer savings behind the wheel than at the hotel check-in desk. But you can still net a free tank of gas (or more) through smart bidding, and drive away smiling even while OPEC does its worst.

In this chapter, you find out about Priceline's rental-car bidding options and walk through a winning bid for a car. You find out how to make sure you're getting the lowest rate, and what to do when you get to the counter to pick up your car. With a little luck and a bit of skill, you'll drive away happy every time.

Figuring Out When to Bid

When you reserve a rental car directly through the rental-car company, your reservation is always fully refundable — you usually don't put down any money in advance. On the other hand, if you win a Priceline bid, you're stuck with the price you named. Priceline bids are nonrefundable.

Rental-car companies run sales *constantly* for dates about a month in advance. They may post coupons on their Web sites, offer free upgrades, or even offer free gas.

So you should never bid on Priceline too far in advance, or you'll risk missing some super-low rate available directly from a rental-car firm. Bidding two weeks or so in advance is a good bet, because if your bid fails, you have a second chance seven days later. For last-minute bids, you can try up to noon on the same day you pick up your car.

Choosing a Car

Before you bid, you need to decide how much to bid. And before you decide how much to bid, you need to decide what kind of car you're bidding for.

Priceline offers 11 types of cars, from 5 major rental agencies: Alamo, Avis, Budget, Hertz, and National. Think of Priceline's cars as fitting into four groups: small, standard, spacious, and special.

For more details on each of Priceline's car types, see Chapter 13.

Small cars

Priceline's economy and compact cars are tiny and cheap. They sip rather than guzzle gas, and they may have two or four doors. Both car classes seat four people and let you put a little bit of luggage — but not too much — in the trunk.

Rental-car companies have no class

Rental-car companies often have a strange idea of what a "guaranteed, prepaid reservation" is. Getting to the rental counter and finding that no cars of your class are available — or even that no cars at *all* are available — is not uncommon.

This happens with all kinds of reservations, not just Priceline. Stand firm and, whatever you do, don't accept a downgrade. For more on what to do in this irritating situation, see Chapter 15.

Standard cars

Priceline's mid-size, standard, and full-size cars are your average, run-of-the-mill, taxicab-type cars. They'll fit four people very comfortably, or two adults with three kids kneeing each other in the back seat, and you'll probably be able to get all your luggage into the trunk.

Selecting full-size will guarantee you a four-door, but otherwise, most full-size cars are identical to standard cars.

Spacious cars

If you need a big, friendly four-door with room for five people of any size, go for premium or luxury cars. These old-fashioned land sharks offer big trunks, roomy back seats, and smooth rides.

Priceline also rents minivans and small SUVs, which I think also fall under "spacious." Minivans seat seven; SUVs have lots of room for luggage.

Special cars

So, you think you're so special? Want to ride down California's Pacific Coast Highway with the wind in your hair, or lug some lumber home from the hardware store? Priceline lets you rent convertibles and pickup trucks.

You'll find convertibles in most cities where the weather's typically good enough — Burbank, not Boise. Pickup trucks are harder to find, because only one of Priceline's partners (Budget) rents out pickups. But if that's what you're looking for, it's still worth a try.

Figuring Out How Much to Bid

The basic rule of Priceline bidding is simple: Find the lowest competing rate, then bid lower.

Figuring out what to bid is a little tricky with rental cars, though, because the lowest rates can sometimes involve coupons you find on rental-car company Web sites or in the Entertainment Book (see the "That's entertainment!" sidebar). You must factor these coupons into other rates before deciding what to bid on Priceline.

That's entertainment!

If you rent cars more than a few times a year, consider buying an Entertainment Book, a coupon book for a specific metro area in the United States or Canada offering discounts on hotels, restaurants, and rental cars. Entertainment Book coupons can knock $20 off the price of a rental, and sometimes Priceline can't beat that savings. Entertainment books for most metro areas cost $25 to $40, and the coupons last a year. Get them at www.entertainment.com.

Checking competing rates

Never bid blindly on Priceline. Priceline will tell you what it thinks prevailing rates are, but it'll usually be wrong. Hunting around for coupons and online specials can pay off with rates lower than even Priceline provides.

Major travel agencies

Priceline owns two "ordinary" car-rental Web sites: BreezeNet.com (www.breezenet.com) and RentalCars.com (www.rentalcars.com). Always check these sites first to find rates Priceline can beat.

The "big three" travel agency Web sites — Expedia, Orbitz, and Travelocity — sometimes have exclusive deals of their own on rental cars. Check all three sites. It'll only take you a few minutes.

Hotwire.com (shown in Figure 14-1) works a little like Priceline in that you don't know which car-rental firm you're getting, and reservations are nonrefundable. But Hotwire shows you prices in advance, making it a great place to check for rates that compete with Priceline's.

Car-rental company sites

Car-rental companies often save the best deals for their own sites. Don't just go straight to the reservations page, though. Scour the car-rental company's home page for a link to deals, specials, or coupons with codes that can get you free upgrades, extra-low rates, or other bonuses (like the free tank of gas offered by Budget in Figure 14-2).

You can't use any discount or upgrade coupons with a Priceline rental.

For a full list of car-rental firm Web sites, see Chapter 20.

Figure 14-1: Hotwire shows you its rates before you put down your money.

Figure 14-2: At the time of this writing, Budget was offering a free tank of gas if you rented through its company — but not if you rented through Priceline.

Weekday versus weekend rates

Most car-rental firms have three sets of rates (see Table 14-1 for an example of the price differences involved):

- ✔ A low *weekend rate* for rentals between 5 p.m. Thursday and 5 p.m. Monday

- ✔ A much higher *weekday rate* for rentals between 5 p.m. Monday and 5 p.m. Thursday

- ✔ A moderately priced *weekly rate* for rentals of five days or more

Table 14-1	Sample Weekday, Weekend, and Weekly Rates			
Rental-Car Company	Weekday Rate	Weekend Rate	Weekly Rate	Weekly Rate Per Day for 7-Day Rental
Hertz	$50.99	$14.99	$130.99	$18.71
Alamo	$33.61	$16.95	$118.95	$16.99
Avis	$50.99	$14.99	$128.99	$18.43

You'll save the most with *Priceline* if you're renting your car between Monday and Thursday. Not only do most car-rental companies offer lower rates on weekends, but they also offer coupons and promotions only good on the weekends. That can make for unbeatable deals.

Priceline can also save you money if you're renting your car for five days or more. You may not save as much per day as you do over weekday rates, but you'll spread out your savings over more days.

Priceline's Best Price Guarantee

Priceline is so confident it can give you the best rates, it guarantees it. If you find a lower rate for the exact same car, same dates, and same pickup location on another travel-agency Web site (no rental-car company Web sites, corporate rates, or AAA rates allowed), Priceline will refund you the difference. To get the refund, you must call Priceline at 800-774-2354 or send an e-mail through its Web site within 48 hours of winning your bid, and before you pick up your car. Tell a customer-service agent your Priceline bid request number and give details of how you found the other rate — offering to send a screenshot of the Web page with the other, lower rate would be great. (See Chapter 3 for details on how to take a screenshot.)

Don't rely on this guarantee. Yes, you can get your money back, but you may have to argue with Priceline extensively before you win. Bidding below what other sites are charging is better.

Choosing a bid amount

How much do you want to save, and how much is realistic? Priceline says you can save up to 25 percent off prevailing rates.

I like to use the Tank of Gas Rule — going through Priceline should save me the price of a tank of gas, at whatever the current price at the pump is.

So here's what to do. Let's say you're renting a car for a week, and the lowest weekly rate you found is $118:

1. **To the lowest rate you can find ($118) add Priceline's $6.95 service fee.**

   Round up to get $125.

2. **Decide how much you want to save.**

   In my case, a Ford Focus has a 13-gallon tank, and gas costs around $2 a gallon. So I wouldn't mind saving $26.

3. **Subtract your savings from the amount in Step 1 ($125 – $26 = $99).**

4. **Divide by how many days you're renting, and round down ($99 ÷ 7 = $14).**

5. **Looks like you're bidding $14 for this rental.**

Making Your First Bid

You know what kind of car you want, and you know how much to bid. It's time to get online and save some money. Go to Priceline's home page, www.priceline.com, and click on Rental Cars to get started.

You're now on the starting page for rental-car bids. Here, you choose your car class and the metro area in which you're picking up the car. On the next screen, you choose a more precise location to pick up your car.

1. **Select the radio button next to the car type you want, such as Compact or Economy.**

   When you select a radio button, you see a brief description of the car type (see Figure 14-3).

   If you're looking for a premium, luxury, convertible, minivan, or pickup, click More, and those options will appear.

2. **Enter the city and state where you want to pick up your car in the Pick-Up/Drop-Off City field.**

   Don't bother worrying about whether you'll get your car at the airport or downtown yet.

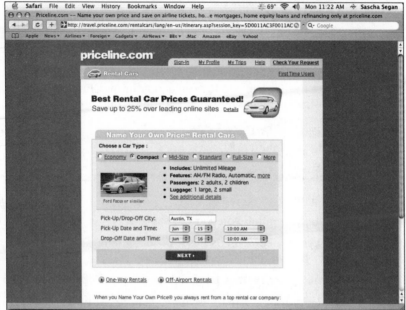

Figure 14-3:
Check out
the options
and choose
your car
class here.

3. **Select your pick-up and drop-off dates and times from the pop-up menus.**

   You must enter times, but don't worry if you're a few hours off.

4. **Click Next.**

   The screen where you choose your rental location and place your bid appears (see Figure 14-4).

5. **Decide whether you want to get your car at the airport or downtown, if downtown is an option.**

   To see what Priceline defines as *downtown,* click on the Details link. You'll see a map showing the area your rental-car company will be in. Believe the map, not the words — *you* may not consider the shaded area to be downtown.

   If you pick up your car at the airport, you still may have to take a shuttle bus to get to the car-rental counter.

6. **If you have a flight reservation, use the drop-down list under What Airline Are You Flying? to pick your airline, and then enter your flight number into the Your Flight Number field.**

   That way, if your flight is delayed, the rental-car firm will know and will (hopefully) keep the rental desk open for you.

   If you don't know your flight number yet, you can always call the rental-car company later and have it attach the flight to your reservation.

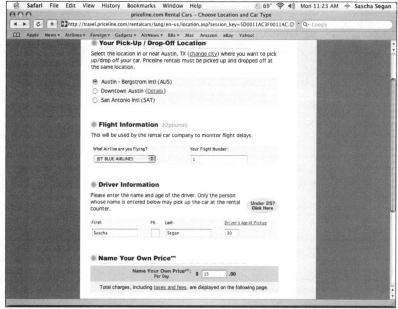

Figure 14-4:
Decide
whether to
pick up your
car at the
airport or
downtown
here.

7. **Enter your price per day in the Name Your Own Price field.**

   For example, if you're renting for seven days and want to pay a total of $99 plus tax, enter $14. (See the "Choosing a bid amount" section earlier in this chapter.)

8. **Click Next.**

   You'll probably see a We Want You to Get Your Car! page like the one shown in Figure 14-5, complaining that you're bidding too low. Ignore it.

9. **Enter your bid again and click Next.**

   Now you see the Please Review Your Request screen (shown in Figure 14-6), the most important screen in your whole bidding process. Pay *really* close attention to the Please Review Your Request screen. Print it out. Read the printout. Walk away from the computer, come back, and read it with a fresh eye. This screen shows what you're committing to. If you're not comfortable with *anything* on this screen, go back and change it. This is your last chance. After this, you'll put in your credit-card number, and then there's no turning back.

   Notice Priceline has added some taxes and fees onto your bid. You have no way around these — no matter how you rent your car, you have to pay these fees.

   Annoyingly, your rental-car firm will probably tack even *more* fees onto your bill when you pick up your car, for things like "concession recovery charges." You can't do anything about those fees, either.

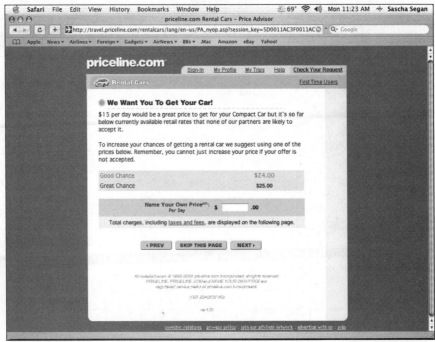

Figure 14-5:
Move along.
Nothing to
see here.

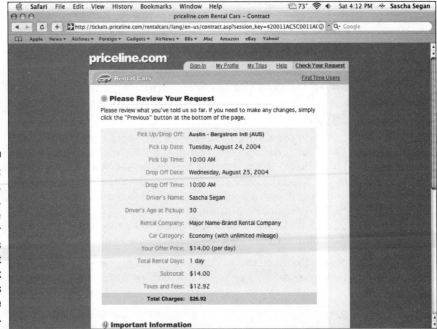

Figure 14-6:
Please,
please,
please
review your
request. This
is your last
chance to fix
any mistakes
before you're
locked in.

10. **If you don't own any credit cards, but only have a debit card or check card, click the appropriate box.**

    Debit cards are ATM cards with a Visa or MasterCard logo on them. Using a debit card will sharply reduce your chances of getting a rental car.

    Rental-car companies like credit cards because they put you on the hook for damages. If they want to charge you extra because you damaged the car, rental-car companies can try to get to you through your credit-card company. But if you use a debit card, they can't do more than drain your checking account.

11. **If you're satisfied with your bid, enter your initials in the field at the bottom of the screen (after reading the "Important Information" section) and click Next.**

    Now you'll see a page where you can enter your credit-card information.

12. **Enter your credit-card details in the appropriate fields.**

    Priceline offers to keep your personal information in a *secure profile*. That means you won't have to reenter your credit-card details every time you bid, and you'll be able to look up your past bids more easily.

    Signing up for a profile also lets you get special "bonus money" coupons through e-mail, which can add value to future Priceline bids.

    For example, a bonus money coupon may add $5 per night to any hotel bid you make of $50 per night or more.

13. **If you don't want to set up a profile, ignore all the stuff under Register Now and SAVE!**

    If you do want to set up a profile, fill out the information under Register Now and SAVE!

14. **If you don't want to get coupons (and don't want to get the additional spam that would arrive with the coupons), *uncheck* the box next to Yes! I Would Like to Receive Exclusive Promotions, Coupons, and Discounts.**

15. **Click Buy My Rental Car Now.**

    Cross your fingers — now you'll find out whether you got a rental car!

When you submit your bid, one of four things will happen.

- ✔ **Your bid will be successful.** Great! If your bid is successful, print out the confirmation page and jump down to "You Won — Now What?", later in this chapter.

- ✔ **Your bid will be nowhere near successful.** If your bid is way too low, you'll see the rebid screen. Jump down to "Bidding Again and Again" later in this chapter and try again.

✔ **Priceline's computers will be jammed.** When this happens, you get a page telling you to check back in 15 minutes or so. Close your Priceline window and wait until you get an e-mail from Priceline (sometimes it takes up to an hour or two). Click on the link in the e-mail, and you'll find out whether your bid succeeded or not. If you don't get an e-mail, go to Priceline's home page and click the Check Your Request link in the upper-right-hand corner to see if Priceline has an answer for you.

✔ **Priceline will let you raise your price.** Very rarely, Priceline will show you a page letting you rebid by raising your price without changing anything else about your bid. (That's such a rare occurrence that I couldn't get a screenshot to show you.) If you're lucky enough to get this page, raise your bid by a few dollars and resubmit it.

Bidding Again and Again

If Priceline rejected your bid, you'll see the Rebid screen (shown in Figure 14-7) asking you to change something about your bid.

Now, most of the options here probably won't be ones you're willing to accept. For example, you probably won't want to change your airport or flight dates to accommodate your rental car.

You can, though, change your car class. If you do, treat it as an entirely new bid — in other words, check competing prices again.

You'll probably find that competing prices for economy and compact cars are about the same. The same goes for prices for full-size and standard cars, and sometimes even prices for mid-size and full-size.

Two drivers, two chances

Most Priceline rentals do not allow additional drivers for free — it tacks on an extra fee if you want a second person to be able to drive your car. (Refer to Table 14-1 for a chart of those fees.)

If you're committed to paying the additional-driver fee, you can always bid again under the second person's name, and have your first bidder become the additional driver. That lets you raise your bid and doubles your chances of winning.

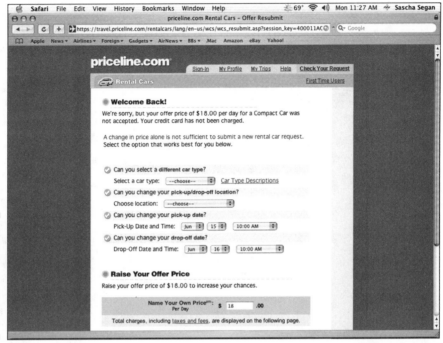

Figure 14-7:
If you change your car class here, you can raise your bid.

If that's the case, switch to the alternate car category and bid a few dollars higher than you did last time. If you're worried, double-check competing rates and make sure that you're still saving money before you put in your bid.

If you're not willing to take a different class of car, or all your possible bids fail, you must wait seven days before bidding again. That's seven days to the minute. If your bid failed at 11 a.m. on Sunday, don't try again at 10:30 a.m. the next Sunday. You must wait until 11:01 a.m.

You Won — Now What?

Congratulations — you got a rental car at a great price! If your bid succeeded, you should see a confirmation page like the one shown in Figure 14-8.

Print out the confirmation page. It'll show the exact location of your rental-car agency, your car class, and your confirmation number.

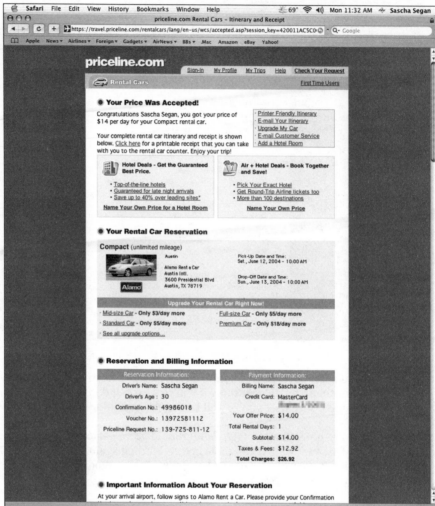

Figure 14-8:
This page
has all the
details you
need to pick
up your car.

Upgrading your car

Priceline will probably also offer you a bunch of possible upgrades. Priceline's upgrade prices are about the same as what you'll inevitably be offered at the rental-car counter, so the only thing you're saving here is time and confusion.

If you do want to take a Priceline upgrade, click on one of the links under Upgrade Your Rental Car Right Now! You'll be taken to the upgrade page, shown in Figure 14-9. There, you'll see the full price you'll pay if you upgrade, and you can agree to upgrade your car.

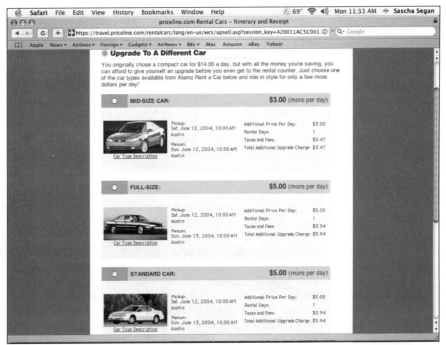

Figure 14-9:
Hmm, the full-size car only costs a little more.

If you agree to an upgrade, it's just as nonrefundable, and just as binding, as any other Priceline bid. In other words, if you agree to an upgrade, the rental-car company *must* give you the upgraded car and not a smaller vehicle.

Picking up your car

Picking up your rental car is the most nerve-wracking part of Priceline bidding, because — to be completely honest — many rental-car counter staffers are jerks.

Overbooking (when a rental-car firm rents out more cars than it has) and *upselling* (when it tries to sell you extras for more money when you go to pick up your car) are obnoxiously common in the rental-car industry. To get what you want, you're going to have to be patient and firm.

First, figure out where your rental-car counter is. Is it in your airport terminal or will you need to take a shuttle bus? Call the rental-car firm's toll-free number (see Table 14-2) and ask.

Table 14-2	Rental Car Toll-Free Numbers
Rental-Car Company	*Toll-Free Number*
Alamo	800-462-5266
Avis	800-230-4898
Budget	800-214-6094
Hertz	800-654-3131
National	800-468-3334

When you get to the counter, hand over your driver's license, a major credit card, and your Priceline confirmation page.

The rental-car staffer will hand you a contract. You'll have to pay extra if you want insurance, a child seat, or an additional driver. You'll also be assaulted by a flurry of possible add-ons: Do you want an upgrade? Do you want a navigation system? How about a mind-bogglingly overpriced tank of gasoline? The choices about the upgrade and navigation system are up to you, but say no to the gas — rental-car companies always charge more than the market rate.

Finally, when you go out to get your car, note any dings or scratches and point them out (in writing) to the rental-car employee. That way you won't get blamed for preexisting problems.

If you have trouble getting the car you paid for, check out the solutions in Chapter 15.

Alas, if you want to keep driving beyond the time you bid for, you won't be able to get extra days at Priceline's rate. Ask when you pick up your car, and you'll probably be able to get extra days — though at a higher rate.

Chapter 15

Fixing Rental-Car Problems

• •

In This Chapter

▶ Correcting mistakes in rental-car bidding

▶ Dealing with missing reservations

▶ Coping with flight delays

▶ Responding to claims that no cars are available

• •

*M*ost non-Priceline rental-car reservations aren't prepaid, so Priceline can be pretty generous about giving refunds on rental cars when things go wrong. That's "generous" by *Priceline's* terms, of course, which means that you can't just ask for a refund because you want one.

If you make a mistake or something goes wrong at the rental-car counter, you can usually count on Priceline to back you up.

Priceline's response to any problem, of course, is for you to call or e-mail its customer-service department. Don't be afraid to call Priceline's toll-free number at any hint of trouble. (For a guide through Priceline's awful voice-mail menus, take a look at Chapter 3.)

The tricky folks to watch out for, in this case, aren't Priceline but the staff at the rental-car counter. They may try to sell you upgrades, try to tack on extra charges, or claim that no cars are available. Know your rights, stick to your guns, and you'll drive away a happy bidder.

I Made a Mistake!

Everybody makes mistakes. Maybe your keyboard stuck and you typed "$144" instead of "$14." Maybe you accidentally punched in "June 5" instead of "May 5." Although Priceline rentals are technically nonrefundable, it's often willing to make a one-time exception if it's obvious you made a stupid error.

E-mail Priceline's customer service with your successful bid request number (it looks like 123-456-789-10, and appears on your winning bid page) and explain how you screwed up. Priceline may cancel the bid, so you can start over. Make sure to get things right this time!

Priceline's so-called one-time exceptions aren't really one-time. It'll probably allow you one screw-up every couple of months. But don't count on it — it's only doing this out of the goodness of its dot-com heart.

Get in touch with Priceline the minute you discover something's wrong. Priceline may require you to resubmit your bid with your fixed price or dates before it gives you a refund. Although it's pretty forgiving about mistakes, it's less forgiving if it thinks you're just trying to get out of a reservation later because your travel plans changed.

Priceline forgives mistakes, but it's much less likely to forgive you if you just didn't know the rules. So if you bid for a mid-size car and you're irritated that you got a two-door, just chalk it up to experience.

I Didn't Hear Back from Priceline!

Sometimes Priceline's computers get jammed up. If you bid for a car and haven't heard back from Priceline in about an hour:

1. **Go to Priceline's home page, `www.priceline.com`.**

2. **Click Check Your Request in the upper-right-hand corner.**

3. **Click Rental Cars.**

4. **Enter your Request Number and the e-mail address you gave Priceline.**

   Your Request Number looks like 123-456-789-10, and should have appeared on the page telling you to wait after you placed your bid. If you don't have your Request Number, click Click Here If You Don't Have Your Number. Priceline will try to find your request based on your e-mail address and credit-card number.

5. **Click Next.**

   You should now see your bid results.

6. **If you don't see your bid results, or if Priceline can't find your request, *don't place another bid;* instead, e-mail Priceline's customer service and explain that your bid seems to have vanished.**

   Only place another bid when you have written confirmation from Priceline that your first bid did not succeed.

Although Priceline will give you a refund if you book a duplicate reservation because of a computer glitch on its end, you're better off just making sure the first bid didn't go through. That way, you avoid having to deal with Priceline's customer-service department again.

Hey, Where's My Reservation?

Prepaid reservations are rare in the rental-car world, so rental-car companies (and staffers) have trouble handling them sometimes. When Priceline's computers don't quite connect to a rental-car company's reservation system, you can show up at a rental counter only to find it has no idea who you are, or that it doesn't know your reservation is prepaid.

To prevent this from happening:

1. **Confirm your reservation the day before you arrive.**

   Call the rental-car company's main reservation number, and say you're just double-checking your reservation.

2. **If the rental-car company says it can't find your reservation, give its customer-service representative the confirmation number (not the Priceline request number) from your winning bid page.**

3. **If the rental-car company *still* can't find your reservation, call Priceline at 800-774-2354.**

   Refer to Chapter 3 for a guide through Priceline's voice-mail menus.

Bring a printout of your winning bid page and bring it with you to the rental-car counter. If a rental-car staffer tries to charge you for your rental, explain that Priceline bids are prepaid and offer to give him Priceline's phone number (800-774-2354).

If you don't have a printout of your confirmation page and the rental-car staffer denies that you have a reservation, your task gets more difficult. You have to call Priceline and put the Priceline customer-service person on the line with the rental-car person. This is something that Priceline and the rental-car company have to work out between them.

If you can't get in touch with Priceline, you don't have a printout of your confirmation page, and the rental car staffer is still intransigent, you're pretty much stuck. Get the staffer's name (if you can) and rent a car elsewhere. If you call Priceline and tell a customer-service representative what happened, Priceline will refund your reservation and possibly give you a credit on your next trip.

My Flight Was Delayed/Cancelled!

Priceline is unusually compassionate about flight delays. If you attach your flight information to your bid (either when you're bidding, or afterward by calling the rental-car company), the rental-car company will hold your reservation for 24 hours after your stated pickup time.

If you get to the airport so late that the rental-car counter is closed, you're responsible for finding your own way to your hotel — but your car will be available when the counter opens in the morning.

If your flight is cancelled and you won't arrive at your destination anywhere near the time you expected, call Priceline. It'll reschedule your rental times to fit with your new flight schedule or give you a refund, if that's impossible.

The Car I Picked Wasn't Available!

It should never happen, but it happens all too often.

Car-rental companies overbook — massively. They take vast numbers of non-prepaid reservations, assuming many will be no-shows. So when everyone *does* show, the car-rental companies run out of cars.

Love Hertz

Wonder why people pay more to rent from Hertz? I asked all five of Priceline's rental firms what they would do if a Priceline customer showed up with a reservation, and no cars of the requested size were available. Their responses:

✔ **Hertz** came through with the customer service that makes them famous: "If the reserved car is not available, Hertz's policy is to provide the customer with a complimentary upgrade to the next car class," spokeswoman Paula Stifter said. "If for some reason Hertz doesn't have any cars available, the customer-service representative will make every attempt to assist the customer in obtaining alternate transportation, including seeking availability with another, nearby rental company. Priceline will refund prepaid rentals, and we normally refund the customer any difference if the other company charges more than the price obtained through Priceline."

✔ **Avis** and **Budget** did almost as well. Their spokesman said that the companies would do what they could to get you one of their cars. That means you should get the upgrade coming to you.

✔ **Alamo** and **National** refused to comment. Uh-oh. Well, deny it or not, they're still responsible for giving you an upgrade or a refund if they don't have your requested car.

Your guaranteed, prepaid reservation doesn't immunize you against the we-have-no-cars disease. But it gives you a legal leg to stand on as well as rights to demand what you paid for. In general, here's the rule: If the car-rental company doesn't have any cars of your selected size available, it must do *one* of the following:

- ✔ Give you a free upgrade
- ✔ Rent you a car from a competitor and pay for your transportation to the competitor's counter
- ✔ Give you a full refund

It can't give you a smaller car than you requested, though sleazier car-rental employees will try. Stand your ground, demand your rights, and call Priceline on the phone if necessary.

If possible, walk away rather than accepting a smaller car. If you walk away, you can get a full refund from Priceline. If you accept a smaller car, you'll end up having to argue with Priceline and will probably only get a partial refund.

The Rental-Car Desk Has No Cars at All!

In extreme situations, like late at night on holidays, you may find yourself standing at a rental-car counter facing a staffer who has no cars on hand. It doesn't change your rights, or what the rental-car company owes you. You can wait around for a car to be returned, but it's still responsible for finding you a car or giving you a refund.

If you walk away because the rental-car desk has no cars, you can always get a refund from Priceline.

Oh No, I'm Late!

Stuck in traffic, or just having too good a time? If you return your car late, you're going to have to pay extra — and you won't get to pay low Priceline rates, either.

Your Priceline rate covers only the exact period you bid for. Spend any more time in your car, and you could be charged for an entire extra day at whatever the car-rental firm's usual daily rate is.

Most rental firms allow a one-hour grace period for late rentals, but that's not set in stone. So make sure to return your car on time — or be prepared to pay.

Part V

More Priceline Products

The 5th Wave   By Rich Tennant

DARRYL LOGS ON TO PRICELINE.COM'S LAST MINUTE VACATION PACKAGE

In this part . . .

Welcome to the backrooms of Priceline's warehouse. Here, you find the unusual merchandise — a little something from Asia, a vacation packager, and even a few guys who want to sell you a mortgage.

Most of Priceline's business comes from selling airfares, rental cars, and hotel rooms in the United States. But these sideshow businesses can still be fun places to shop, and can still save you big bucks.

If you don't live in the United States (or don't have a credit card with a U.S. billing address), go straight to Chapter 18. There, you find all the secrets of how to bid on Priceline.com from anywhere in the world.

Chapter 16

No Bidding Required: Buying Priceline Vacations

- -

In This Chapter

▶ Figuring out whether Priceline vacations are really a bargain

▶ Knowing how to buy a Priceline package

- -

Priceline's air-and-hotel vacations eliminate most of the mystery from your trip. Unfortunately, they also eliminate most of the savings.

With Priceline vacations, you buy an airline ticket and a hotel room together. *The good news:* You get to pick your exact hotel (and sometimes your exact flight), and you find out the price in advance. *The bad news:* Priceline charges for that knowledge.

Bidding for airfare and a hotel separately will almost always end up costing less than buying a vacation. But Priceline competes well with other ordinary travel agencies, such as Expedia, that sell air-and-hotel vacations.

In this chapter, I show you how to gauge whether Priceline offers the best rate for your air-and-hotel vacation, and you'll find out how to buy vacations from Priceline. If bidding seems like too much of a risk for you, Priceline's vacations just may provide the savings you need with the assurances you want.

Judging Priceline's Package Prices

When you're bidding for airfare or hotels, you know you'll get a great deal from Priceline. But as far as I can tell, Priceline doesn't heavily discount the hotels on its packages. Here are my rules for Priceline packages:

✔ You can *always* do better by bidding a hotel and airfare separately.

✔ If the package has a mystery flight, the package will be somewhat cheaper than the competition.

✔ If the package tells you what flight you're on, just treat Priceline as an average travel agency. It may be the cheapest — but then again, it may not.

I compared more than a dozen successful Priceline airline and hotel bids with packages set up for the same itineraries. Mystery flights made all the difference with Priceline packages. I found savings of $40 to $200 per person over Expedia when Priceline offered mystery flights. But when the flights *weren't* a mystery, Expedia and other competitors such as Southwest Airlines beat Priceline pretty often.

Expedia and other major travel agencies have one other big advantage over Priceline vacations — a large stock of 1- and 2-star hotels that don't participate with Priceline.

For example, although Priceline handily beat Expedia's price for a trip from Kansas City to New York City staying in 3- and 4-star hotels like the Sheraton Manhattan, Expedia undercut Priceline by offering 1- and 2-star hotels like the Belnord and West End Studios — not luxury lodging by any means, but definitely ways to save money if you're on a tight budget.

Checking Out Priceline's Hotels

Because you can pick your exact hotel with Priceline packages, you can check out the hotel in advance and make sure it's *exactly* what you want. Priceline helps you by showing you a page of hotel details while you're shopping. That page explains a hotel's amenities, but it doesn't give a truly honest opinion on whether the hotel is worth staying at.

For real consumer opinions, go to TripAdvisor (www.tripadvisor.com), and type your hotel and city name into the Search box in the upper-left-hand corner. You'll get a page of reviews from average travelers like yourself, telling you whether your hotel is really worth putting down money for.

You can also go to Epinions.com (www.epinions.com), another consumer review site. Type your hotel and city name into the Search For box. When you get to the page for your hotel, scroll down past the ads until you see Read Reviews. That's the juicy stuff.

Apples and oranges

You can't use Priceline's lists of vacation-package hotels to figure out which hotels you'll get if you bid for a hotel alone. Different hotels belong to the two different Priceline services, and they charge different rates for bidding and for air-and-hotel vacations.

For an expert's view, go to www.frommers.com. Type your hotel and city into the Search In box in the upper-left-hand corner of the screen, and you'll get a page that will link you to Frommer's expert review of your hotel (if there is one).

Buying a Vacation

With air-and-hotel vacations, you get to pick out your hotel and see your price before putting down your money. The vacations are just as nonrefundable as tickets and hotels you bid for, but less mystery and worry are involved.

Starting to buy your vacation

To buy a vacation:

1. **Go to Priceline's home page,** www.priceline.com.

2. **Click on Vacation Packages near the top of the screen.**

   The screen shown in Figure 16-1 appears.

   Priceline's "Best Deal Destinations" are the ones it has the most low fares to, but Priceline has good deals to other locations, as well.

3. **Pick your destination from the Choose a Destination box.**

   If you don't see your U.S. destination listed, look for it in the drop-down list. If you're traveling to Canada, Europe, the Caribbean, or Mexico, click the appropriate link.

4. **Type the name of your home city into the Departure City field.**

Figure 16-1:
Start
buying your
vacation
package on
this screen.

5. **Select your departure and return dates using the drop-down lists.**

6. **Select the number of hotel rooms you'll need from the Rooms drop-down list.**

7. **Choose how many adults, children between 2 and 17 years old, and infants under 2 are coming along using the Passengers drop-down list.**

Ignore the Rental Car box, even if you want a rental car. You'll get a chance to add one later.

8. **Click Next.**

You'll see Figure 16-2, below.

Choosing your vacation options

When you get ready to choose your vacation options, you'll see the difference between Priceline vacations and ordinary Priceline bidding. The deals look great — you can see all the options and the prices. Just remember, you'll save even more if you bid.

Figure 16-2:
So many
possibilities!
Pick your
favorite
hotel from
this list.

You should now see Figure 16-2. This page shows all your vacation options. Using the Sort By buttons, you can sort by price, star rating, hotel name, or hotel location.

The big, red prices are per-person prices. The little gray prices below them show what you'll really pay for your vacation. If you have two people, the real price will be double the big, red per-person price.

The star levels on this page follow the same rules as star levels when you're bidding for hotels (see Chapter 10 for more information). You'll also get a chance to see all of a hotel's amenities in detail in a few moments.

Hotels on this page aren't necessarily near downtown. It's up to you to double-check your hotel's location. In Figure 16-2, for example, the Sheraton New Orleans is in a great location a block from the French Quarter, but the La Quinta New Orleans Causeway is several miles away from most New Orleans attractions.

Click on a Choose button to pick a hotel, and you'll see Figure 16-3, where you discover more details about your vacation.

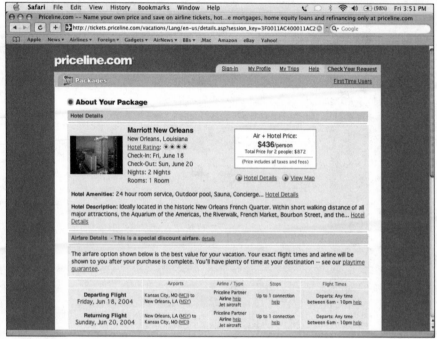

Figure 16-3:
When you
bid on a
Priceline
vacation,
you can see
all kinds of
details about
your hotel.

Look next to Airfare Details. If you see the words *This is a special discount airfare* in red, smile. That means you're saving money. You won't know your exact airline or flight times, but you'll probably get a lower price than you would with another package-holiday company.

If you have a special discount airfare, the airlines and terms will be exactly the same as if you had bid for a flight — you'll just know the price in advance. To find out about Priceline's airline partners and other details, see Chapter 5.

If Priceline shows you your exact airline and flight on this screen, its price won't be so great. You may be able to get a better deal somewhere else.

If you're bidding on a package for one of the next two weekends, you should see a line about the Playtime Guarantee in the area below Airfare Details. Priceline's Playtime Guarantee ensures you'll spend at least 44 hours at your destination for a two-night trip and 64 hours for a three-night trip. That means if you book for Friday and Sunday, the worst-case scenario is a flight that lets you spend from 2 p.m. Friday to 10 a.m. Sunday at your destination, or 8 p.m. Friday to 4 p.m. Sunday. That's not so bad. The guarantee only applies to weekend trips over the next two weeks, though, and only if you see the Playtime Guarantee line on this page.

To find out more about your hotel, click on Hotel Details. You'll see a full list of your hotel's amenities and a map of where it is. Compare the map to one in a reliable travel guidebook to make sure you're where you want to be.

Adding a rental car

Scroll down, and you'll see Figure 16-4. This is your chance to add a rental car to your trip.

Just like with the mysterious flights, the rental cars here have the same rules and restrictions as if you were bidding:

- ✔ They'll come from any one of five major rental-car firms.

- ✔ You'll have to pick up and drop off the car at the airport your flight arrives at.

- ✔ You can't specify whether the car-rental counter will be in your airport terminal, or whether you'll need to take a shuttle bus to get there.

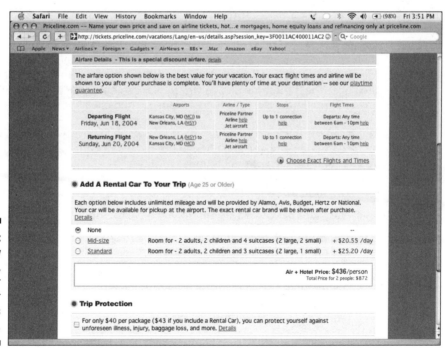

Figure 16-4:
You know your hotel, but your rental-car firm remains a mystery.

To find out about Priceline's car categories and its other restrictions, read Chapter 13.

To add a rental car, click the radio button next to the size of rental car you want.

Deciding on insurance

Also on this screen, you can decide whether you want to buy trip insurance. Priceline's trip insurance for packages covers your airfare, hotel, and car rental all together, but it has the same restrictions as all of Priceline's insurance (see Chapter 3). That means you'll get your money back if you're called up for jury duty or come down with a deathly illness and can't travel, but not if your airline goes bankrupt or if a chronic illness flares up.

You can also buy independent trip insurance from a company like Travel Guard, which offers more comprehensive and flexible coverage for about the same price as Priceline's insurance (see Chapter 3 for more information).

If you want to buy Priceline's trip insurance, click the box under Trip Protection.

Sealing the deal

After you've chosen all your options, click the Next button at the bottom of the page. You'll then see a page where you can enter the names of the people on your trip. Enter the passengers' names, then click Next.

You'll see the Package Summary page, shown in Figure 16-5. This is your last chance to double-check and change the details of your vacation. Make sure you're comfortable with the following things:

- ✔ **The total price for your vacation, shown in red at the top of the page.**
- ✔ **The dates of your vacation:** Do you have the right month? The right days?
- ✔ **The hotel you're staying in:** Are you sure you know where it is, and are you comfortable with the location?
- ✔ **Your airline flights:** If you're using a special discount airfare, are you willing to fly anytime during the period listed? Is Priceline giving you the Playtime Guarantee? (If it is, you should see *Backed by our Playtime Guarantee* next to Airfare Details.)
- ✔ **Hotel restrictions:** Do you understand you can't guarantee a room with one bed, a room with two beds, or a handicapped or nonsmoking room?

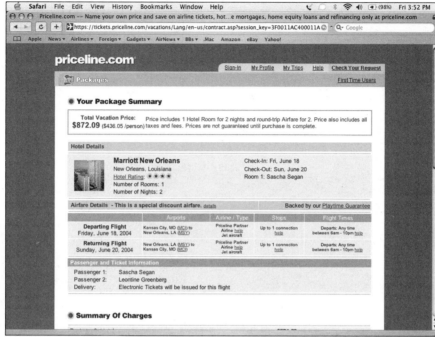

Figure 16-5:
Read this page closely — it's your last chance to change things.

If you're comfortable with your options, enter your initials in the box at the bottom of the screen and click Next. You'll see a page where you can enter your credit-card details. Enter them and click Buy My Vacation Now. Within a few seconds, you'll see a page confirming your vacation details. Print it out — you're on your way!

Chapter 17

Bidding for Mortgages

. . . .

. . . .

*P*riceline is great for hotel rooms, and dandy for rental cars. But *mortgages?* What are these people thinking?

Name-your-own-rate mortgages may sound like a crazy idea, but Priceline is crazy like a fox. By partnering with a Florida-based mortgage bank, EverBank (formerly known as First Alliance), Priceline offers loans with extremely low rates and extremely little human contact — perfect mortgages for cheapskates and misanthropes.

In this chapter, I explain exactly what kind of beast Priceline Mortgage is and walk you through the first steps of applying for a mortgage with this company.

I am not a financial expert. In fact, I'm in the market for my first home myself (and very well may get the mortgage through Priceline). Although I can and do walk you through Priceline's process, if you're in the market for a mortgage you should absolutely read *Home Buying For Dummies,* 2nd Edition, and *Mortgages For Dummies,* both by Eric Tyson, MBA, and Ray Brown (both published by Wiley).

The First National Bank of Priceline?

Priceline Mortgage is not a bank. It's essentially a mortgage broker; it shops around your mortgage to various banks and comes back with the best offer.

But Priceline Mortgage is more than half owned by EverBank, a Jacksonville, Florida–based bank that's been selling mortgages for about 40 years. EverBank handles first mortgages, second mortgages, and home refinancing.

Priceline Mortgage: Better than ever

In the past, some home buyers have complained about Priceline Mortgage's slow service. An EverBank loan officer explained to me that the company wasn't entirely prepared for the huge boom in home refinancing business when interest rates dropped in 2002 and 2003, so the loan officers became utterly overworked. By mid-2004, he said, they'd fixed the problem and even separated their refinancing and purchase teams, making sure that loans for actual home purchases got special priority.

If you call Priceline Mortgage on the phone, you'll get an EverBank loan officer who'll try to sell you an EverBank mortgage. You don't get to name your own rate on the phone; the process works just like with any other mortgage bank.

If you apply for a Priceline mortgage online and name your own rate, EverBank gets first crack at your application. If EverBank can't match your terms, Priceline Mortgage sends out an application with LendingTree (www.lendingtree.com) and sees if any of LendingTree's bank partners will match the rate.

After you agree to a loan, Priceline Mortgage is out of the picture. You're then dealing with a loan officer from EverBank, or from the LendingTree member bank that matched your rate.

You're not locked in to a Priceline mortgage the way you are with an airline ticket or hotel room. (That'd be kind of scary, because we're talking a 30-year commitment here!) But you do pony up a nonrefundable $395 application fee. If EverBank or a LendingTree partner agrees to a mortgage on your terms, you'll pay the $395, and the money will be applied to the closing costs. But if you decide to back out of the loan, you lose the $395.

If nobody can match your terms, you pay nothing.

Preparing to Bid for a Mortgage

Don't jump in to bidding for a mortgage on the spur of the moment. Bidding on Priceline should be the *last* step in your mortgage search. You should already know what kind of loan you want, how much money you need, and how much other lenders are offering.

If you don't know whether you want a 30-year fixed-rate mortgage or a 15-year adjustable-rate mortgage, what *points* are, or other details of how mortgages work, stop here. Put down this book, go read *Mortgages For Dummies* (Wiley), and come back.

Understanding Priceline's mortgage options

Priceline offers three main mortgage options — pre-approvals, purchase money, and refinancing:

- ✔ If you don't have a purchase contract on a house yet, come to Priceline for a *pre-approval.* Priceline will check your credit and send you a letter showing that you're eligible for a mortgage, which can give you a leg up with sellers.

- ✔ If you're trying to buy a house and you have a purchase contract already, you're looking for *purchase money.*

- ✔ If you just want to take advantage of low interest rates to pay off an old mortgage with a slightly cheaper new mortgage, you're trying to *refinance.*

For both purchases and refinancing, Priceline sells both fixed- and adjustable-rate mortgages with terms from 10 to 30 years. **Remember:** Decide what kind of mortgage you want before you start bidding.

Getting your information in order

Before you start working with Priceline Mortgage, get the following information ready:

- ✔ The type of purchase (primary home, secondary home, and so on)
- ✔ The amount you want to borrow
- ✔ The purchase price of your home
- ✔ The amount of your down payment
- ✔ The number of years you're looking for in a mortgage
- ✔ Your expected closing date on the property
- ✔ The property's location
- ✔ Your Social Security number (and your spouse's, if you're applying together)
- ✔ Your employer's name, address, and phone number, and how long you've been working there (ditto for your spouse, if you're applying together)
- ✔ How much money you made last year (ditto for your spouse, if you're applying together)
- ✔ Your outstanding debts, such as loans and credit cards
- ✔ Your assets (such as cash and bank accounts)

If you're refinancing, Priceline will also need to know:

- ✔ How much your home is worth
- ✔ When it was built
- ✔ How big your existing mortgage is
- ✔ How much is still outstanding
- ✔ The length of your existing mortgage
- ✔ How much you pay each month for your mortgage
- ✔ How much is left to pay on your existing mortgage

Deciding How Much to Bid

First of all, don't pay any attention to the mortgage rates on Priceline's home page. Those rates are for Jacksonville, Florida, and they may not apply to where you live. Use a site like HSH Associates, Financial Publishers (www.hsh.com) to find mortgage rates in your area instead.

When you bid, undercut the lowest rates you found elsewhere for the same mortgage type and term length that you will be bidding for by a quarter to a half of a percentage point. For example, if the best rate you found elsewhere is 6 percent with no points, try 5.75 percent with no points, or 5.5 percent with one point.

Placing Your Bid

To bid for a mortgage with Priceline Mortgage, you enter your rate first. Then you fill out a mortgage application, and Priceline gets back to you within six business hours. Here's how it goes:

1. **Go to** www.pricelinemortgage.com.

2. **Scroll down to the box marked Name Your Own Rate — Mortgages (see Figure 17-1).**

3. **Using the drop-down lists, choose:**

   - Whether you're purchasing or refinancing
   - The length and type of your mortgage
   - The rate you want
   - The number of points you can pay
   - How much money you need

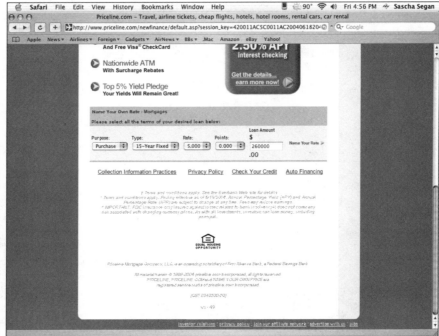

Figure 17-1:
Sure, the
drop-down
lists let you
choose
a 4.375
percent
mortgage,
but try to
have some
self control.

4. **Click Name Your Rate.**

   The screen shown in Figure 17-2 appears.

5. **Scroll down to Get Started Here.**

   Now you're filling out a loan application. Answer the various questions by using the drop-down lists, and click Next.

   If you answer No to "Do you have a signed purchase/sales agreement?" you'll be shunted to Priceline's preapproval section. It can't give you a loan if you don't have a purchase agreement.

6. **On the next page, you have to fill out all sorts of probing personal questions; answer all the questions and click Next.**

7. **You see a page with nosy questions about your employment status and income — fill out all of these and click Next when you're done.**

   The only tricky thing on this page is the way you enter your income. You have to click on the little icon of the calculator next to the words *Click on the calculator to total your monthly income.*

   Then a pop-up window will appear with a form where you can enter your income. Enter your various forms of income, and click Calculate. The pop-up will go away, and the original form will reappear, with the income field filled in.

Figure 17-2:
Let the loan
application
begin.

If the pop-up doesn't appear, make sure you don't have any pop-up blockers or other ad-stopping software turned on.

8. **Now you fill out a form with all the details of your bank accounts and debts; click Next when you're done.**

   Nosy, I know, but the mortgage guys need to know this stuff.

9. **You see a form asking for details about the house you're buying; fill it out and click Next.**

   If any of the items on this form confuse you (like whether you should put the property taxes in an escrow account), go check out *Home Buying For Dummies* and *Mortgages For Dummies* (both published by Wiley).

   Finally, it's time for Priceline to show you the money. You see the screen shown in Figure 17-3.

10. **Priceline will offer you some rates EverBank thinks you'll qualify for; you can pick one of its rates using the radio buttons, or stick with your own rate.**

    If EverBank likes the rate you originally named, it'll only show one radio button — click it.

    Priceline will also give you the option of locking down your closing costs at a fixed amount, or paying $900 plus whatever the title and settlement fees turn out to be. Pick your choice and click Next.

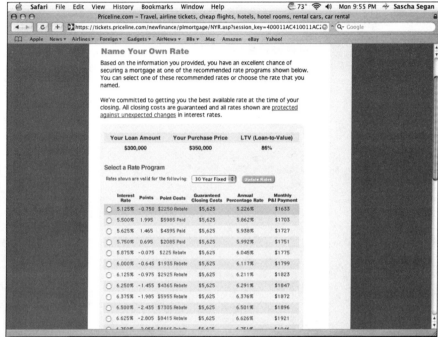

Name Your Own Rate

Based on the information you provided, you have an excellent chance of securing a mortgage at one of the recommended rate programs shown below. You can select one of these recommended rates or choose the rate that you named.

We're committed to getting you the best available rate at the time of your closing. All closing costs are guaranteed and all rates shown are protected against unexpected changes in interest rates.

Your Loan Amount	Your Purchase Price	LTV (Loan-to-Value)
$300,000	$350,000	86%

Select a Rate Program

Rates shown are valid for the following: 30 Year Fixed ◆   [Update Rates]

Interest Rate	Points	Point Costs	Guaranteed Closing Costs	Annual Percentage Rate	Monthly P&I Payment
5.125%	-0.750	$2250 Rebate	$5,625	5.226%	$1633
5.500%	1.995	$5985 Paid	$5,625	5.862%	$1703
5.625%	1.465	$4395 Paid	$5,625	5.938%	$1727
5.750%	0.695	$2085 Paid	$5,625	5.992%	$1751
5.875%	-0.075	$225 Rebate	$5,625	6.045%	$1775
6.000%	-0.645	$1935 Rebate	$5,625	6.117%	$1799
6.125%	-0.975	$2925 Rebate	$5,625	6.211%	$1823
6.250%	-1.455	$4365 Rebate	$5,625	6.291%	$1847
6.375%	-1.985	$5955 Rebate	$5,625	6.376%	$1872
6.500%	-2.435	$7305 Rebate	$5,625	6.501%	$1896
6.625%	-2.805	$8415 Rebate	$5,625	6.626%	$1921

Figure 17-3:
Priceline didn't agree with my first bid of 5 percent, but it has lots of other rate options for me.

There's no such thing as a free lunch in home finance. Depending on where you live, Priceline's fixed closing costs may or may not be a good deal. Your best bet is to print out Priceline's list of fees (available through a link on the page where Priceline asks you about locking down your closing costs) and take them to a financial advisor who can tell you what the fees are likely to be. Then you can decide whether Priceline's fixed-fee option is the best one for you.

11. **Now you have to fill out a form with a bunch of nosy questions about your financial status, semi-incomprehensible questions like "Are you a co-maker or endorser on a note?"** (*Translation:* **Have you co-signed a loan for somebody else?**); **when you're done, click Next.**

    If you don't know the answers, consult a banker.

    If you don't want to answer the questions about race, sex, and ethnicity, select Information Not Provided from those menus.

12. **Time to lock it down! You now see the mortgage terms you're agreeing to, shown in Figure 17-4. Study this page carefully, enter your credit-card details, and click Lock In My Rate.**

    You're now committed to paying Priceline's $395 deposit if it comes back with a loan, either through EverBank or a LendingTree partner.

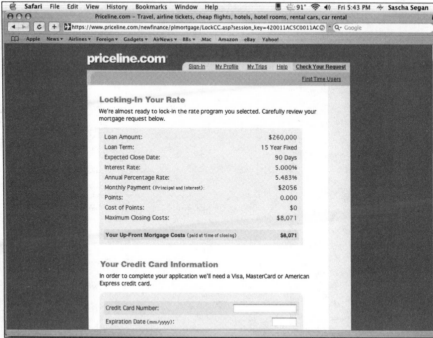

Figure 17-4:
Make sure
this is really
what you
want before
plunking
down your
$395.

Now What? Waiting to Hear whether Your Bid Has Been Accepted

After you've placed your bid, it's time to wait. Within two business days, Priceline will send you an e-mail with a link in it. Click on the link, and you'll see a Web page announcing one of three things:

- ✔ **Your bid has been rejected.** No, you can't get a 2 percent mortgage with no points, no matter how good your credit is. You can try again in seven days, though.

- ✔ **Your bid has been accepted.** Congratulations! You just got a mortgage on your terms. Your acceptance page will include a phone number where you can contact the bank making your loan, whether it's EverBank or someone else. Give your new loan officer a call and find out what you need to do next.

- ✔ **Priceline made a counteroffer.** If EverBank or one of LendingTree's banks can come close to your terms (for example, it may add a few points to what you proposed), you'll see a page with the proposed terms. You don't owe any money yet. You can accept the terms, pay $395, find out who your lender is, and move ahead — or you can walk away.

Guarantee? What guarantee?

Priceline Mortgage offers a $500 best-price guarantee. It says if you can find a competing first mortgage with the same interest rate and terms, and lower points or closing costs, *on the same day* as you accept a Priceline Mortgage offer, it'll kick you $500 — the value of Priceline's $395 deposit plus another C-note for your troubles.

That sounds good, but it also sounds like a consumer nightmare. Not only do you have to find the competing rate within one business day, you must send in a sheaf of arcane paperwork to get your $500. Don't count on this guarantee as a cushion.

The home-finance process isn't over, but this is where I have to leave you. You now have a loan — but you still have to fill out a lot of forms, send a lot of packages back and forth, get your new property appraised, close your home purchase and your loan, and much more.

One piece of advice I can give you from the experiences of others: Watch these lenders like a hawk. Although EverBank says it's lessened its caseloads and sped up its loan process during the past year, take no chances. Be persistent, return paperwork promptly and call your loan officer frequently.

As for the money you saved on your loan — maybe you can buy an airline ticket and a hotel with it!

Chapter 18

Using Priceline around the World

In This Chapter

▶ Knowing the rules and regulations where you live

▶ Figuring out how to bend the rules and put Priceline to work for you

*P*riceline is such a great idea, it's no wonder the rest of the world has picked up on it.

In Canada, people sneak into the U.S. Priceline site and save big bucks. They're not supposed to, but Priceline doesn't seem to mind too much.

Europeans have their own site, which lets them bid for hotels in U.K. pounds — but they can use the U.S. site, too, by bending the rules a bit.

Priceline sites in Singapore, Hong Kong, and Taiwan are for everyone. They're designed for Asians to bid on airfares and hotels, but they're also open to Europeans and Americans who need cheap airline tickets from Singapore, Hong Kong, and Taiwan to other destinations.

All five Priceline sites — the U.S. site, the U.K. site, the Hong Kong site, the Singapore site, and the Taiwan site — offer the same hotels at the same prices. The site you decide to use is just a matter of which one you feel most comfortable with.

In this chapter, I show you how to bend the rules and bid on Priceline no matter where in the world you live. After all, no matter where you live, chances are you're looking to save some money.

Priceline for Canadians

Canadians aren't supposed to use Priceline. But Priceline doesn't seem to mind if they do. Hundreds, if not thousands, of Canadian bidders have bagged huge savings on Priceline, and Priceline cheerfully takes their money and puts them on flights, in hotel rooms, and behind the wheels of cars.

Technically, it's not where you live that matters; it's the billing address of the credit card you use. So if you're a Canadian who, somehow, receives your credit-card bills at a P.O. box in the United States, you're fine with Priceline. But we'll assume for now that you get your credit-card bills in the country where you lay your head at night.

The secret: The credit card

If you live in Canada and you want to use the U.S. Priceline site, you must find a Canadian credit card that works with Priceline. That's tricky, because Priceline rejects many Canadian credit cards out of hand.

American Express cards work more often than any other Canadian credit card. If none of your other cards work, sign up for the American Express Air Miles card at www.americanexpress.ca. It has no annual fee, and you get reward points for buying anything — even Priceline tickets.

Whether you're bidding on flights, hotel rooms, or rental cars, bid just like an American does. (*Remember:* You're bidding in U.S. dollars, not in Canadian dollars). When you get to the final screen, where you fill in your name and address, fill it out as shown in Figure 18-1:

- ✔ **Enter your real name, street address, and phone number.**

- ✔ **For state, use California.** The abbreviation for California, CA, is the same as the international postal abbreviation for Canada.

- ✔ **Use zip code 99999.**

Pricelining hotels

Using Priceline for hotels is easiest, because you can book rooms anywhere in the United States, Canada, Europe, or Asia with Priceline.

Go ahead and book hotels the same way U.S. residents do. Remember, once again, that all prices are in U.S. dollars.

Keep in mind one uniquely Canadian quirk: If you book a Canadian hotel room, Priceline won't charge the usual 7 percent goods and services tax (GST). Instead, your hotel will probably add the GST in a separate charge on your credit-card bill. Don't be surprised when it pops up.

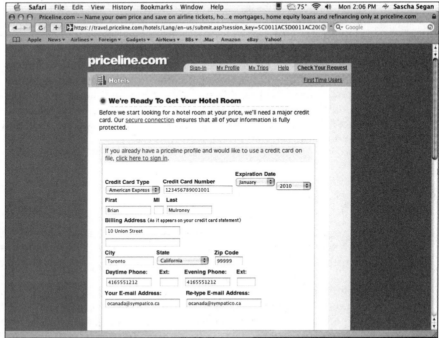

Figure 18-1:
Toronto,
CA — get it?
CA means
California,
but also
Canada.

Pricelining airfares and cars

Priceline only sells airline tickets that depart from the United States. But Canadians can still find bargains by driving across the border and booking flights from the cities listed in Table 18-1.

Table 18-1	**U.S. Airports Bordering Canada**
U.S. Airport	*Canadian Region*
Buffalo, New York	Southern Ontario/Toronto
Rochester, New York	Toronto (via ferry)
Detroit, Michigan	Southern Ontario
Burlington, Vermont	Southern Quebec/Montreal
Plattsburgh, New York	Southern Quebec/Montreal
Seattle, Washington	Vancouver/Victoria

Book Priceline flights using the same credit-card trick I explain earlier. You'll most likely find savings from Detroit and Seattle, because the other airports listed in Table 18-1 are pretty small. But hey, they're still worth a try.

Only book e-tickets on Priceline. Priceline cannot send paper tickets to a Canadian address. It'll try to send paper tickets to the quasi-fake address you put on the credit-card information page, and then you'll be up a creek. Fortunately, Priceline will always say on the Please Review Your Request screen if you have a chance of getting paper tickets on the route you selected. If you do, stop and don't complete your bid.

Priceline for Europeans

Europeans have a Priceline of their very own: Priceline.co.uk. Priceline.co.uk sells Name Your Own Price hotels all over the world, as well as ordinary, not-so-cheap airline tickets and car rentals.

Priceline.co.uk looks like it's only for Brits, but when I asked the Priceline U.K. team if other Europeans could use the service, they told me only that they don't promote the service outside the United Kingdom or claim that others can use it. That's a far cry from saying others *can't* use it — they're just saying that if you're outside the United Kingdom, you're using the site at your own risk.

Europeans can also use the U.S. Priceline site, as long as they're willing to bend the rules.

Europeans on Priceline.com

Europeans who want to try bidding on the U.S. Priceline site may want to do it to get U.S. domestic flights and rental cars that they can't book on the U.K. site, or to get extra bids when they're trying to get hotel rooms.

The trick: Credit cards and addresses

The trickiest part of bidding on Priceline.com as a European is finding a credit card that will work. Priceline rejects most European credit cards out of hand — which credit cards work and which ones don't seems to be entirely unpredictable. When you find a card that works, it will continue to work, so stick with that card for all your bidding.

Bidding help for Europeans

The bulletin board Cleverbidding.com (www. cleverbidding.com) exists to help Europeans bidding on Priceline.co.uk. Alas, Cleverbidding. com is much quieter than BiddingForTravel.com (www.biddingfortravel.com) or Better Bidding.com (www.betterbidding.com). If you're just looking for recent bid results and hotel lists, turn to one of the two more popular boards, grab a calculator, and convert the U.S. dollar prices into pounds for your Priceline U.K. bids. (Use the exchange rates at www.oanda.com to translate currencies.) But the folks on Clever bidding.com may be able to help you with spe-cific bidding questions and strategies to use on Priceline U.K., especially because the moderators of BiddingForTravel.com shun any discussion of the U.K. site.

American Express cards have the greatest chance of working, so if you have one, go for it. If you don't have an American Express card, consider getting a no-fee card such as the Blue Card from www.americanexpress.co.uk.

Bid on Priceline.com just like an American does. When you get to the page where you enter your credit-card details, though, try to mangle your address to look more "American":

- ✔ **If you live in Germany, use Delaware as your state, because DE stands for both Delaware and Deutschland.** Everyone else (including U.K. resi-dents) should use California.

- ✔ **If your country uses numeric postcodes (like 1001), put your postcode in the Zip Code field.** Otherwise, use a zip code of 99999.

- ✔ **Add your country to the city field.** If you live in London, for example, enter your city as "London UK." If you live in Amsterdam, enter "Amsterdam NETHERLANDS."

- ✔ **Try to mangle your phone number so it fits into 11 digits, not starting with a zero.** For instance, if your London phone number is 020 7823 4567, enter your phone number as 207-823-4567.

If your bid doesn't go through properly, don't walk away. Try tweaking the address some more — for instance, remove the country name from the city line, or try a different permutation of your phone number. Sometimes finding the key that fits in Priceline's lock takes a few tries.

Bidding for airfares and rental cars

Buy U.S. domestic flights and rental cars on Priceline the same way Americans do. As long as you stick to domestic and not international flights, all your tickets will be e-tickets. That's good, because Priceline can't send paper tickets to a European address.

If you're booking rental cars on Priceline, they don't come with insurance, and insurance can be very costly. If you don't know what insurance you need, talk to a knowledgeable travel agent to hear about your other options before renting a car through Priceline.com.

Bidding for hotels

Because Priceline.co.uk lets you bid on hotels without all the hassle, why would you ever want to turn to Priceline.com for hotels? One word: *rebids*.

The prices of hotels on Priceline.com and Priceline.co.uk should be about the same, because Priceline uses exchange rates set by the global travel booking service Worldspan.

But you can use Priceline.com to keep bidding when you run out of bids on Priceline.co.uk. If you turn to Priceline.com after you've exhausted your bids with Priceline.co.uk, Priceline will let your bids go through — it won't recognize them as duplicates.

Bidding on Priceline.co.uk

Bidding for hotels on Priceline.co.uk works almost exactly like Priceline.com. You bid for the same kinds of star levels, in the same zones, and get results in the same way. You'll find only a few differences:

- You start bidding at Priceline.co.uk (shown in Figure 18-2) instead of Priceline.com.
- You bid in U.K. pounds instead of U.S. dollars.
- If you live outside the United Kingdom, enter your country into the County field on the credit-card form.

Ignore everything on Priceline.co.uk except for hotels. You can't bid for flights, and you can't bid for rental cars. It'll sell you flights and rental cars, sure, but at normal, run-of-the-mill prices. You can get great deals on Priceline for flights and rental cars, but they're only as good as the deals you'll find on Opodo.co.uk, Expedia.co.uk, or other major travel-agency sites.

Getting help with Priceline.co.uk

Priceline.co.uk has its own toll-free number if you need help with your hotel bids. Call 0800 074 5000 (toll-free) in the United Kingdom, or +44 800 074 5000 (not toll-free) from any other country. To cut through Priceline's voice-mail menus and talk to a Priceline customer-service representative, here are the steps to take (as of this writing):

1. **Choose option 1, "calling regarding an offer you have already submitted."**

2. **Enter your Priceline bid request number and hit the # button on your phone.**

3. **Enter your phone number and hit the # button on your phone.**

4. **Wait through about a minute of babble.**

5. **Choose option 4, "for all other requests."**

6. **Choose option 1, "for further assistance."**

   Victory! You're now on hold for a real, human operator.

Using Priceline Asia

Priceline's Hong Kong–, Singapore-, and Taiwan-based sites work slightly differently than Priceline U.S. and Priceline U.K. That's because they aren't run entirely by Priceline — they're a joint venture between Priceline and Hutchison Whampoa, a Chinese mega-corporation.

Priceline Hong Kong/Singapore/Taiwan (I just call them Priceline Asia from here on in) let you bid for airfares and hotels. For hotels, they share the same database and prices with Priceline U.S. and Priceline U.K., though they have a few quirks all their own.

Priceline Asia spokesman Ray Li told me, "Priceline Asia shares the same hotel database with U.S. Priceline. Participating hotels offer the same rates for all Priceline points-of-sale."

The Asia sites charge a fixed service fee of HK$75 or S$16.50 (about $9.75 in U.S. dollars) for hotel and airline reservations. Priceline U.S.'s fee for booking hotels varies — in many cases it'll be lower than Priceline Asia's, and in some cases higher. But I still suggest you use Priceline U.S. to book hotels if you can, because of its U.S.-based tech support. (Do you really want to be calling Hong Kong for help?)

For airfares, you can get super-cheap, name-your-own-price round-trips with Priceline Asia from Hong Kong, Singapore, Taiwan, and sometimes Macau to anywhere in the world. If you're flying to other Asian destinations, you can even demand nonstop flights.

Best of all, anyone in the world can bid on Priceline Asia. If you're buying airline tickets, you need to have a mailing address in Hong Kong, Singapore, or Taiwan. They won't send the tickets to anywhere else. But you don't need to live there — you can use a hotel, a friend, or a business acquaintance for the mailing address.

Priceline Asia for U.S. residents

Why should Americans use Priceline Asia? After all, we have our own Priceline, and it's just dandy.

But Priceline Asia offers hotels in cities like Bombay, Osaka, and Auckland that Priceline.com doesn't cover. If you're looking for a cheap room in an Asian city that's beyond Priceline.com's reach, Priceline Asia just may be able to scratch your itch.

Also, if you're planning a multicity trip to Asia, Priceline Asia's name-your-own-price airline tickets are definitely worth taking a look at.

If you want to visit, say, Hong Kong and Tokyo, a conventional ticket from the United States to Hong Kong, to Tokyo, and back can cost $1,200. Multicity tickets including both Southeast Asia and Australia can be even more expensive — over $2,000 in many cases.

Simple round-trips to Hong Kong and Singapore, though, are pretty cheap — as low as $700 from major U.S. gateways. Even if you're buying tickets through a regular travel agency, getting a round-trip from the United States to Hong Kong, and then another round-trip from Hong Kong to your other Asian destination, if you intend to visit both cities, can be much cheaper.

Priceline makes those multicity trips even cheaper. Book a ticket by normal means as far as Hong Kong or Singapore, and then use Priceline Asia to connect to your second destination. You'll save.

Bidding for airfares on Priceline Asia

Almost all the recommendations, strategies, and warnings in the rest of this book also apply to Priceline Asia. Start bidding using the yellow Name Your Own Price box on Priceline.com.hk (shown in Figure 18-3), Priceline.com.sg, or Priceline.com.tw. Ignore the various Priceline "specials" on the home page, unless you see a "lucky money" link — it will work like bonus money does on the Priceline U.S. site (see Chapter 4 for more information).

In the following sections, I cover what's different on Priceline Asia.

Origination cities

Because Priceline Hong Kong and Priceline Singapore tickets can only start in Hong Kong or Singapore, you can't use the city-changing tactics I explain in Chapter 6 to get extra bids.

You can still use strategies based on impossible destination airports, though. (See Chapter 6 for an explanation.)

Service fees

Priceline Hong Kong charges a HK$75 service fee for each airline ticket Priceline Singapore charges S$16.50. As of this writing, Priceline Taiwan wasn't up and running yet, but I expect it'll charge about the same.

Figure 18-3:
Name your own price here to bid for airfares or hotels.

Nonstop flights

For most routes within Asia — including flights as far as Australia — you can start out by searching for nonstop and direct flights only. Go, Priceline Asia!

Priceline sometimes uses confusing language, so look under "Select More Connections" on the page where you enter your bid amount, shown in Figure 18-4. If the first check box is Yes, If Non-Stop or Direct Flights Are Unavailable, I Am Willing to Make 1 Connection Each Way, you're headed for nonstop/direct flights (as long as you don't check that box).

If the first check box is I Am Willing to Make 2 Connections Each Way, you can't guarantee nonstop flights, just like with Priceline U.S.

Paying by phone

Priceline Asia requires a credit card, just as Priceline U.S. does. But because many Asians bid from insecure Internet cafes where they may not want to punch in their credit-card numbers, Priceline offers an extra option for payment: You can call a special phone number and enter your credit-card number. After you've entered your credit-card number, Priceline will put your request through its system and e-mail you when it has a response.

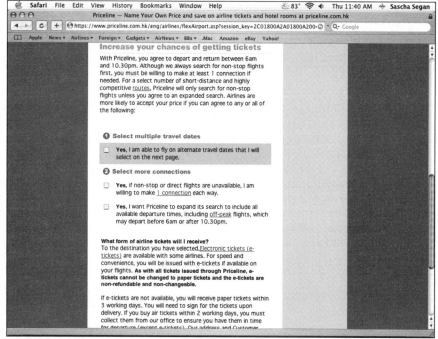

Increase your chances of getting tickets

With Priceline, you agree to depart and return between 6am and 10.30pm. Although we always search for non-stop flights first, you must be willing to make at least 1 connection if needed. For a select number of short-distance and highly competitive routes, Priceline will only search for non-stop flights unless you agree to an expanded search. Airlines are more likely to accept your price if you can agree to any or all of the following:

❶ Select multiple travel dates

☐ **Yes, I am able to fly on alternate travel dates that I will select on the next page.**

❷ Select more connections

☐ **Yes,** if non-stop or direct flights are unavailable, I am willing to make 1 connection each way.

☐ **Yes,** I want Priceline to expand its search to include all available departure times, including off-peak flights, which may depart before 6am or after 10.30pm.

What form of airline tickets will I receive?
To the destination you have selected, Electronic tickets (e-tickets) are available with some airlines. For speed and convenience, you will be issued with e-tickets if available on your flights. **As with all tickets issued through Priceline, e-tickets cannot be changed to paper tickets and the e-tickets are non-refundable and non-changeable.**

If e-tickets are not available, you will receive paper tickets within 3 working days. You will need to sign for the tickets upon delivery. If you buy air tickets within 2 working days, you must collect them from our office to ensure you have them in time for departure (except e-tickets). Our address and Customer

Figure 18-4:
If you don't check that "1 connection" box, you won't have to change planes.

Billing address and delivery address

Unlike Priceline U.S., Priceline Asia accepts credit cards from 29 countries including most Asian nations, the United States, Canada, and major European countries.

When you complete your bid, you'll have to fill out a separate form with a delivery address and contact phone number in Hong Kong, Singapore, or Taiwan.

Priceline Asia books e-tickets whenever possible, but sometimes they come up with paper tickets. You have no control over whether you get paper or e-tickets. If you get paper tickets and are flying more than three days after bidding, the tickets will be sent to your delivery address in Hong Kong, Singapore, or Taiwan.

Priceline Hong Kong bidders can buy flights two days in advance rather than three, but they have to go pick up their paper tickets at Priceline's Hong Kong office.

In other words, if you don't have anyone to deliver your tickets to in Hong Kong, Singapore, or Taiwan — a hotel, a friend, a business contact — don't bid for airline tickets on Priceline Asia.

No immediate response

Priceline U.S. almost always responds to your bid request immediately. Priceline Asia can take up to an hour. It'll send you an e-mail with a link to see if you won your bid.

Deals, specials, and surprises

Priceline Asia runs special promotions much more often than Priceline U.S. does. For example, in June 2004, Priceline Hong Kong handed out HK$100 in hotel bonus money to everyone who booked airline tickets from Macau, as shown in Figure 18-5. By July, it had moved on to an even cooler promotion, where everyone who booked a hotel stay through its site got a randomized, automatic discount — sometimes nothing, sometimes 40 percent off their stay, and sometimes their entire stay for *free*.

Priceline Singapore, meanwhile, was giving away a free MP3 player to everyone who spent at least S$1,200 on airline tickets during June (as if most Singaporeans need *another* MP3 player).

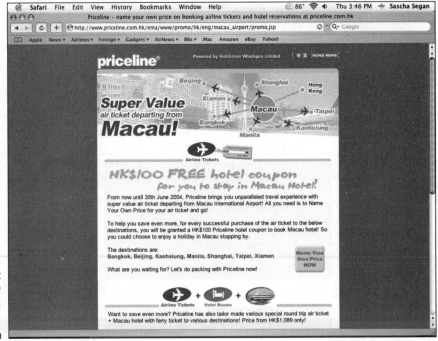

Figure 18-5:
I have no idea if you'll be able to bid for tickets from Macau when you read this. Priceline will probably be running a different crazy promotion by then.

These deals are great, and there's almost never a catch. Priceline Asia is just trying to drum up business.

Bidding for hotels on Priceline Asia

To start bidding for hotels on one of the Asian Priceline sites, first click on the orange Hotels tab on your site's home page. Then scroll down to "Where do you want to stay?" Pick your destination from the drop-down list in the large yellow box, enter your dates of travel, and click Name Your Own Price.

If your destination isn't listed in the drop-down list, click Other Destinations.

Past this point, hotel bidding works pretty much like it does on Priceline U.S. The zones are the same, the hotels are the same, the prices are the same, and the rebidding strategies are the same. However, a few differences do exist, and I go into these in the following sections.

More Asian cities than Priceline.com

Priceline Asia lets you bid for a slew of Asian cities that were (as of this writing) not available through Priceline.com.

- **Australia:** Brisbane, the Gold Coast, Perth, and Cairns
- **China:** Guangzhou
- **Guam**
- **India:** New Delhi and Mumbai
- **Indonesia:** Jakarta
- **Japan:** Yokohama, Osaka, and Sapporo
- **Macau**
- **Malaysia:** Kota Kinabalu, Langkawi, and Penang
- **New Zealand:** Auckland and Christchurch
- **The Philippines:** Cebu and Manila
- **South Korea:** Pusan
- **Sri Lanka:** Colombo
- **Taiwan:** Kaohsiung

Bidding for these cities works just the same as bidding for anywhere else. They have the same kinds of zones and the same star levels. They just don't appear on Priceline's main U.S. site.

No 2½-star hotels

Other than the extra cities, the biggest difference between Priceline Asia and Priceline U.S. is that Priceline Asia does not have a 2½-star level. That means you can't bid for 2½-star hotels in the United States if you're using Priceline Asia. If you bid 2 stars, you may get upgraded to a 2½-star hotel, but you can't count on that.

No same-day bidding

You also can't bid for same-day hotels on Priceline Asia. You can bid for next-day hotels in Asian cities; for everywhere else, you must bid two days in advance.

Service fees

Priceline Hong Kong charges a HK$75 service fee for each hotel booking (which can include several rooms and nights). Priceline Singapore charges S$16.50. As of this writing, Priceline Taiwan isn't fully up and running yet, but I expect it'll charge about the same.

Paying by phone

Just like with airfare bookings (see "Bidding for airfares on Priceline Asia," earlier in this chapter), you can enter your credit-card number over the phone when you're bidding for hotels on Priceline Asia. After you've entered your credit-card number, Priceline will put your request through its system and e-mail you when it has a response.

No immediate response

Priceline U.S. almost always responds to your bid request immediately. Priceline Asia can take up to an hour. It'll send you an e-mail with a link to see if you won your bid.

Getting help with Priceline Asia

To get help with a bid you made on Priceline Asia, first e-mail Priceline's customer-service staff at the following addresses:

✔ **For help with airline tickets,** e-mail `airline.cs@priceline.com.hk` or `airline.cs@priceline.com.sg`.

✔ **For help with hotels,** e-mail `hotel.cs@priceline.com.hk` or `hotel.cs@priceline.com.sg`.

✔ **For other questions,** e-mail `general.cs@priceline.com.hk` or `general.cs@!priceline.com.sg`.

You usually get a response within a few hours.

If e-mailing doesn't work, call Priceline. To contact Priceline Asia by phone, call 3163-0808 from within Hong Kong or +852 3163-0808 from outside Hong Kong. Priceline uses one phone number in Hong Kong for all its Asian customer service. Priceline's customer-service staff is on duty from 8 a.m. until midnight, Hong Kong time.

Part VI
The Part of Tens

"Okay, how many of you signed up for the Priceline.com salmon fishing excursion?"

In this part . . .

Need some cash? In this part, I lend you a few ten-
ners. I dig into my expertise as a travel writer to tell
you the best zones for nabbing hotels in 20 popular U.S.
and foreign cities. You get a summary of Priceline bidding
tips that you can refer back to later. And you find out
which other Web sites you should check to make sure you
don't overbid on Priceline.

Chapter 19

Ten Rules for Bidding

In This Chapter

▶ Knowing what to expect

▶ Getting the most out of your bids

▶ Practicing patience with Priceline

Do you only have 15 minutes to find out about Priceline? I've boiled down the best lessons from this book into the ten tips in this chapter. These tips are the keys to Priceline, things no bidder should head online without knowing. And I've summed them up in a handy, easy-to-read list. If you're in a hurry, let these tips guide your bidding.

Know Priceline's Restrictions

Priceline has some oddball rules, and you're signing on to them when you put your money down. So make sure you agree to the rules before you bid. The most important rules relate to the following:

- ✔ **Nonrefundability:** Assume Priceline reservations are totally nonrefundable and nonchangeable under any circumstances. That isn't *strictly* true — you can get out of hotel and car reservations in some circumstances — but being prepared to lose your money if you don't use your reservation is always a good idea.

- ✔ **What Priceline can't promise you:** If you absolutely need a window seat, a nonsmoking hotel room, or a room that sleeps three people, don't use Priceline. Or use Priceline, but don't be disappointed if you don't get what you want.

For a full rundown of Priceline's rules and your rights, see Chapters 2 and 3.

Research Competing Prices

Yeah, yeah, I know — Priceline has a Best Price Guarantee that will refund the difference if you find a lower rate than Priceline's. But the guarantee is full of restrictions, and it's a pain to use, so just make sure you're getting the best price before you bid.

That means checking at least three major online travel agencies; checking airline, hotel, or car-rental Web sites (all of which may have lower prices than the travel agencies); checking Priceline's competitor Hotwire.com; and checking the bidding watchdog bulletin boards, BiddingForTravel.com and BetterBidding.com.

Yes, I know that's a lot of work. But it pays off. Only after you've scoured the Net do you really know how low you should bid on Priceline.

Low-fare airlines like Southwest Airlines (www.southwest.com), Independence Air (www.flyi.com), Allegiant Air (www.allegiant-air.com), Virgin USA, and JetBlue (www.jetblue.com) don't participate with Priceline. They may have prices on their own Web sites that Priceline can't match. So make sure to check the low-fare airlines' Web sites if one of them covers your route.

Ignore Priceline's Price Suggestions

Priceline has many ways of trying to get you to bid higher. Ignore them all. Its "suggested retail prices" for hotels are usually higher than you can find on hotel-chain Web sites — and far higher than what you'll pay by bidding.

When you're bidding for a car, it may say you have a "good chance" at a certain amount, but trust me, you have a good chance if you bid *lower*. When you're bidding for airfares, you'll almost always get shunted through a page whining about how you're bidding much lower than published fares. Well, yeah, that's the *point*. You're *supposed* to be bidding much lower than published fares.

Pay attention to the lowest rates you find on airline, hotel, and car-rental Web sites — ignore what Priceline says are the lowest retail rates.

Priceline's suggestions about "best days to fly" and "best deal airports" are actually useful — they're based on the inventory Priceline has in its computers.

Remember That Last-Minute Flights Are Best

Domestic leisure airfares are at all-time lows. That means if you're buying your tickets at least three weeks in advance, you can usually get spectacularly low domestic airfares from airlines or conventional travel agencies. Often, the airlines and travel agencies will beat Priceline's rates.

On the other hand, last-minute airfares on many routes are still quite expensive (although a low-cost carrier on the route may have low last-minute fares). That's where Priceline serves up the biggest discounts. So if you need to fly off to Omaha tomorrow (but don't care what time of day you fly), you'll find big savings on Priceline.

Don't wait until the last minute just to get a low airfare on Priceline. If you see a low fare somewhere else way in advance, grab it. After all, you can guarantee fares you see elsewhere, but Priceline is always a little bit of a gamble.

Study the Zone Maps and Hotel Lists

Remove the mystery from Priceline hotel bidding by checking out the hotel lists on BiddingForTravel.com and BetterBidding.com. Those two sites list all the hotels that thousands of other Priceline bidders stayed in recently. You may still get a hotel that isn't on the lists, of course, but the lists give you a great idea of the hotels you're most *likely* to get in any given zone.

Speaking of zones, pay very close attention to the zone maps when bidding for hotels on Priceline. Don't bother with the zone names — the *maps* are what are important. If you don't understand the map for a particular city, bone up by checking out a travel guidebook (such as the *For Dummies* series of travel guides or Frommer's Travel Guides, both published by Wiley). Knowing, for example, that the Charlestown neighborhood is across the river from downtown Boston or that Priceline's Las Vegas Strip Vicinity zone includes areas not actually on the Strip can save you a lot of grief.

Be a Happy Pessimist

Someone once told me that pessimists were happier than optimists because when good things happen to pessimists, they're always pleasant surprises.

TIP

Be a happy pessimist when bidding on Priceline. Prepare for the worst — a one-connection flight at an odd time of day, a hotel on the edge of your chosen zone, or a car that's a long shuttle-bus ride from your airport terminal. *Remember:* You agreed to accept all these things when you bid on Priceline.

Chances are good that you'll get exactly what you really want: a nonstop flight; a great, convenient hotel; or a spiffy rental car. But by expecting the worst, you'll be prepared for anything Priceline throws at you, and you'll be even more thrilled when you get what you want.

Check, Check, and Check Again

Priceline is pretty forgiving when it comes to mistakes made in hotel and car bidding. It's a lot less forgiving when it comes to mistakes in airline bidding. So try not to make mistakes.

Before you put in your credit-card details, you always see a Please Review Your Request screen (like the one shown in Figure 19-1), showing your travel dates, your bid amount, and the terms of your bid (which hotel zones you're bidding for, whether you agree to fly on a prop plane, and other details).

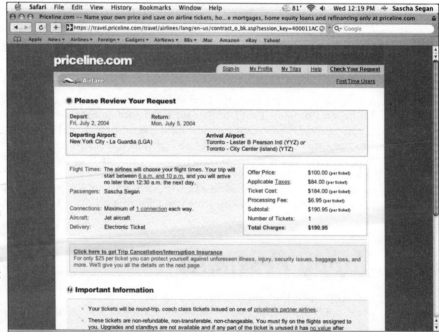

Figure 19-1:
Make sure
to review
your request
before
you place
your bid.

Study this page intently. Print it out, walk away from the computer, and look at the printout. This is what you're agreeing to, and this is your last chance to change things. Have you checked everything three times? Great. Put in your pennies and see what you won.

Maximize Your Rebids

For hotels and airlines, don't bid the maximum possible amount on your first try. Instead, check out Chapter 6 (for airfares) and Chapter 10 (for hotels) to find out about rebids. You may have 2, 4, or even 15 chances to bid for the same trip before you have to wait your 3 or 7 days to bid again. That means you can start low and work your way up, making sure you don't pay more than you absolutely have to.

When you're ready to rebid, keep these tips in mind:

- ✓ **If you're traveling with another adult and sharing a hotel room, you always have two chances.** Just use the other person's name and credit card.

- ✓ **If you're bidding for 4-star hotels, adding hotel zones that don't have any 4-star hotels lets you nab another bid.** You don't have any chance of getting a hotel in your "new" zone, if it doesn't have any 4-star hotels. But because Priceline demands that you change something in your bid so you can raise your price, adding the "free" non-4-star zone satisfies Priceline and lets you raise your bid for the zone you really want. (The same advice applies to other star levels as well.)

- ✓ **If you're bidding for airline tickets, adding airports that don't have any flights to your destination (or from your originating city) lets you bid again without really changing your options.** For example, if you live in Los Angeles and want to fly out of LAX, you can change your originating city to Santa Monica (or any of dozens of other cities in the area) and still fly out of LAX.

Be Patient

Bidding can be very exciting. You may be tempted to get caught up in the thrill of offers and counteroffers, bid higher and higher, or use sneaky, risky tactics to increase your available bids.

Don't.

Take a deep breath and sit back. If you have a few more weeks to bid, don't jump in to any risky strategies. ***Remember:*** Risky strategies should be a last resort, not something to do when you still have plenty of options.

Think about how much money you're really willing to spend, not about proving a point to Priceline. After all, if you've bid up to within $50 of another commercial airline fare, is the mystery of Priceline really worth that small a savings?

Also, if you don't get a response from Priceline a few seconds after you bid, don't panic. Its computers may be jammed up. Give it an hour or two to e-mail you with a response to your bid. If you have a spam-blocker, remember to check your spam box — your e-mail program may be filtering out Priceline's e-mail as spam. You can also see if Priceline has an answer for you by clicking on the Check Your Request button in the upper-right-hand corner of Priceline's home page.

Share the Wealth

The Priceline watchdog sites, BiddingForTravel.com and BetterBidding.com, rely on people like you to report their winning bids. That way, future bidders (including yourself) can know which hotels are available at what prices, and how the trends run in Priceline airfares.

In other words, BiddingForTravel.com and BetterBidding.com will only be there if you contribute. So contribute. Check out the two sites — BiddingFor Travel.com is much bigger and better organized; BetterBidding.com is friendlier though sloppier.

Pick your favorite and post your bid history, including:

- ✔ Bid amounts
- ✔ The airports, hotel star levels and zones, or car classes you bid for
- ✔ Which bid succeeded
- ✔ The lowest retail price you found elsewhere for your airline ticket, hotel room, or car rental
- ✔ Whether you got a counteroffer and how you responded to it

If you bid more than once before succeeding, post all your bids in your message. That way, other bidders will know you didn't overbid, and they won't try to undercut you by much.

Chapter 20

Ten Web Sites to Check before You Bid

*B*efore you bid on Priceline, you have to shop around. Priceline may very well have the lowest prices — but you may be able to find better deals elsewhere, and at the very least, you need to check out the competition to know what to bid on Priceline. In this chapter, I fill you in on ten Web sites that are great resources whenever you're planning to travel.

BiddingForTravel.com

Whenever you're planning a trip, start at BiddingForTravel.com (`www.bidding fortravel.com`). The ultimate resource for Priceline bidding is run by Sheryl Mexic, a former business administrator who quit her job to provide Priceline advice full-time. BiddingForTravel.com chronicles the results of tens of thousands of Priceline bids.

Start by reading the FAQ for hotels, airline tickets, or rental cars. If you want help with your bidding, fill out the bidding assistance form and post your request to the appropriate category: "Hotels," "Car Rentals," or "Airline Tickets–Bidding Related Questions."

Use BiddingForTravel's hotel boards to see what other bidders have been paying for hotels recently. BiddingForTravel's hotel lists show most of the hotels Priceline offers in the most frequently bid zones, though new ones are always cropping up.

Each time you win a bid, post the result on BiddingForTravel.com so other bidders can benefit from your experiences. And when you're done with a Priceline trip, post a hotel review or a complaint on BiddingForTravel.com for the same reason.

Priceline.com, as well as hotels, airlines, and car-rental agencies, generally hate BiddingForTravel and don't support the board at all. Sheryl lives on commissions from bookings made through links on her board, so make sure to book through her links to keep her valuable service going. She also takes donations to help with the cost of hosting the board on the Web.

Some bidders find BiddingForTravel.com's rules too strict. In that case, head over to BetterBidding.com (www.betterbidding.com). It's a much smaller site, with much less information, but it seems friendlier to some people.

Orbitz.com

One of the "big three" online travel agencies dominating business in the United States (the other two are Expedia and Travelocity), Orbitz (www.orbitz.com) came second to Priceline for providing low car-rental rates in Consumers Union's independent tests. It didn't fare as well with hotels or airfares, but Orbitz is still worth a look. It's owned by five major airlines, so sometimes you'll find exclusive airfares here.

Orbitz's flexible airfare search (shown in Figure 20-1) is the site's best feature. The flexible search option lets you hunt for a weekend trip in a month of your choice, lets you check a spread of a few days around your preferred dates, or lets you just search for the cheapest time to travel in a 30-day period. That makes Orbitz top-notch for indecisive or flexible folks looking for a cheap time to travel.

Expedia.com

Expedia (www.expedia.com) probably has the most oddball "exclusive" air-fares and hotel rates of any travel Web site. Because of Expedia's network of exclusive deals, you can't use it to gauge rates to bid against, but you can find some great rates on here.

In Consumers Union's independent tests, Expedia came second to Priceline for providing low airfares; it didn't do so well with hotels or car rentals.

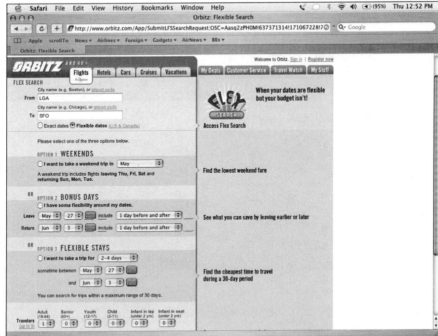

Orbitz: Flexible Search

Figure 20-1:
Flexible
travelers will
love Orbitz's
search
functions.

When you're browsing Expedia, keep an eye out for "Expedia Special Rate" hotels and airfares. These super-low-priced deals usually have huge change or cancellation penalties.

Travelocity.com

Travelocity (www.travelocity.com) came in third for providing low airfares and car-rental rates in Consumers Union's independent tests. Beyond the usual search functions and exclusive deals, Travelocity has two very cool features: Dream Maps and published fare listings.

To get to the Dream Maps, click the Flights link near the top of Travelocity's home page. Then click Dream Maps, which should be right under the Search Flights button.

A Dream Map like the one in Figure 20-2 shows how far you can get on a set budget. Have only $300, and don't know where that can take you? Check it out on the Dream Map. *Remember:* The Dream Map won't show low-fare airlines like Southwest or Independence Air, so it's not comprehensive.

Figure 20-2:
Travelocity's
Dream Map
shows you
how far you
can go on
your budget.

Travelocity's published fare listings show all the fares airlines have in their computer systems — whether or not they're available on the dates you want. From Travelocity's Flights page, click Fare Listings in the Flight Tools box on the right-hand side of the screen. If flights on your chosen dates are too expensive, check out the published fare listings — they may show fares that are much lower if you change your dates.

Travelweb.com

Travelweb (www.travelweb.com), owned by Priceline, is the only Web site whose hotel star ratings match up with Priceline's. If a hotel is a 3-star hotel on Travelweb, it'll be a 3-star hotel on Priceline. (There's one exception: Travelweb doesn't have a 2½-star rating, so Priceline's 2½-star hotels show up on Travelweb as 3-star hotels.) That makes Travelweb critical for figuring out what hotels you may get on Priceline.

Consumers Union didn't test Travelweb, but the site's tight relationship with the Hyatt, Hilton, Marriott, Intercontinental, and Starwood chains gives it lots of exclusive low rates. (Those five hotel chains used to own Travelweb before Priceline took it over.)

SideStep

SideStep (www.sidestep.com) taps directly into hotel, airline, and car-rental reservation systems to offer you rates that are often as low as what hotels and airlines post on their own sites. Most importantly, SideStep includes several major airlines that don't show up on any other tool. You can book Southwest, JetBlue, and Hooters Air flights through SideStep — no other major search engine tracks these airlines.

SideStep lets you search for hotels on its Web site, but to look for airfares and car rentals, you must download a separate program from www.sidestep.com. The program plugs in to your copy of Internet Explorer, adding a SideStep button to your toolbar. You can click this button to activate SideStep, or set SideStep to automatically open side-by-side with another travel Web site you're searching (as in Figure 20-3).

Antivirus programs and spyware detectors sometimes complain about SideStep. Ignore their warnings. SideStep isn't spyware, and it doesn't carry viruses.

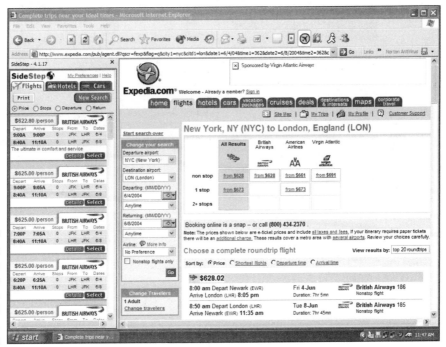

Figure 20-3: SideStep opens up next to other travel Web sites.

Hotwire.com

As Priceline's main competitor, Hotwire.com (www.hotwire.com) has one big advantage over Priceline: You can see the prices of hotels and airline tickets before you buy. Figure 20-4 shows the results of a Hotwire hotel search.

Otherwise, Hotwire is a lot like Priceline. You pick hotels by zone and star level. You control your arrival and departure airports for flights, but not your flight time, routing, or airline. And you can tell Hotwire where you want a rental car, but the car company is always a surprise.

Priceline usually beats Hotwire's prices, but every once in a while, Hotwire pulls out a really great price.

If you're bidding on Priceline, you're probably comfortable giving up some control over your travel in exchange for a great price. So always check Hotwire before you bid, and never bid above Hotwire's price. *Remember:* You can always turn to Hotwire if Priceline fails you!

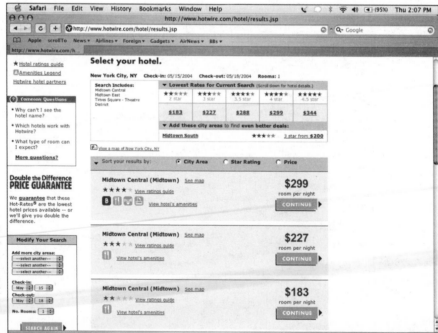

Figure 20-4: Hotwire shows you prices but not names of hotels.

Hotwire's hotel star ratings are more generous than Priceline's. Many Hotwire 4-star hotels are 3-star hotels on Priceline.

Also, the prices Hotwire shows for hotels don't include taxes and fees. Compare Hotwire prices to the amount you're *bidding* on Priceline, not to the final amount you'd pay after taxes.

Airline Web Sites

All of Priceline's participating airlines have their own Web sites with exclusive low fares. Often, the fares on their sites can beat any online travel agent — including Priceline.

Use one of the travel-agency sites earlier in this chapter to find out who flies on the route you're looking for, and then compare the lowest price you find against the airline's own price.

Alaska Airlines, ATA, AirTran, Frontier, Independence Air, JetBlue, Northwest, Southwest, and Spirit *do not* sell tickets through Priceline. If the only flights on your route are on those airlines, you probably won't be able to get a ticket on Priceline.

Here are the Web sites of major U.S. airlines:

- ✔ **AirTran Airways:** www.airtran.com
- ✔ **Alaska Airlines:** www.alaskaair.com
- ✔ **Aloha Airlines:** www.alohaair.com
- ✔ **America West Airlines:** www.americawest.com
- ✔ **American Airlines:** www.aa.com
- ✔ **ATA:** www.ata.com
- ✔ **Continental Airlines:** www.continental.com
- ✔ **Delta Air Lines:** www.delta.com
- ✔ **Frontier Airlines:** www.flyfrontier.com
- ✔ **Hawaiian Airlines:** www.hawaiianair.com
- ✔ **Independence Air:** www.flyi.com
- ✔ **JetBlue Airways:** www.jetblue.com

- **Midwest Airlines:** www.midwestairlines.com
- **Northwest Airlines:** www.nwa.com
- **Southwest Airlines:** www.southwest.com
- **Spirit Airlines:** www.spiritair.com
- **United Air Lines:** www.united.com
- **US Airways:** www.usairways.com

Hotel Web Sites

Along with Travelweb, hotel Web sites have the rates on which you should base all your Priceline bids.

When you've found a hotel you like with an online travel agency Web site, check the room rates on the hotel's own Web site. Here is a list of a whole bunch of sites for hotel chains Priceline uses around the world (keep in mind that this list is nowhere near complete — I'm only hitting the big chains here):

- **AmeriHost Inn:** www.amerihostinn.com
- **Baymont Inns:** www.baymontinns.com
- **Candlewood Suites:** www.candlewoodsuites.com
- **Courtyard by Marriott:** www.courtyard.com
- **Crowne Plaza Hotels:** www.crowneplaza.com
- **Days Inn:** www.daysinn.com
- **Doubletree Hotels:** www.doubletree.com
- **Embassy Suites Hotels:** www.embassysuites.com
- **Fairfield Inn:** www.fairfieldinn.com
- **Four Points Sheraton:** www.fourpoints.com
- **Hampton Inn:** www.hamptoninn.com
- **Hilton:** www.hilton.com
- **Hilton Garden Inn:** www.hiltongardeninn.com
- **Holiday Inn:** www.holiday-inn.com
- **Homewood Suites by Hilton:** www.homewoodsuites.com
- **Howard Johnson:** www.hojo.com

- **InterContinental Hotels & Resorts:** www.ichotelsgroup.com
- **Kimpton Hotels:** www.kimptongroup.com
- **Knights Inn:** www.knightsinn.com
- **Marriott:** www.marriott.com
- **Motel 6:** www.motel6.com
- **Novotel:** www. novotel.com
- **Ramada:** www.ramada.com
- **Red Roof Inns:** www.redroof.com
- **Renaissance Hotels & Resorts:** www.renaissancehotels.com
- **Residence Inn:** www.residenceinn.com
- **Ritz-Carlton:** www.ritzcarlton.com
- **St. Regis Hotels & Resorts:** www.stregis.com
- **Sheraton Hotels & Resorts:** www.sheraton.com
- **Sofitel:** www.sofitel.com
- **SpringHill Suites:** www.springhillsuites.com
- **Staybridge Suites:** www.staybridge.com
- **Super 8 Motels:** www.super8.com
- **TownePlace Suites:** www.marriott.com/towneplace
- **Travelodge:** www.travelodge.com
- **Villager:** www.villager.com
- **W Hotels:** www.whotels.com
- **Westin Hotels & Resorts:** www.westin.com
- **Wingate Inn:** www.wingateinns.com

Priceline also uses these hotel chains in Europe:

- **Dorint Hotels & Resorts:** www.dorint.de/home_uk.html
- **Etap Hotel:** www.etaphotel.com
- **Hotel Formule 1:** www.formule1.de
- **Ibis:** www.ibishotel.com
- **Mercure:** www.mercure.com
- **Suitehotel:** www.suite-hotel.com

Car-Rental Web Sites

Priceline gets all its cars from Alamo, Avis, Budget, Hertz, and National, five of the nation's biggest car-rental firms. (The other big ones are Dollar, Enterprise, and Thrifty — but Priceline doesn't get its cars from these companies.) Just like hotel chains and airlines, the car-rental firms sometimes offer exclusive low rates on their own Web sites. If you see a good rate elsewhere on the Web, it's worth checking out the appropriate site:

- **ACE Rent A Car:** www.acerentacar.com
- **Advantage Rent-A-Car:** www.arac.com
- **Alamo Rent a Car:** www.alamo.com
- **Avis Rent A Car:** www.avis.com
- **Budget Rent A Car:** www.budget.com
- **Discount Car & Truck Rentals:** www.discountcar.com
- **Dollar Rent A Car:** www.dollar.com
- **Enterprise Rent-A-Car:** www.enterprise.com
- **Fox Rent A Car:** www.foxrentacar.com
- **Hertz:** www.hertz.com
- **National Car Rental:** www.nationalcar.com
- **Payless Car Rental:** www.paylesscarrental.com
- **Rent-A-Wreck:** www.rentawreck.com
- **Thrifty Car Rental:** www.thrifty.com

Chapter 21

Ten Top Domestic Hotel Cities

In This Chapter

▶ Knowing the top U.S. cities for bidding on Priceline hotels

▶ Finding the best neighborhood zones for tourists

*C*hoosing the right hotel zone can make the difference between a cheerful, convenient trip and one where you're stuck slogging to and from some distant hotel.

I'm here to help. Four times a year, Priceline announces its most popular hotel zones. I combined those lists with information from BiddingForTravel.com and Frommer's Travel Guides to create this list of top Priceline hotel zones. Bid these zones with confidence!

Boston

Beantown is compact, but Priceline's zones sprawl out into the suburbs. Your best bets are the Back Bay–Copley zone and the Downtown Boston–Charlestown zone:

✔ **Back Bay–Copley:** Shop 'til you drop in Boston's most fashionable hotel zone. Most of the hotels here cluster around Copley Place near Newbury Street, Boston's top street for shopping. Back Bay is a safe, central, upscale area great for strolling. Although Priceline's zone map appears to stretch all the way back to Fenway Park, I couldn't find any hotels on that end of the zone. But even if you do get dropped back there, it's a nice neighborhood.

✔ **Downtown Boston–Charlestown:** Some parts of Boston's most central zone are less charming and a bit less safe than Back Bay, but you can't beat the location. No matter where you end up in this zone, you're practically on top of at least one major Boston attraction. A few hotels here are in Charlestown, near Bunker Hill and across the Charles River from downtown. Ferries and buses connect Charlestown to the rest of the city, but if you get a Charlestown hotel and you're out in downtown late at night, you may want to take a taxi back.

The World Trade Center and Cambridge zones also provide easy access to Boston attractions by public transportation. Avoid the Boston area's other zones unless you know where you're going — they can be pretty far-flung.

Chicago

Priceliners find favorable winds in this city, where a knot of convenient zones surrounds downtown. The following three zones are your best bets:

- **North Michigan Ave.:** This zone actually sprawls more than half a mile on either side of Michigan Avenue, Chicago's top shopping street. It's Priceline's most popular Chicago zone, because it surrounds the city's best shopping and entertainment district. Chicago's flashiest, fanciest hotels are all here. Looking for the Swissotel, the Sheraton, or the Drake? This zone's 3- and 4-star hotel possibilities blow away all other Chicago zones.

- **River North Area:** An itty-bitty, teeny-tiny zone north of downtown, River North should by all rights be part of the North Michigan Ave. zone. River North is a prime location, packed with top-notch shopping, eating, and entertainment, all within walking distance from the rest of central Chicago. The 2½- through 4-star hotels here are all class acts, too.

- **The Loop–Grant Park:** Chicago's central downtown zone is actually less desirable than the zones north of it, because many Chicagoans avoid this area at night and on the weekends. It's not unsafe — just deserted. Still, you're right by the Sears Tower and the Art Institute, and a quick bus or elevated-train ride from all the attractions of River North and North Michigan Avenue.

You can also try the Lincoln Park zone for a comfortable residential area with good public-transit connections to downtown.

Las Vegas

Bidding for Las Vegas hotels on Priceline can be tough. Vegas hotels generally don't release many rooms to Priceline, and you can often find better rates through other discounters.

If you bid on the Las Vegas Strip Vicinity zone, your hotel could be up to half a mile east of the Strip!

If you won't have your own car, bid for 5-star hotels only. All of Vegas's 5-star hotels are top Strip joints like the Bellagio and the Venetian, so you're guaranteed to get a prime seat in the middle of the action.

Miami

Chock full of Art Deco buildings, pastel colors, beautiful beaches, top restaurants, and supermodels, South Beach is *the* place to be in Miami. Priceline has a strong stock of South Beach hotels.

Priceline's one vice in Miami: The South Beach zone includes areas about ten blocks north of what's normally considered South Beach. Your hotel may be a little ways from the heart of the action, but you'll still be only a quick bus or cab ride away from all the hoppin' happenings.

New Orleans

In New Orleans, the French Quarter zone actually delivers as advertised. Bid here, and you'll get a hotel in New Orleans's historic French Quarter, home to the longest-running continuous party in American history — about 300 years and counting.

If you're comfortable with a little urban adventure, expand your chances by including the Central Business District, Convention Center, and Garden District zones. The Central Business District and Convention Center zones include top-notch hotels right across the street from the French Quarter, but safety is a concern, because both may drop you half a mile away from the French Quarter in New Orleans's somewhat dodgy modern downtown. The Garden District zone includes the genteel and beautiful Garden District, a ten-minute trolley ride from the French Quarter.

New York City

It's hard to go wrong in the Big Apple with Priceline. Just try not to underbid — this is the nation's most expensive hotel town, and even 3-star hotels usually go for $90 or more. New York's zones are tightly packed, and all are close to attractions, so you really can't go wrong, but start with the following zones:

- **Midtown West:** Jam-packed with hotels and attractions, New York's most touristy zone surrounds Times Square, Rockefeller Center, and the theater district.

- **Upper Midtown–Central Park South:** This narrow zone right by Central Park and next to both of the Midtown zones boasts some of New York's most posh hotels.

- **Upper West Side:** A quieter, more "local" and family-oriented residential area than Midtown, the Upper West Side often delivers hotels for cheaper prices than the Midtown zones.

✔ **Midtown East:** I recommend bidding the three preceding zones before bidding this very central zone, near Grand Central Station. Midtown East is a business area, within walking distance of Times Square — but it's quite a bit quieter than Times Square.

Just across the river from Manhattan, in Jersey City, hotel rates drop by 60 percent. Subways, trolleys and ferries link Jersey City, New Jersey, with Manhattan, making this otherwise depressing town a haven for bargain-hunters enjoying the lights and sights of the big city. I wouldn't recommend Jersey City to night owls — the commute late at night can be a chore, and may involve calling a cab — but for families on a very tight budget willing to trek a little to get into town, the spacious and cheap rooms here are fabulous. If you want to bid for Jersey City, scroll down to the bottom of the New York City zone map and click the Newark-Meadowlands link. Then pick Jersey City as your only zone. Or just enter Jersey City on Priceline's home page.

Oahu

The difference between the two Waikiki zones — Waikiki North and Waikiki South — is pretty subtle:

✔ **Waikiki North:** Waikiki's flashiest resorts and classiest hotels are in this zone, which includes the Ewa Waikiki neighborhood and part of Mid-Waikiki. The Hilton Hawaiian Village, Hawaii Prince Hotel, Outrigger Reef, and Sheraton Waikiki all serve up deluxe beach vacations, and lower-class hotels will still land you in the midst of the buzz.

✔ **Waikiki South:** Hotels in the Diamond Head area of Waikiki and in part of Mid-Waikiki fit into this zone; you'll also find kid-friendly Kuhio Beach here. Many of the hotels in this zone are a bit older than the resorts in Waikiki North, but they're still proud and luxurious. For instance, Resort-level bidders may get the classic Sheraton Moana Surfrider.

If you're not too picky, just bid both, and you'll double your chances of success!

Only Resort-level hotels guarantee beach access.

Orlando

When you're bidding on the Disney World Vicinity zone in Orlando, keep an eye on that word *Vicinity.* Although the Walt Disney World Swan and Dolphin participate in Priceline as Resort-level hotels and you can nab a slew of Downtown Disney hotels in this zone, you may also get a hotel that is close to Disney but not in the park. Hotels here range from 1-star motels all the way up to gorgeous resorts with private lakes and nature trails.

All the hotels I've seen in this zone offer free shuttles to the Disney parks, but Priceline doesn't *guarantee* a shuttle.

San Francisco

The City by the Bay puts on its best face in the downtown zone of Union Square East–Embarcadero, which lands you amongst top-notch dining, classy shopping, and the famous cable cars.

Although the Union Square West zone also has many classy hotels, you have a slight risk of being stuck on a less savory block. The Fisherman's Wharf zone is fine if you like a purely touristy atmosphere. Avoid the Civic Center Area zone, which is seedy.

Washington, D.C.

If you're looking for the traditional D.C. tourist experience, the White House–Downtown and Convention Ctr–Capitol Hill Area zones land you smack in the middle of it, amongst Washington's monuments and historic sites.

If you prefer to focus on Washington's restaurants and nightlife, the Georgetown–Foggy Bottom and Dupont Circle–Woodley Park zones are in D.C.'s trendiest residential areas.

For bargain hunters, the otherwise utterly dull Crystal City zone offers very cheap hotels and a quick subway connection to downtown D.C.

Chapter 22

Ten Top International Hotel Cities

. . . .

In This Chapter

▶ Finding the top cities for bidding Priceline.com hotels outside the United States

▶ Knowing the best neighborhood zones for tourists

. . . .

*P*riceline assigns fewer, bigger zones to international cities than it does to U.S. cities, which burns bidders by reducing the number of free rebid zones and preventing you from nailing down the exact location of your hotel before you buy. But bidding is still worthwhile, because the savings on hotels in other countries can be spectacular.

I combined four of Priceline's most-popular-zone lists, cross-referenced them with the hotel lists on BiddingForTravel.com, and mixed in my own expertise as a writer for Frommer's Travel Guides to give you these suggestions for finding hotels in cities outside the United States. Bid these zones, and you can't go wrong.

Amsterdam

Amsterdam's City Centre and Museum Quarter zone is big, but it isn't bad. Yes, it stretches well beyond the historic city center. But all the neighborhoods it contains are winners. You'll probably get a hotel smack in the center of Amsterdam, amongst the museums and canals.

At worst, you'll end up in either one of Amsterdam's hippest residential areas (De Pijp) or one of its classiest 'hoods (the Oud Zuid). Both areas are a short and entertaining tram ride from all the tourist attractions, and both expose you to real Amsterdammers rather than to the ravenous mobs of tourists who flock the center of town.

Bidding Amsterdam takes a little bit of urban adventurousness. In this case, though, the big zone is a bonus. If you don't end up with a hotel in the center of town, you'll be at somewhere like the 4-star Bilderberg Garden Hotel on a peaceful, tree-lined street, and you'll thank Priceline for getting you out of the insane bustle of central Amsterdam.

The City Centre South zone isn't anywhere near the city center. Avoid it.

Barcelona

I wouldn't bid for Barcelona hotels on Priceline. Priceline's zones are just too large, and you're too likely to get hotels far from the city center. For the $100 and up I've seen bids succeeding at, I'd rather get a budget hotel in a location I choose than take the risk of being exiled out to a business district on the city's fringe.

If you're going to bid, though, bid Barcelona East. You may get lucky and get a hotel near the central Plaça de Catalunya. But you may also get a hotel all the way out in the new Diagonal Mar neighborhood, a dull business district requiring a trek on the Metro from the historic city center.

The Barcelona West and Suburbs zone, meanwhile, includes huge stretches of the western suburbs. I've seen bidders end up with hotels that aren't even in Barcelona at all. That zone is a loser at any price.

Hong Kong

You're sure to get a hotel in a great location if you bid the Tsim Sha Tsui zone, which covers the very tip of the Kowloon peninsula opposite Hong Kong Island. Restaurants, shops, and hotels fill Tsim Sha Tsui, Hong Kong's most touristy neighborhood. Most hotels sit at the end of the peninsula or abut Nathan Road, Hong Kong's "golden mile" for shopping.

If you're considering bidding either of Priceline's Hong Kong Island zones (creatively named East Hong Kong Island and West Hong Kong Island), you may get a hotel as far west as Western or as far east as North Point. Neither area is considered central. Sticking with a 5-star bid in those areas maximizes your chances of getting a centrally located hotel.

The correct pronunciation of Tsim Sha Tsui is *Chim-Sha-Choi.*

London

The Mayfair-Soho zone is the London of dreams and fantasies. Covent Garden, Piccadilly Circus, Buckingham Palace, Trafalgar Square — most of London's big-name tourist destinations cluster in this zone, and if it's your first time in London, you should, too.

Kensington–Earls Court–Knightsbridge is another solid choice. Along with the three neighborhoods named, this zone also includes Chelsea. Hotels here scatter across some of London's wealthiest neighborhoods, near Harrod's and the Victoria & Albert Museum.

The Houses of Parliament and the Tate Britain art museum tempt bidders in the Westminster zone. One hotel here (the Marriott County Hall) lies on the "wrong" (or south) side of the Thames River, but it's a luxurious place with incredible views of the city, so don't despair if you win a room there.

Although most of the hotels in the Bloomsbury–Marble Arch zone and The City–Financial District zone are terrific, those zones also include some seedy areas near the King's Cross, St. Pancras, and Euston Tube stations that may deter non-urbanites.

Montreal

Montreal's main zone — creatively called Montreal — covers much of the city, but the hotels cluster downtown. If you bid for a 3- or 4-star hotel, chances are you'll get a hotel smack in the modern city center, perfectly positioned for shopping on St. Catherine Street and a short walk or bus ride from Old Montreal.

Bid 2½ stars, and you may get a hotel downtown or one in Westmount, an upscale neighborhood a short subway ride away from the city center. Montreal's public transportation is so convenient that you can bid any star level with confidence, as long as you make sure not to overbid.

Paris

Paris is gorgeous, and part of the fun in visiting the City of Light is discovering neighborhoods you wouldn't have known about otherwise. I generally bid all four of the following zones:

- **Opera Quarter East–Les Halles:** Bidding this zone guarantees you a hotel near the Louvre, the Opera, and the center of town, but parts of this area lack charm and look unappealingly modern. Still, this area is great for first-time tourists who just want to hit major attractions. Three-star hotels dominate Priceline's inventory here.

- **St. Germain–Latin Quarter–Montparnasse:** This zone stretches about 2 miles south of the Seine along the Left Bank. No longer bohemian, this is probably Paris's prettiest zone, with the largest concentration of pre-19th-century buildings.

- **Champs Elysees–Opera Quarter West:** Great restaurants, top-notch hotels and proud shopping streets pack this district, which spans much of the Right Bank. You won't necessarily get a hotel near the Arc de Triomphe, but you'll get a place in a solid neighborhood that feels very Parisian. Your hotel may be a 20-minute Metro ride from the Louvre.

- **Eiffel Tower–Grenelle-Montparnasse:** This zone sprawls from the Eiffel Tower all the way down to the southwest edge of the city, through peaceful residential neighborhoods and a high-rise business district or two. Nothing makes this zone better than any of the others, but if you fail in bids elsewhere, hotels here are just fine. *Remember:* You'll probably need to ride the Metro to get to the center of town.

Rome

Bidding for hotels in Rome can be frustrating. Priceline's 3-star inventory includes some unacceptable hotels, so you're stuck with 4- and 5-star hotels, both of which can require pretty high bids ($100 or more) for success. This city is one in which booking a charming, small hotel using a travel guide like *Frommer's Rome* by Darwin Porter and Danforth Prince (published by Wiley) or *Italy For Dummies,* 2nd Edition, by Bruce Murphy and Alessandra de Rosa (published by Wiley), may save you some trouble.

If you're going to bid, though, most of Rome's main attractions are in the Central zone. Hotels here are generally close to bus and subway lines and within a short stumble of some sort of historic monument, whether it's the Colosseum, the Pantheon, or the Spanish Steps.

Rome's Vatican City zone is another good bet for 4-star hotels. All the hotels I've seen here are within walking distance of the Vatican and a short bus or subway ride from the historic center of Rome.

San Juan

Priceline only offers one zone in Puerto Rico's capital. That hasn't stopped bidders from snapping up 3-star, Boutique-level, and Resort-level hotels. Most of the 3-star hotels are in the city, not at the beach. Resorts have beach access. The super-prestigious Water Club crops up now and then; for a while it was a 5-star hotel, then a Boutique-level hotel. **Remember:** Some hotels in this zone are quite far from the cruise port, if that's important to you.

Toronto

Priceline's Downtown Toronto zone includes downtown and midtown Toronto, from the Expo Center to the Cherry Street docks and from the harbor all the way up past Bloor Street. Most hotels are quite near Yonge Street, Toronto's main street.

Buses, subways, and trams crisscross the Downtown Toronto zone, so you won't need a car if you're staying here. You can bid this zone with confidence.

 If you have a car or you're willing to take a bus to the subway, also try the Don Valley zone. That'll probably get you a hotel near Eglinton Avenue between the Don Valley Parkway and Yonge Street in a residential part of Toronto that isn't terribly walkable but has perfectly good bus service and is a ten-minute drive from downtown.

Vancouver

The Vancouver zone swallows all of central Vancouver, so you're not spoiled for choice here. The good news: All the hotels I've seen in this zone are in the central Downtown, Yaletown, and West End neighborhoods.

BiddingForTravel's Vancouver hotel list includes some terrific luxury hotels, like the Sheraton Suites Lesoleil, which made Condé Nast's Gold List of top hotels. Bid 4-star, and you can't go wrong.

Glossary

alternate airport: An airport with no commercial jet service (or no service by a Priceline.com airline partner), near a major airport, that can be used to generate extra bids for the larger airport. For instance, Hagerstown, Maryland, is an alternate airport for the Washington, D.C., area. You can find a list of alternate airports on BiddingForTravel.com. *See also* BiddingForTravel.com.

bankruptcy: Chapter 11 bankruptcy is a legal dodge to let companies (such as airlines) get out of debts and renegotiate contracts. If a company declares bankruptcy, it's in shaky financial shape, sure, but airlines go in and out of bankruptcy all the time and keep flying.

Best Price Guarantee: Priceline guarantees that if you find the exact same air ticket, hotel room, car, cruise, mortgage, or vacation on another Web site for less, it'll give you *some* money back. Don't rely on these guarantees; they have loopholes (for instance, Hotwire.com and many super-discounted hotel rates don't count), and they're generally pretty difficult to take advantage of.

BetterBidding.com: An online discussion group where you can see which hotels and flights Priceline bidders have won recently and how much money they've paid, as well as get advice on bidding strategies. BetterBidding.com is friendlier and more informal than BiddingForTravel.com. *See also* BiddingForTravel.com.

bid grid: My own invention, a chart listing all the bids you plan to make. Creating a bid grid before making your first bid helps you maximize your bids, pay as little as possible, and not get caught up in the excitement of Priceline bidding.

bid number: *See* request number.

bidding: Entering a price you hope Priceline will accept.

BiddingForTravel.com: An online discussion group where you can see which hotels and flights Priceline bidders have won recently and how much money they've paid, as well as get advice on bidding strategies. BiddingForTravel. com is much bigger and more efficient than BetterBidding.com. *See also* BetterBidding.com.

bonus money: An electronic coupon sent out by Priceline that adds value to a bid. Priceline sometimes sends bonus money coupons by e-mail or makes them available through links on partner Web sites.

Boutique-level hotel: A quirky hotel that usually doesn't belong to a major chain. It may have small rooms and unusual amenities (like pet goldfish in every room). Priceline rates Boutique-level hotels in between 3 stars and 4 stars.

bumping: An airline practice where the airline sells more tickets than it has seats available and then tells a few people they'll have to take the next plane. If you can get *voluntarily* bumped, you can reap a free ticket and usually only be delayed by a few hours.

car classes: Priceline rents 11 different types of cars and trucks, from economy all the way up to minivans. The most important factor: If you want a four-door vehicle, you must rent a car that's full-size or larger.

codesharing: A misleading airline-industry practice where one airline's flights pretend to be another's, for marketing reasons. For instance, you can buy a ticket on United and end up on a US Airways plane.

connection: Stopping and potentially changing planes on your way to your destination. Priceline demands that you accept one connection each way, but it asks your permission before you have to accept two connections.

counteroffer: After you bid, Priceline often suggests a guaranteed price at which you'll be able to get your ticket or room; this is a counteroffer. Priceline will usually accept a bid slightly lower than the counteroffer. Keep in mind that you have no guarantee that the price will still be available when you decide to accept it.

direct flight: A flight that may have one stop, but no change of planes. *See also* nonstop flight.

distressed-passenger rates: Lower hotel rates for people who are unexpectedly stuck in the airport overnight.

e-ticket: Not a ticket at all; when you have an e-ticket, your details are stored in the airline's computer, and you don't need a paper ticket. Still, you should bring a printout of your Priceline acceptance page and confirmation number in case the computers go down.

force majeure: When all bets are off. In the case of a terrorist attack, a war, or a catastrophic natural disaster, airlines are no longer required to get you where you're going.

free rebid: To make a second bid on Priceline, you must add a hotel zone or airport. Adding hotel zones or airports where you couldn't possibly get a room or a flight is a *free rebid*. For hotels, that means adding a zone where your chosen star rating isn't available; for airports, it means adding an airport with no commercial service or no jet service (or no service by a Priceline.com partner airline).

high season: The time of year when the most people are traveling to a particular destination; also the time when fares and rates are highest.

Hotwire.com: Priceline's number-one competitor. Hotwire.com doesn't tell you exactly what hotel you're staying in or what flight you'll be on (similar to Priceline), but Hotwire does tell you the price of your hotel or flight in advance (unlike Priceline).

impossible airport: An airport with no commercial airline service, an airport only served by non-Priceline airlines, or an airport with such limited service that there's no way to get to your destination Finding impossible airports can get you plenty of free rebids when you're bidding for airfares.

jet-only: A flight where you don't have to get on a prop plane for any portion of the trip. The smallest jets are 37 seats, and they offer smoother and quieter rides than prop planes. Priceline always searches for jet-only flights first.

low season: The time of year when fewer people are traveling to a particular destination; also the time when fares and rates are lowest.

misrating: When Priceline gets the star level of a hotel wrong. Usually, if you're in a misrated hotel and can prove it's missing some of Priceline's promised features, you can get a refund from Priceline.

Name Your Own Price: More like "Guess Our Price." Priceline knows what prices it'll accept for hotels and airfare. Your game is to guess as close to Priceline's price as possible.

non-jet: A propeller plane, with as few as 18 seats. Non-jet flights make some people nervous. Priceline will always ask your permission before putting you on a prop plane.

nonrefundable: Technically, when you bid through Priceline, your money is nonrefundable, which means you can't get it back for any reason. However, this policy isn't what it seems. Priceline often refunds your tickets if you made a gross mistake on a bid, if you have a health emergency, or if a hotel doesn't offer the amenities Priceline promises. You just can't be sure it'll be that nice.

nonstop flight: A nonstop flight is a flight that — you guessed it! — doesn't stop between the origin and the destination. Priceline never guarantees non-stop flights, but sometimes you get lucky. You can request nonstop flights (on certain routings) on Priceline Asia, but you have to start out in Asia. *See also* direct flight.

off-peak flight: Also known as a *red-eye flight,* this is any flight leaving between 10 p.m. and 6 a.m. Priceline will ask your permission before putting you on an off-peak flight.

one-stop flight: A flight where you have to get off and change planes once. *See also* direct flight.

one-way flight: A flight that only goes one way, not back to your point of origin. You can't bid for one-way flights on Priceline. *See also* throwaway ticketing.

opaque fares: Fares that are hidden from the customer at the time of purchase, as Priceline's fares are.

open-jaw flight: A flight that goes from Point A to Point B to Point C, and then from Point C directly back to Point A. You can't bid for open-jaw flights on Priceline. Sometimes referred to as a *three-legged flight.*

out-of-pocket maximum: The maximum you're willing to pay, including all taxes and fees. If you're asking for help on BiddingForTravel.com, this is one of the pieces of information it'll ask you for.

overbidding: When you bid more than you had to. If you overbid, Priceline won't tell you; it'll just take your money. So it's up to you to bid as low as possible and still succeed. You can avoid overbidding by doing lots of research before using Priceline.

overbooking: A travel-industry practice of selling more tickets (or rooms, or cars) than actually exist, betting that some people will be no-shows. If every-one does show up, airlines will bump you, hotels will walk you, and car-rental agencies will try to put you in a different class of car than the one you asked for. You can't do anything to stop overbooking, but you can avoid being bumped or walked. *See also* bumping *and* walking.

Playtime Guarantee: If you book a vacation package on Priceline for two or three nights over one of the next two weekends, it guarantees you'll have either 44 hours (for a two-night trip) or 64 hours (for a three-night trip) at your destination. If you bid for the flight alone, you'd have a chance of getting a flight out late Friday night and a return flight early Sunday morning — which makes for a lousy weekend.

Priceline Asia: A group of three Web sites — based in Hong Kong, Singapore, and Taiwan — that sell Name Your Own Price hotels around the world and Name Your Own Price airline tickets departing from Hong Kong, Singapore, or Taiwan. Anyone can use these sites, but you need a delivery address in Hong Kong, Singapore, or Taiwan if you're buying airline tickets.

Priceline Cruises: A spin-off of Priceline that sells cruises, Priceline Cruises is run by National Leisure Group, a big cruise travel agency. Priceline Cruises is *not* Name Your Own Price and only has the lowest prices as often as any other travel agency does.

Priceline Mortgage: A joint venture between Priceline and EverBank, a Florida bank, this site lets you Name Your Own Rate for mortgages. The mortgages are then sold to you by EverBank or by another bank Priceline finds through LendingTree, a mortgage-comparison service.

Priceline U.K.: A version of Priceline for European residents to use, it only sells Name Your Own Price hotels — not Name Your Own Price airfares or car rentals.

Priceline.com: A positively brilliant, often infuriating service for saving huge amounts of money on airfares, cars, and hotel rooms.

rebidding: Using several bids to start low and then come up to meet Priceline's lowest acceptable price.

red-eye flight: *See* off-peak flight.

request number: Also known as a *bid number,* it appears in the form 123-456-789-10 on winning bid pages, counteroffer pages, and rebidding pages. Write down this number — it's critical if you need to get customer service from Priceline.

Resort-level hotel: A hotel with a pool and some kind of nearby activity, like skiing, golfing, or tennis. In Priceline's star-rating system, Resort-level hotels fall in between 4 and 5 stars.

round-trip flight: A flight that goes from Point A to Point B and back to Point A again. This is the only kind of flight you can bid for on Priceline.

Rule 240: Airline slang for the section of an airline's Contract of Carriage that details what the airline owes you if your flight is delayed or cancelled. Generally, Rule 240s (which vary from one airline to the next) say that the airline must get you on the next available flight to your destination.

run-of-house room: The most common type of hotel room or whatever's available at the time.

shoulder season: The time of year that's neither high season nor low season. *See also* high season *and* low season.

star level: The quality of a hotel, measured by amenities like room service and whether the place has a pool. Priceline lets you bid for hotels in eight star levels: 1-star, 2-star, 2½-star, 3-star, Boutique, 4-star, Resort, and 5-star. One and 2-star hotels are motel-like; 3- and 4-star hotels are generally upscale chains, and 5-star hotels are truly luxurious — but also very rare. If you're looking for some luxury, a 4-star hotel is generally the way to go; if you just want a clean place to lay your head, a 2- or 2½-star hotel will probably satisfy you. The only star level that guarantees a pool is Resort.

suggested retail price: What Priceline *says* the going non-Priceline rate for a hotel is. Ignore Priceline's suggested retail prices. They're usually much higher than the special rates you can get on hotel-chain Web sites, so they're not a good gauge of what you should bid. (Priceline isn't trying to fool you — it just gets its suggested prices from a computer system that doesn't have the chains' lowest rates.)

taxes and fees: Always added onto your bids, they can range anywhere from about $10 for a cheap hotel in the United States to more than $100 for an international airline ticket. For airline tickets, Priceline will always try to estimate taxes and fees before you pay, and it's pretty honest. For hotel rooms, it'll tell you the exact taxes and fees you'll have to pay before you hand over your credit-card details.

three-legged flight: *See* open-jaw flight.

throwaway ticketing: A tactic of turning a round-trip ticket into a one-way by only using half of it. It works if you use the first half, but not the last half. If you miss a leg of a flight, your airline will automatically cancel the rest of your ticket. *See also* one-way flight.

two-stop flight: Dreaded by travelers, a flight with two connections. Priceline will ask before sending you on one of these journeys. Two-stop flights are often necessary if you're going from a smaller U.S. city to Europe.

underbidding: When you bid unrealistically low. There's no virtue in under-bidding by too much. You won't get your airfare or hotel room, and hey, Priceline's got to make its money somehow.

upselling: A car-rental industry practice of trying to strong-arm you into buying upgrades, extra insurance, or tanks of gas when you come to pick up your car. Stand firm — you don't have to say yes to any of the salesperson's gambits, and the deals being offered usually aren't very good.

vacation package: A booking that includes an airline ticket, a hotel room, and sometimes a car. It's not an escorted tour, it's just a way to book your air and hotel together. If Priceline hides the details of your airline flights, booking a vacation package will usually be cheaper than booking the same package on another Web site. But it'll almost always be more expensive than bidding for your airfare and hotel room separately.

walking: When hotels sell more rooms than they have, they send patrons to another hotel nearby. Unlike *bumping,* walking is never fun; check in early to avoid getting walked. *See also* bumping.

zone: A section of a city, as defined by Priceline, for hotels. A hotel's zone and its star level are the two main things you control when bidding for hotels. Sometimes Priceline's zones stretch far beyond the boundaries of the city they're named for, so check out the maps on Priceline's Web site. Priceline's zone names are often misleading, but its maps never lie.

Index

first-floor rooms, 39
5-star hotels, 152–153
flexible travel plans, 31
flight
  cancellations, 130–131
  delays, 130
  times, 86–87
  vacation packages, 71
flying standby, 36
force majeure events, 50, 303
foreign services
  from Canada, 255–258
  credit card, need for, 73–74
  from Europe, 258–261
  foreign sites, 74–75
  using U.S. site outside U.S., 74
foreign travel
  layovers, 84
  passport and visa requirements, 123
  Priceline, 13–15
  regulations affecting travelers'
    rights, 49
  zones, hotel, 156
four-door rental-car categories, 208
4-star hotels, 149–150
Frankfurt, 32
free rebid
  airline tickets, 99–104
  alternate cities, 102–103, 112
  described, 303
  ITA Software's flight search, 100
  non-jet-only airports, 103
  two-connection-only airports,
    103–104
  zones, hotel, 154, 157–159
French Quarter zone, New Orleans, 291
frequent-flier miles, 36–37
frequent-guest hotel programs,
  40, 183, 184
Frommer's Rome (Porter and
  Prince), 298
full-size cars, 204

• G •

Golden, Fran Wenograd (*Cruise
  Vacations For Dummies 2005*), 45
grid, airfare bid
  airport, choosing, 96
  described, 91, 301
  free rebids, 99–104
  maximum bid, picking, 97–99
grid, hotel bid
  simple, 163–164
  star level or zone, changing, 164–165
  switching bidders, 164
group air travel, 110
GST (goods and services tax), 256
guarantee, price
  airfare, 301
  car rentals, 216
  hotel rooms, 176
  mortgage rate, 253
guessing price, 10, 11–12

• H •

hand controls, cars with, 42
Hawks, John (executive director of
  Consumer Travel Rights Center),
  59, 60
Hertz car-rental company
  customer service, 40
  Mexico, driving into, 41
  minimum age, 42
  rental-car problems, 230
  sample car models by class, 202–203
high season, 31, 303
Holden, Greg (eBay expert), 21–23
Home Buying For Dummies (Tyson and
  Brown), 245
Hong Kong
  hotel zones, 296–297
  Priceline in, 13, 14, 75, 266, 268

● *P* ●

• *U* •

Notes

Notes

Notes

Notes

FOR DUMMIES®

A world of resources to help you grow

HOME, GARDEN & HOBBIES

Feng Shui FOR DUMMIES
A Reference for the Rest of Us!
0-7645-5295-3

Gardening FOR DUMMIES
A Reference for the Rest of Us!
0-7645-5130-2

Guitar FOR DUMMIES
A Reference for the Rest of Us!
0-7645-5106-X

Also available:

Auto Repair For Dummies
(0-7645-5089-6)

Chess For Dummies
(0-7645-5003-9)

Home Maintenance For Dummies
(0-7645-5215-5)

Organizing For Dummies
(0-7645-5300-3)

Piano For Dummies
(0-7645-5105-1)

Poker For Dummies
(0-7645-5232-5)

Quilting For Dummies
(0-7645-5118-3)

Rock Guitar For Dummies
(0-7645-5356-9)

Roses For Dummies
(0-7645-5202-3)

Sewing For Dummies
(0-7645-5137-X)

FOOD & WINE

Cooking FOR DUMMIES
A Reference for the Rest of Us!
0-7645-5250-3

Cookies FOR DUMMIES
A Reference for the Rest of Us!
0-7645-5390-9

Wine FOR DUMMIES
A Reference for the Rest of Us!
0-7645-5114-0

Also available:

Bartending For Dummies
(0-7645-5051-9)

Chinese Cooking For Dummies
(0-7645-5247-3)

Christmas Cooking For Dummies
(0-7645-5407-7)

Diabetes Cookbook For Dummies
(0-7645-5230-9)

Grilling For Dummies
(0-7645-5076-4)

Low-Fat Cooking For Dummies
(0-7645-5035-7)

Slow Cookers For Dummies
(0-7645-5240-6)

TRAVEL

Italy FOR DUMMIES
A Travel Guide for the Rest of Us!
0-7645-5453-0

Hawaii FOR DUMMIES
A Travel Guide for the Rest of Us!
0-7645-5438-7

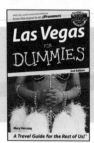

Las Vegas FOR DUMMIES
A Travel Guide for the Rest of Us!
0-7645-5448-4

Also available:

America's National Parks For Dummies
(0-7645-6204-5)

Caribbean For Dummies
(0-7645-5445-X)

Cruise Vacations For Dummies 2003
(0-7645-5459-X)

Europe For Dummies
(0-7645-5456-5)

Ireland For Dummies
(0-7645-6199-5)

France For Dummies
(0-7645-6292-4)

London For Dummies
(0-7645-5416-6)

Mexico's Beach Resorts For Dummies
(0-7645-6262-2)

Paris For Dummies
(0-7645-5494-8)

RV Vacations For Dummies
(0-7645-5443-3)

Walt Disney World & Orlando For Dummies
(0-7645-5444-1)

Available wherever books are sold. Go to www.dummies.com or call 1-877-762-2974 to order direct.

FOR DUMMIES®

Plain-English solutions for everyday challenges

COMPUTER BASICS

0-7645-0838-5

0-7645-1663-9

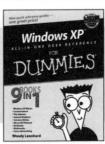

0-7645-1548-9

Also available:

PCs All-in-One Desk Reference For Dummies
(0-7645-0791-5)

Pocket PC For Dummies
(0-7645-1640-X)

Treo and Visor For Dummies
(0-7645-1673-6)

Troubleshooting Your PC For Dummies
(0-7645-1669-8)

Upgrading & Fixing PCs For Dummies
(0-7645-1665-5)

Windows XP For Dummies
(0-7645-0893-8)

Windows XP For Dummies Quick Reference
(0-7645-0897-0)

BUSINESS SOFTWARE

0-7645-0822-9

0-7645-0839-3

0-7645-0819-9

Also available:

Excel Data Analysis For Dummies
(0-7645-1661-2)

Excel 2002 All-in-One Desk Reference For Dummies
(0-7645-1794-5)

Excel 2002 For Dummies Quick Reference
(0-7645-0829-6)

GoldMine "X" For Dummies
(0-7645-0845-8)

Microsoft CRM For Dummies
(0-7645-1698-1)

Microsoft Project 2002 For Dummies
(0-7645-1628-0)

Office XP For Dummies
(0-7645-0830-X)

Outlook 2002 For Dummies
(0-7645-0828-8)

Get smart! Visit www.dummies.com

- **Find listings of even more *For Dummies* titles**

- **Browse online articles**

- **Sign up for Dummies eTips™**

- **Check out *For Dummies* fitness videos and other products**

- **Order from our online bookstore**

Available wherever books are sold. Go to www.dummies.com or call 1-877-762-2974 to order direct.

FOR DUMMIES®

The advice and explanations you need to succeed

SELF-HELP, SPIRITUALITY & RELIGION

0-7645-5302-X

0-7645-5418-2

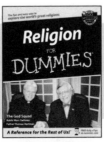

0-7645-5264-3

Also available:

The Bible For Dummies
(0-7645-5296-1)

Buddhism For Dummies
(0-7645-5359-3)

Christian Prayer For Dummies
(0-7645-5500-6)

Dating For Dummies
(0-7645-5072-1)

Judaism For Dummies
(0-7645-5299-6)

Potty Training For Dummies
(0-7645-5417-4)

Pregnancy For Dummies
(0-7645-5074-8)

Rekindling Romance For
Dummies
(0-7645-5303-8)

Spirituality For Dummies
(0-7645-5298-8)

Weddings For Dummies
(0-7645-5055-1)

PETS

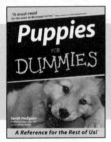

0-7645-5255-4

0-7645-5286-4

0-7645-5275-9

Also available:

Labrador Retrievers For
Dummies
(0-7645-5281-3)

Aquariums For Dummies
(0-7645-5156-6)

Birds For Dummies
(0-7645-5139-6)

Dogs For Dummies
(0-7645-5274-0)

Ferrets For Dummies
(0-7645-5259-7)

German Shepherds For
Dummies
(0-7645-5280-5)

Golden Retrievers For
Dummies
(0-7645-5267-8)

Horses For Dummies
(0-7645-5138-8)

Jack Russell Terriers For
Dummies
(0-7645-5268-6)

Puppies Raising & Training
Diary For Dummies
(0-7645-0876-8)

EDUCATION & TEST PREPARATION

0-7645-5194-9

0-7645-5325-9

0-7645-5210-4

Also available:

Chemistry For Dummies
(0-7645-5430-1)

English Grammar For
Dummies
(0-7645-5322-4)

French For Dummies
(0-7645-5193-0)

The GMAT For Dummies
(0-7645-5251-1)

Inglés Para Dummies
(0-7645-5427-1)

Italian For Dummies
(0-7645-5196-5)

Research Papers For
Dummies
(0-7645-5426-3)

The SAT I For Dummies
(0-7645-5472-7)

U.S. History For Dummies
(0-7645-5249-X)

World History For Dummies
(0-7645-5242-2)